Byzantine Chant
Tradition and Reform

Byzantine Chant
Tradition and Reform

Acts of a Meeting held at
the Danish Institute at Athens, 1993

Edited by C. Troelsgård

Monographs of the Danish Institute at Athens
Volume 2

BYZANTINE CHANT
Tradition and Reform

© Copyright: The Danish Institute at Athens, Athens 1997

General editors: *Søren Dietz & Signe Isager*
Graphic design and Production by: *Freddy Pedersen*

Printed in Denmark on permanent paper
conforming to ANSI/NISO Z39.48-1992

The publication was sponsored by:
The Danish Research Council for the Humanities
The Carlsberg Foundation and
The Eleni Nakou Foundation

Monographs of the Danish Institute at Athens
Volume 2

ISBN 87-7288-733-8
ISSN 1397-1433

Distributed by
AARHUS UNIVERSITY PRESS
University of Aarhus
DK-8000 Århus C
Fax (+45) 8619 8433

73 Lime Walk
Headington, Oxford OX3 7AD
Fax (+44) 1865 750 079

Box 511
Oakville, Conn. 06779
Fax (+1) 860 945 9468

The cover depicts an ornament from the musical Anthology
MS Copenhagen IGLM 3,8°, written around A.D. 1800
by monk Ioasaph of the Pantokrator Monastery, Mount Athos.

Contents

Foreword

Christian Troelsgård

Byzantine chant is inevitably associated with the word 'tradition'. Even if this concept in itself is vague and imprecise, we cannot avoid using it when we speak about the history of the chant so closely connected with the Byzantine rite. It seems that this tradition was maintained through a continuous and complex interplay between two different modes of transmission, written and oral, the pen and the memory, but many aspects of these processes still deserve a closer examination. How was the education of the singers? How was the notation used? How stable can a oral tradition stay over a long period? And which were the reasons behind developments and reforms of both the musical notation and the chanted repertories?

This volume includes papers read at a Dano-Hellenic Symposium held at the Danish Institute at Athens, November 11-14, 1993, under the main theme 'Byzantine Chant - Tradition and Reform'. The individual papers do not only present studies on various aspects of the transmission of Byzantine and Post-byzantine chant from the 11th-20th centuries, but they also demonstrate a wide range of various approaches, drawing on disciplines as different as ethnomusicology, palaeography, codicology, philology, neumatic and formulaic analysis.

In many respects, it is the merit of Dr. phil. Jørgen Raasted (1927-1995) that this meeting could be held and brought to a successful conclusion. Jørgen Raasted was a person who, more than anyone else, linked Greek and Danish scholars of Byzantine music together, and he was the teacher of a significant num-

ber of both Greek and Danish scholars in the field. His open-minded attitude as a scholar established new perspectives of combining a thorough knowledge of the medieval musical manuscripts with the experiences of Greek scholars and their being at home with the living chant tradition. Now, we have a firm basis for a continuation of the collaboration along this line, and, therefore, this volume is dedicated to his memory. Also another contributor to this volume, prof. Marios Mauroïdis, is no longer among the living; both these inspiring colleagues are severely missed.

The different dates and styles of the Greek quotations and texts included in this volume have called for the use of different conventions in accentuation and orthography, and following no single style has been applied throughout. Due to technical problems in the very last phase of the production of the book, the modal signatures, neumes, and great hypostaseis in the table on pages 192-94 have been drawn by hand by the editor, who is responsible for any error that might have resulted thereby.

I would like here to express my gratitude to the then director of the Danish Institute at Athens, Dr. phil. Søren Dietz, who supported the idea of a 'medieval' double-symposium right from the beginning (a symposium on Byzantine and Latin philosophy in the Middle Ages was held along with the one on Byzantine music). Without his help, and the assistance of the staff of the Danish Institute at Athens, the practical performance of the meeting would not have been possible.

I also thank prof. Gregorios Stathes,

who enriched the symposium with a live performance of Byzantine chant. In the great hall of the University of Athens, designed by the Danish architect Chr. Hansen (1803-1883), a concert sponsored by the Athenian University and the Institute of Byzantine Musicology of the Greek Church took place. Prof. Stathes delivered a brief account on the life of the Byzantine composer Parthenios Meteorites (last quarter of the 18th cent.) and with the Χορός Ψαλτών Βυζαντινής και Μεταβυζαντινής Μουσικής he performed a selection of Parthenios' works.

Finally, I would like to thank the Carlsberg Foundation for its financial support, without which the symposium could not have been held. We are most grateful to the Danish Research Council for the Humanities, the Carlsberg Foundation and the Eleni Nakou Foundation for supporting the production of the publication.

Copenhagen, August 26, 1997

Koukouzeles' Sticherarion[1]

Jørgen Raasted

In 1469, when Ioannis Plousiadinos – in Venice – finished his beautiful copy of the Kalophonic Sticherarion Sinai 1234, he was well aware that the collection of Kalophonic Stichera ultimately went back to Koukouzeles, and that this earliest collection contained compositions and arrangements both by Koukouzeles himself and by others. The heading of the Sinai manuscript (Sinai 1234, 1r) speaks quite clearly about Koukouzeles' work as a redactor and a composer of Kalophonic Stichera:

Ἀρχὴ τῶν στιχηρῶν τοῦ ὅλου ἐνιαυτοῦ, ἀπ'ἀρχῆς τῆς ἰνδίκτου... ποιήματα διαφόρων ποιητῶν· συνετέθεσαν οὖν σαφέστατα παρὰ τοῦ μαΐστορος· καὶ ἐκαλλοπίσθη– σαν τὰ παλαιὰ μόνα, τὰ δὲ νέα ἀσάλευτα μένουσιν.

Koukouzeles composed numerous melodies in kalophonic style – long compositions taking up several manuscript pages in contrast to the rather few lines of, for instance, a Sticheron in the old, non-kalophonic tradition. Apart from acknowledging his rôle as a composer of a considerable part of the kalophonic repertory, scholarship has credited Koukouzeles with many activities in the transmission and development of Byzantine Chant. Let me mention, however briefly, some of the most important:

(a) He is supposed to be the one who organized the collection of the Ordinary Chants, the so-called ἀκολουθίαι – and, probably, the small beginners' book (the one often referred to as the "ἀρχὴ μέση τέλος") with its concomitant propaedeutic material. This includes a list of ἠχήματα arranged according to modes, with incipits (mostly of Stichera) fitting to the various Echemata-endings of each mode.

(b) Following the example of Ioannis Glykys he composed his famous Lehrgedicht, the Μέγα Ἴσον.

(c) He is connected with the growing use of the Great Ὑποστάσεις, the "red subsidiary signs".

(d) Two colophons in Heirmologia from the early 14th century point towards some connection with Koukouzeles. The earlier – St Petersburg 121, from 1302 – describes itself as an ἔργον ἰωάννου παπαδοπούλου τοῦ ἐπι– λεγομένου κουκουζέλη. The other manuscript (the Heirmologion Sinai 1256, from 1309) was written by Irini, daughter of Theodor Hagiopetritis – but it quotes, apparently, the colophon of its model: τέλος. δόξα τῷ θεῷ. ἀμήν. χεὶρ ἰωάννου παπαδοπούλου τοῦ κουκουζέλη. On the strength of these colophons and comparisons with other 14th-15th cent. Heirmologia, Oliver Strunk claimed that Koukouzeles made a revision of the Heirmologion[2].

(e) My final point – the topic of this paper – deals with the Sticherarion. Are there any traces of a connection between Koukouzeles and the Sticherarion tradition since the end of the 13th or the beginning of the 14th century? The question was opened in the West by Strunk in a couple of papers from the 1960es[3]. In order to understand Strunk's reasoning, you must remember that some Stichera from the Oktoechos were so well known that their melodies were normally not written down in the earlier Sticheraria. It is thus not until the Koukouzelian or Post-Koukouzelian period that we find melodies for the full set of Stichera Anastasima and the ordinary Dogmatikon for Saturday evening. Apparently, this feature is to be found only in the cyclically arranged Oktoechos, where all songs of a mode are grouped together. In earlier manuscripts, as you know, the normal procedure was to arrange the songs systematically, with sections comprising pieces for all eight modes for each genre (Alphabetika, Anabathmoi, Anatolika, or whatever). Now, it was in the cyclical Oktoechos of a few late Sticheraria that Strunk found a number of musical idioms which he knew from Koukouzeles' revision of the Heirmologion. To use Strunk's cautious wording: in some of these manuscripts there seemed to be "a significant relation of some kind" between the Stichera Anastasima and Dogmatika of the Oktoechos and the Heirmologion of Koukouzeles[4]. My present lecture follows these ideas which Strunk put forward a generation ago and extends their implications to the central repertory of the Sticherarion. I use the term of "a central repertory" to mark the distinction between these Stichera and the Anastasima and Dogmatika which Strunk dealt with and which he called "the marginal repertory."

The codex A 139 sup in the Biblioteca Ambrosiana in Milan is one of the manuscripts that contain the "marginal" repertory of the Oktoechos. In 1992 the MMB published a facsimile edition of the Ambrosianus[5]. Before I go on, I shall permit myself to quote the last few lines of my introduction to the facsimile edition:

Did Koukouzeles ever establish a version of the complete Sticherarion? It is not unreasonable to think so; a Koukouzeles who revised the Heirmologion and initiated a collection of the Ordinary Chants – the '-Akolouthiai' – may as well have had his ideas about how to normalize the tradition of the Sticherarion. At present, however, we do not know for sure whether Koukouzeles produced his own version of the Sticherarion, nor have we any means to define in what respect the entire Ambrosianus A 139 sup might represent or reflect a Koukouzelian Sticherarion. If Koukouzeles ever revised the central parts of the Sticherarion, chances are that his interventions in the melodies of the central and stable repertory were far less conspicuous than in the marginal repertory on which Strunk focussed.

Strunk's probings into the manuscript sources for the "marginal" repertory led him to "a tentative classification, based in some instances on comparisons of a few test pieces only"[6]. He divided his sources into the following four groups:

1. *Allied to Ambrosianus gr. 733:*
   Iviron 953
   Sinai 1471

2. *Allied to the "Codex Peribleptus" [N]:*

Example 1
Oktoechos, Protos, endings in "marginal" repertory: Inventory

	1	2	3	4	5	6	7	8
A1:	c	c	c	b	a	c	b	a
A2:	c	c	c	b	d	c	b	a
A2a:				b	d	c	b	a
A3:				a	b	c	b	a
A4:				a	ba	c	a	a
A4a:				bc	a	cb	a	a
A5:				a	ba	bc	a	a
A6:	c	c	c	bc	a	bc	a	a
A7:	c	c	c	b	a	bc	a	a
B1:			a	EF	D	F	D	D
B2:			a	EF	D	EF	D	D
C1:	a	GF	EF	G	a	EF	D	D
C2:	a	GF	EF	G	a	bc	a	a
D:	G	GF	Ga	a	GFE	F	E	D

Example 2
Oktoechos, Protos, endings in "marginal" repertory: Distribution

MS:	A1	A2	A2a	A3	A4	A4a	A5	A6	A7	B1	B2	C1	C2	D
1471										x3	x2	x4		
953						Nr9				x2	x2	x4		
17							Nr8					Nr1	x3	
71							Nr8			Nr19		x5		x2
1228			Nr8					x3				Nr17	x4	
139		x2	Nr3	Nr8				Nr9						
1230		x2	Nr3	Nr8				—						
386	Nr9				Nr8				x7					
1493	x4				Nr8									
N	x8				Nr8									
386v	x4													
1493v							Nr1?	Nr2						
1228v							Nr17							

ΕΣΠΕΡΙΝΟΣ ΤΟΥ ΣΑΒΒΑΤΟΥ: **ἀναστάσιμα**: 1 Τὰς ἑσπερινὰς ἡμῶν εὐχάς, 2 Κυκλώσατε λαοί, 3 Δεῦτε λαοὶ ὑμνήσωμεν. **θεοτοκίον δογματικόν**: 8 Τὴν παγκόσμιον δόξαν. **ἀπόστιχον**: 9 Τῷ πάθει σου χριστέ

ΟΡΘΡΟΣ ΤΗΣ ΚΥΡΙΑΚΗΣ: **ἀναστάσιμα**: 17 Ὑμνοῦμέν σου χριστέ, 18 Ὁ σταυρὸν ὑπομείνας, 19 Ὁ τὸν ἅδην σκυλεύσας, 20 Τὴν θεοπρεπῆ

Dionysiou 564 [386]
Vatopedi 1493

3. *Allied to Ambrosiana gr. 44* [now: A 139 sup]:
Sinai 1230

4. *More or less independent:*
Naples II.C.17
Laura Γ.71
Sinai 1228

Of Strunk's four groups, Nos. 2 and 3 display, as I have already mentioned, "a significant relation of some kind" with the Koukouzelian Heirmologion.

Of these two groups, Group 3 (A 139 and Sinai 1230) is the one which Strunk found to be "most deeply involved – involved almost to the point of virtual identity"[7].

My present lecture takes its starting point in Strunk's observations on the "marginal" repertory and extends their implications to the central repertory of the Sticherarion. My main source material is the eleven manuscripts that Strunk mentioned; but I have supplied with some others that were easily accessible in the microfilm collection of the MMB. As you will understand, my material is certainly not complete – but I consider it to be sufficient for my present purpose.

I have gathered my documentation in four examples of musical variants, to demonstrate -at least in principle – what kind of material I dispose of in my hypothetical reconstruction of Koukouzeles' non-kalophonic Sticherarion.

In order to get a more solid foundation I have – as a first step – collated the entire Protos section in the manuscripts used by

Strunk. To make our lives more easy, I have looked at the final cadences, only.

Let us first have a look at EXAMPLE 1, the inventory of the 14 different ways in which the Protos melodies end in the nine Stichera of the "marginal" repertory. The main distinctive grouping is between the endings which I have marked A1-A7 (ending high, on a) and the rest, mostly ending *low*, on D[8].

EXAMPLE 2 shows the *distribution* of our 14 cadential formulas in 10 out of Strunk's 11 manuscripts[9]. You see how nicely my diagram supports Strunk's less explicit remarks: The *low* types (the endings that I call B C and D) – those to the right of my vertical double stroke – are *not* found in any of the manuscripts that belong to Strunk's Groups 2 and 3, the ones where Koukouzeles' supposed influence is most strongly marked. On the diagram you find the Koukouzelian candidates below the first horizontal stroke. You can immediately see, that these two groups of Strunk's differ clearly from each other. Each of them has its own preferences: The first two manuscripts on my diagram (A 139 sup and Sinai 1230), i.e. Strunk's Group 3, use 4 different endings. The other 3 (Strunk's Group 2) use 2 others. The only exception to this picture is the ending A7; it occurs no less than 7 times in Dionysiou 386 – but as you see at the bottom of the diagram, four of these have as alternative readings the ending A1, the favourite ending in the other members of Group 2[10].

To conclude this part of my exposé: My diagram certainly *does* confirm Strunk's observations on the melodic tradition for the marginal repertory, especially as to his Groups 2 and 3 -those groups which Strunk found to come especially close to the ways of Koukouzeles' Heirmologion.

The next logical step will be to have a look at the central repertory of the Oktoechos – the types of songs known as ἀνατολικά, ἀλφαβητικά, and ἀναβαθμοί. The Protos section of the cyclical Oktoechos comprises 24 such items. Again, I have collated only their endings. (See EXAMPLE 3).

This central repertory is transmitted in all Sticheraria that contain an Oktoechos, thus also in the numerous manuscripts of the older type where the melodies are arranged systematically, after *genre*. To get an idea of this older tradition I have collated the Vienna manuscript which was reproduced as vol. I of the MMB. This manuscript was written, in 1217 or 1221, by one Ioannis Dalassenos and is therefore normally referred to by the siglum "D". I have included, also, the relevant data from two other manuscripts which from my earlier experience seem to be related to our "Koukouzelian" tradition, Athens 888 and the Copenhagen Sticherarion NkS 4960,4°.

Example 3 shows, beyond any doubt, that Strunk's observations on the *marginal* Oktoechos are also valid when we turn to the *central* part of the repertory. We could not know that in advance – but we have now reasons to believe that Koukouzeles made his imprint on the *entire* Oktoechos.

We can also, at least tentatively, find a place for the "newcomer" Athens 888. In all 5 Stichera, it has the "Koukouzelian" readings – either together with the five other members of Strunk's Groups 2 and 3, or joining the readings of Group 3.[11] Notice, however, that in No. 22 it sides with Strunk's Group 2. It is thus, without any doubt, to be classified as a third member of Group 3, together with the Ambrosianus and Sinai 1230.

As for the Copenhagen Sticherarion (NkS 4960,4°), the picture is more unclear. I notice, however, that it *never* sides with Group 2 – whereas it shares some readings with Group 3.[12]

The first group in Strunk's tentative classification[13] consisted of Sinai 1471 and Iviron 953. In Example 3, these two manuscripts normally follow the readings of Dalassenos ("D").[14] Strunk's Group 1 is thus closer to the old, non-Koukouze-

Example 3/1
Nos. 12, 13, 14a, 14c, 22 (slight deviations marked with parenthesis)

[**ἀλφαβητικά**: 12 Γυναῖκες θεοφόροι, 13 Ἰδοὺ πεπλήρωται.
    ἀναβαθμοί: 14a Ἐν τῷ θλίβεσθαί με, 14c Ἁγίῳ πνεύματι τιμὴ καὶ δόξα.
    ἀνατολικόν: 22 Ὀδυρόμεναι μετὰ σπουδῆς.]

12:

1a
α νε στη   ο κυ ρι ος
EF abc a   GF Ga FE DE
(D) 1471 953 17 71 1228 4960 + 386v 1493v Nv

1b
α νε στη   ο κυ ρι ος
a a G   cb c b aG
(139) (1230) 888 386 1493 N

2a
ο πα ρε χων   τω κο σμω   το με γα ε λε ος
C D EF D   EF a GF   EF G a EF D D
(D) 953 17

2b
ο πα ρε χων   τω κο σμω   το με γα ε λε ος
C D EF D   EF G G   G G a EF D D
71 1228 (4960) + 386v 1493v Nv

2c
ο πα ρε χων   τω κο σμω   το με γα ε λε ος
C D EF D   EF G G   G a ba cb a a
1471

2d
ο πα ρε χων   τω κο σμω   το με γα ε λε ος
E F ab a   G a GF   EF G a EF D D
139 1230 888 386 1493 N

lian tradition than his Groups 2 and 3. As we shall see in a moment, the picture does not change when we leave the Oktoechos and turn to the rest of the Sticherarion. Before doing so, however, it might be useful to recapitulate the main result of what we have done until now.

Starting from Strunk's observations on a connection between Koukouzeles' Heirmologion and the marginal repertory of the Oktoechos, we corroborated his observations and extended them to cover also the central Oktoechos repertory. As I said, we could not know in advance what would come out of this investigation – but we have now found reasons to believe that Koukouzeles made his imprint on the *entire* Oktoechos, not only on its marginal repertory. The inevitable question, of course, is now: What about the rest of the Sticherarion, the Menaia and the Triodion+Pentekostarion?

For the Menaion I have – at random – taken a Sticheron from the month of November (see EXAMPLE 4). Once more, we see the same grouping of the Koukouzelian manuscripts as before. Here, as in Example 3, Athens 888 is always connected with Ambrosianus 139 and Sinai 1230, i.e. with Group 3, the subgroup which in Strunk's eyes came closest to Koukouzeles' Heirmologion.

Also in this Example I have added a few more manuscripts to my material –

Example 3/2

```
13:
         ϙ̣..   ⁖     ᾿     ᾿
   ⎧ 1   και  πρε  σβευ  ε     D  1471  953  17  71  4960    + Nv
   ⎪     EF   ab   a    G
   ⎨
   ⎪     ⌐    ⁖    ᾽ᴧ   ᾿
   ⎩ 2   και  πρε  σβευ  ε     1228  * 139  1230  888  386  1493  N
         a    bc   a    G


14a:
   ⎧        ϖ̃ ᾽ᵛ
   ⎪ 1a   οδυνων         D
   ⎪       a GF
   ⎪
   ⎪        ᷄ ᷆᾽
   ⎪ 1b   οδυνων         1471?  953
   ⎨       a GF
   ⎪
   ⎪        ᷄̃ ᴧ
   ⎪ 1c   οδυνων         17 . 4960   *  139  1230  888
   ⎪        G E
   ⎪
   ⎪        ᷄̄⌐
   ⎩ 1d   οδυνων         71  1228  * 386  1493  N  + 17v
           GFE

   ⎧        ᷆᾽   ᾽̃   ϙ̣..
   ⎪ 2a   κυ   ρι   ε    D  1471  953
   ⎪      Ga   F    CD
   ⎪
   ⎪        ᷆᾽   ᾽ᵛ   ϙ̣..
   ⎨ 2b   κυ   ρι   ε    71  4960  *  139  1230?  888  386  1493  N + 17v
   ⎪      FG   F    CD
   ⎪
   ⎪        ᷆ᴗ   ᾽᷅   ᷄᾽
   ⎩ 2c   κυ   ρι   ε    17  1228  + (386v) (1493v)
          F    ED   CD

                  (14a continues next page!)
```

again based on previous experience over the years. You find now, also, Athens 883, Paris 262, and Ottobonianus 380.

Of these, the *Ottobonianus 380* clearly belongs to Strunk's subgroup 1 (Sinai 1471 and Vatopedi 953). In the Oktoechos, this group was closer to the old, non-Koukouzelian tradition than subgroups 2 and 3. The same is true in the present Sticheron from the Menaion for November.

Athens 883: Already Tillyard was aware of the close relationship between Athens 883 and the codex Neglectus, the manuscript "N". Example 4 shows clearly that 883 is a member of Strunk's Group 2.[15]

NB One detail about Athens 883: Its *date*: In the catalogue – and hence in literature until now – this Sticherarion is dated "*12th* century". Its evident connection with one of our "Koukouzelian" subgroups makes this early date absolutely impossible. It must be late 13th century, at the earliest, but probably 14th.! The mistake is understandable, however. For the text is written in an archaizing type of script, a *scrittura mimetica* – a term that I know from Giancarlo Prato.

Finally some words about the Paris manuscript *Ancien fonds grec 262*. When I first saw this manuscript – 30 years ago – I was struck by its peculiarities: The nota-

Example 3/3

```
        ˋˏ    ˏˏ   ˗
3a      σοι  κρα  ζω        D 1471 17 (71) 1228 4960  *  139 1230? 888
    D   FE   D    D

        ˎ˰    ˀ    ˗
3b      σοι  κρα  ζω        953  *  386 1493 N
    D   F    D    D

        ˏˏ    ˏˏ   ˗
3c      σοι  κρα  ζω        (386v) (1493v)  Nv?
    C   FE   D    D


14c:
        ˗     ˗    ˶    ˀ
1a      τη   τρι  α    δι   D 1471 953 (17) 71 1228
    E   F    ab   a

        ˗     ˗    ˶    ˀ
1b      τη   τρι  α    δι   386  1493 N
    E   F    ab   a

        ˗ı   ˗    ˶    ˀ
2       τη   τρι  α    δι   4960  *  139 1230 888
    a   a    bc   a


22:
        ˀˑˑ   ˶    ˏ    ˏˇ
1       δω   ρου  με   νος  D 1471 953 17 71  *  888 386 1493 N
    EF  ab   a         G

        ˗    ˶    ˏˀ   ˏˇˑ
2       δω   ρου  με   νος  1228  *  139 1230 + 17v    (not in 4960)
    a   bc   a         GF
```

tion looked 13th or 14th century to me. But the writing was unnatural and old-fashioned, and the scribe often used iota subscriptum or even adscriptum. Furthermore, some mistakes in the copying of the text showed clearly that the scribe must have followed the lay-out of his model as closely as humanly possible, page by page – producing, as it were, a diplomatic replica of his model. Special difficulties were caused by the repetitions of vowels for melismatically sung ornaments. Here neumes and text fit so badly together that we may infer that the neumatic ductus of the model differed greatly from what we actually find in the Paris manuscript. Add to this that Paris 262 contains a number of textual variants written in its margins, quite against normal practice in Sticheraria.

30 years ago I made a hypothesis about the model: It was written in Round Notation – hence the vowel repetitions for the melismata – but the oldfashioned way of text writing, so carefully imitated by the scribe, suggests that it must have been a very early Round Notation . My hypothesis, then, was that Paris 262 represented an attempt to save the tradition of a very old manuscript in Round Notation – a manuscript which maybe was considered to be of special importance. I did not ask, at the time, about the reason for this procedure. In short, I asked about the *quid*, but not about the *cui bono*.

It would be wonderful, of course, if I could now produce – as a white rabbit from a tophat – some indication that it was *Koukouzeles* who wanted – for his revision work – a copy of this "venerable Sticherarion of special importance". Of course, I can *not*! Paris 262 is defective and does not any longer contain the Protos section of its Oktoechos, so for the moment my bold and daring hypothesis rests *exclusively* on the variant distribution in line 7 of my Example 4, with manu-

Example 4
A Stricheron for the Anargyroi (November 1), transcribed from A 139 sup, 38v

1	Την	χα	ριν	των	ι	α	μα	των	2	εκ	θε	ου	ει	λη	φο	τες
	D	a	a	a	a	G	a	EF		G	a	bc	a	G	bc	a

3	αν	αρ	γυ	ρως	τα	πα	θη	4	των	ψυ	χων	και	των	σω	μα	των	η	μων
	D	D	EF	D	EF	a	G		G	a	bc	a	bc	a	EF	a	G	bG a

5	θερ	μως	θε	ρα	πευ	ε	τε	6	παγ	κοσ	μι	οι	αν	αρ	γυ	ροι
	a	bc	a	G	bc	a	G		a	GF	EF	G	a	EF	ED	D

7	ο	θεν	δι'	υ	μων	χρι	στος	τοις	πι	στοις
	D	a	a	Ga	a	EF	a bc	a	a	b

8	την	δε	δο	με	νην	ευ	ρω	στι	αν	χα	ρι	ζο	με	νος
	G	a	b	c	b	a	G	a	a	bG	a	GF	F	

9	φω	στη	ρας	α	πλα	νεις	υ	μας
	EF	a	a	a	b	c	G	a

	α	να	δει	κνυ	σι	τη	οι	κου	με	νη
	G	G	a	G	G	a	E	FE	D	D
							[G	a	FE	D]

10	αυ	τω	πρε	σβευ	σα	τε	11	σω	θη	ναι	τας	ψυ	χας	η	μων :—
	a	a	EF	a	G	G		a	GF	EF	G	a	EFE	D	D

4 καὶ τῶν σωμάτων	b a EF a G:	D (1471) 953 380 • 139 888 4960
	a GF EF a G:	71 1228 • 386 1493 N 883 1230 262

4 ἡμῶν + 5 θερμῶς	bG a + a bc:	1471 953 • 139 1230 888 4960 + Nv 262v
	aF G + a bc:	D 380 71 1228 • 386 262 + 1493v 883v
	aF G + G bc:	1493 N 883 + 386v

7 ὅθεν δι' ὑμῶν	D a a a a:	D 1471 953 380 71 1228 4960
	D a a Ga a:	139 1230 888 386 1493 N 883 262
	bc a a Ga a:	386v 1493v Nv 883v

8 εὐρωστίαν	a Ga a a:	(D) (1471) (953) 380 71 1228 • (139) 1230 888 (262) + 1493v Nv
	a EF a a:	386 1493 N 883 4960

9 ὑμᾶς	Petasthe on accented syllable:	D 1471 953 380 1228 • 139 1230 888 4960 262
	Apoderma on accented syllable:	386 1493 N 883
	Kratema on accented syllable:	1493v 883v

script 262 siding with all seven members of our two "Koukouzelian" subgroups. It is a hypothesis, however, which deserves to be followed up.

The last step in my tedious investigation of musical variants is again inspired by one of Oliver Strunk's observations. He pointed out that there was a stylistic tendency in the Koukouzelian readings to use a higher register than the older tradition. We have already met this feature a number of times:

(a) In the endings of the *marginal* Protos Stichera – [Examples 1 and 2] – the MSS of subgroups 2 and 3 preferred *high* endings (on a), in contrast to the *low* endings (on D) found in the other MSS.

(b) In the material which I produced

from the *central* Oktoechos repertory [Example 3], there are several cases where one or both Koukouzelian groups prefer a high bc a for the lower ab a of the older tradition – or high ab instead of low EF. We thus find in No. 12 the words ὁ παρέχων sung in low position (C D *EF* D) in the old groups (readings 2a, 2b, 2c), but in high position (E F *ab* a) in the six Koukouzelians which constitute subgroups 2 and 3. In the same example [Ex.3, Nos. 14c and 22] we find E F ab a in the older tradition, against a a *bc* a in subgroup 3.

A perusal of Tillyard's volume of Pentekostarion transcriptions confirms Strunk's notion about Koukouzeles' tendency to use a higher register than we find in the older tradition. Comparing Tillyard's data on all Protos Stichera of the Pentekostarion I found a number of cases where D had the low position, whereas a high position was preferred by the Koukouzelian manuscript N or another of the recent manuscripts used by Tillyard. Typical was the pair EF *ab* a versus a *bc* a – and a case of low ending (on D) *versus* high ending on a. But there were also a few cases which went the other way round – with an older form in high position and a low position in manuscripts of the Koukouzelian group.

The overall picture, however, is thus clear: There are indubitable traces of Koukouzeles *in the entire Sticherarion*, and these are most particularly to be seen in two groups of 14th century manuscripts:

1) Ambrosianus A 139 sup, Athens 888 and Sinai 1230;
2) Dionys. 386, Vatop. 1493, Athens 883, and the *codex Neglectus* (N).

So, it certainly looks as if there really was a Koukouzelian revision of the entire Sticherarion, parallel to that of the Heirmologion.

Equally clear, it seems, is the fact that nonKoukouzelian readings can be found even in the most "Koukouzelian" of these manuscripts – and, *vice versa*, that Koukouzelian readings may be found also in manuscripts which do not belong to these two groups. This, however, by no means invalidates my construction. We would have no reason, in fact, to expect a clear and closed manuscript tradition where there must have been thousands of Sticheraria – many of them provided with musical variants. We can be sure that most musical manuscripts were manufactured by professional scribes, many of them singers who had their own tradition and might be influenced by it at any moment of the copying process. Of course, also the presence of musical variants in the models to be copied may be reflected in the copies, in unpredictable ways. As we have seen, such variants are one of the characteristic traits of Group 2.

I have now presented my case – a reasoning on variant distribution that I hope have convinced you that an extended search in the many Sticheraria copied after the end of the 13th century may enable us to isolate a number of direct or indirect witnesses to a Koukouzelian revision of the Sticherarion.

From the seven manuscripts which I have dealt with here, we have already formed a good idea of what features we can expect from a "Koukouzelian" Sticherarion:

I am sure, for instance, that the Oktoechos Part of Koukouzeles' Sticherarion was cyclically arranged and contained also the Anastasima and the ordinary Dogmatika, one for each mode.

There must also have been a collection of Stichera Dogmatika and of Stavrotheotokia. It is as yet unsettled, which pieces these two collections contained.

Typical for most of the manuscripts of Groups 2 and 3 is their interest in *ascriptions*. Normally, each Sticheron will be provided with an indication of who wrote it (text? or melody? probably both!). The manuscripts, however, do not agree completely in their ascriptions. So, we can be sure that Koukouzeles' Sticherarion was provided with ascriptions, but we still do not know his choice in every case.

Similarly, the Koukouzelian Sticherarion must have been lavishly provided with musical variants. These interlinear variants seem to be predominantly found in manuscripts of Group 2, (Example 4). We still do not know exactly what tradition or traditions they represent.

Now, Strunk claimed that it was Group 3 (especially Sinai 1230) that came closest to the Koukouzelian habits which he – Strunk – had found in the Heirmologion. Now, if Group 3 represents the real Koukouzeles Sticherarion – what, then, shall we think about Group 2? I just mentioned its many musical variants. Is that also a Koukouzeles product – may be a kind of second edition? Or is it rather a local group, constituted on the basis of a Sticherarion of the Koukouzelian type? At present I cannot tell. I ask myself, however: Would it not have been really strange, if Koukouzeles felt compelled to stick ever after to his choices once he had completed a revised Sticherarion? Wouldn't we rather expect him to go over his product again and again – and during this constant process of revision to *re*introduce older melodic turns which he had originally dropped? Or, still assuming that both groups are Koukouzeles, we may turn the chronology upside down and place Group 2 chronologically earlier than Group 3. In this case, we can choose between two solutions, depending on where we place the Heirmologion revision in terms of relative chronology – before or after his first revision of the Sticherarion.

There is no need to go on with these speculations now. I am sure that you have got the message and can follow my need for a clarification of the relationship between our two groups.

An important aspect of our complex – in a way the most interesting of them all – is the influence of the Koukouzelian revision on other branches of the Sticherarion tradition. Ever since the late 13th or the early 14th cent. – the unknown date of Koukouzeles' work on the Sticherarion – any copyist of a Sticherarion might have wanted to include some – perhaps many – Koukouzelian features and turns into his product. As you see, the problem is interesting as well as enormously difficult to handle in an intelligent way.

After all these discussions about small and inconspicuous melodic variants, I am sure that you are sitting with a quite simple question on your lips: What about the music? I mean: The aim of our reconstructing the Koukouzelian version of the Sticherarion must ultimately be to understand its underlying principles. Now, when trying to "understand" the reasons behind his revision, I think that we ought to distinguish between two fields. One is the field of contents and repertory. This implies, for instance, the constitution of a full Oktoechos, including the Anastasima and the Ordinary Dogmatikon and Apostichon for each mode, and the arranging of the Oktoechos in eight cycles, one for each mode. Also, the inclusion of a collection of Stavrotheotokia, and – in all likelihood – also a remodelling of the series of Stichera Dogmatika.

Quite another field is the remodelling of melodies, the choice between the variants of tradition and the introduction of melodic turns and features hitherto more or less unknown. The latter question, of course, is simply to ask for – and if possible to define – a special Koukouzelian *idiom*. The former question deals, as it were, with his *aesthetic ideals*[16]. Are we able to reconstruct some components of his aesthetics? It is my firm belief that we shall some day be able to define the reason for his choice of reading in a tradition which was at the same time stable and unstable. Stable in outline and in many details which had been kept unchanged over centuries. But in many other details capriciously unstable and, in the eyes of Koukouzeles, obviously in need of some kind of "uniformification".

The reconstruction of Koukouzeles' Sticherarion is more within reach than it was a year ago when we published the facsimile-edition of the Ambrosianus. It must be much further advanced before we can even dream of answering some of the questions now raised.

Additional note: As mentioned below, note 1, Professor Stathis has drawn my attention to the manuscript Athens EBE 884. Its colophon (fol 390v) runs as follows:

+ Ἀθανάσιος τὴν μελουργὸν πυκτίδα
  Ταύτην ἐμαῖς χερσὶ γέγραφα κοσμίως
  Ἐξ ἀντιγράφου πάνυ διωρθωμένου
  Ὄντος κἀκείνου τοῦ πάλαι κουκουζέλη:+

+ Ἐξ ἀντιγράφου γέγραφα τὸ πυκτίον
  Ἀθανάσιος τοῦ κουκουζέλη τόδε:-
  Ἔτους ϛωμθ᾽

In both of the alternative colophons Athanasios claims that he has copied ἐξ ἀντιγράφου τοῦ κουκουζέλη. So much is clear. In the first colophon, this model is said to be πάνυ διωρθωμέ-νον. The implication of the last verse of this colophon is not clear to me. What exactly does τοῦ πάλαι κουκουζέλη mean? And what is implied by the word κἀκείνου? Anyhow, EBE 884 must represent Koukouzeles' revision of the Sticherarion, his διώρθωσις.

Before I left Athens, I had a chance to inspect the manuscript. I was immensely curious to find out to which of my two groups it belonged – or whether it did not fit into the picture at all. The latter case would mean, of course, that my method had been wrong. The result was quite clear: At the 25 variant places that I had used above, the readings of EBE 884 fitted 100% to the readings of the second of my groups (Dionysiou 386, Vatopedi 1493, Athens 883, and the so-called *codex Neglectus*. So, finally, we have a means to study Koukouzeles' revision directly, without having to rely on reconstructions and hypotheses.

I have not yet found time for a careful study of this new source. To get an idea of the connection between the two groups of Koukouzelian Stichera, I have compared the readings of EBE 884 and the Ambrosianus A 139 sup (facsimile:

MMB XI, 1992), but only for one melody (Τὰ τῆς ψυχῆς θηρεύματα, used on April 1). In Copenhagen we have collated almost one hundred versions of the standard Stichera for the month of April. We can therefore say with considerable certainty, that when the two Koukouzelian groups have the same reading, this is normally the reading of the majority of the tradition. When the two MSS *disagree*, it is mostly Athens 884 which has the old, traditional majority readings.

According to its colophon, the *Ambrosianus* was written in October 1341 (ϛων᾽), and thus slightly later than the Athens MS which is dated ϛωμθ᾽. It was written by two scribes: Leon Padiates wrote the text, and the Hieromonachos Athanasios wrote the lines of music (ὁ τόνος καὶ ἡ τοῦ μέλους κατάρτη-σις). As you see, the scribe of EBE 884 and the neumator of the *Ambrosianus* are homonyms. Is this the same Athanasios? Stathis was inclined to think so, I am more hesitant. The maximum distance between the two MSS is no more than one year: The Athens MS was written in 6849, the Ambrosianus in 6850. But in the older MS some neumes (e.g. the Kratema and the Hypsele) are written with forms which are a little more "modern" than those of the more recent one. This is why I hesitate to ascribe both products to the same Athanasios.

Bibliography

Amargianakis, G. 1977
An Analysis of Stichera in the Deuteros Modes, Cahiers de l'Institut du Moyen-âge Grec et Latin (CIMAGL) 22-23, Copenhagen.

Raasted, J. 1981
The interlinear variants in Byzantine musical manuscripts, Actes du congrès international des études byzantines, Athénes 1976, Vol. II Art et archéologie, Athens.

Raasted, J. 1992
Ed. together with Lidia Perria, Monumenta Musicae Byzantinae XI. Sticherarium Ambrosianum, Pars Principalis & Pars Suppletoria. Hauniae.

Strunk, O. 1977
Essays on music in the Byzantine world, ed. K. Levy, New York.

Notes

NOTE 1

In a discussion with Gregorios Stathis I learned – on the very evening before I was to read the present paper – about an Athens manuscript (EBE 884) which I must confess that I had overlooked, and which settles many of the questions raised in my communication. I have decided, however, to print my communication in the shape in which it was read. For details on Athens 884, see note at the end of this paper.

NOTE 2

Strunk 1977 199-201.

NOTE 3

Oliver Strunk, Melody construction in Byzantine chant, Actes du XIIe congrès international d'études byzantines (Belgrade 1963), 365-73; reprinted in Strunk 1977 191-201. Idem, P. Lorenzo Tardo and his Ottoeco nei MSS. melurgici. Some observations on the Stichera Dogmatika, originally published (in Italian) in the Bollettinmo della Badia Greca di Grottaferrata 21, 1967, 21-34), reprinted in Strunk 1977 255-267.

NOTE 4

Strunk 1977 197.

NOTE 5

Raasted 1992.

NOTE 6

Strunk 1977 196.

NOTE 7

Strunk 1977 197.

NOTE 8

The ending C2 begins like C1, but has the high ending – like the one called A5.

High and low endings might also be grouped after their treatment of the last three syllables:

To the high endings A1, A2, A3 correspond the low ending D.

To high A4 and A4a corresponds low B1

To high A5, A6, A7 (+ C2) we see the low parallels B2 and C1.

NOTE 9

I have not a microfilm copy of Ambrosianus gr. 733.

NOTE 10

The 139-group contains 4 or 5 stichera. Their endings are not used by the three MSS of the other group. – For No. 8 (the Dogmatikon Τὴν παγκόσμιον δόξαν), the c b a ending is used by the first group, the c a a by the second. – Dionysiou 386 has a predilection for the ending A7 – which ends with bc a. This ending is used in 7 out of 9 cases. For No. 8 he prefers the c a a ending (A4) – and only in No. 9 (the Apostichon Τῷ πάθει σου χριστέ) do we meet ending A1 – which is the favourite of Neglectus and Sinai 1493. But notice, that the same ending – A1 – is given as alternative reading in 386, no less than 4 times.

NOTE 11

No. 14a, readings 1c + 2b + 3a; No. 14c, reading 2.

NOTE 12

Nos. 14a and 14c.

NOTE 13

Example 1, subgroup 1.

NOTE 14

The only exception is to be found at the end of No. 14a, where 1471 (as usually) join with D, whereas 953 reads as subgroup 2.

NOTE 15

Like the other members of Group 2 it has many musical variants, written in red by the scribe. As I demonstrated at some length at the 15th Byzantine Congress (Athens, 1976), a number of MSS contain such first-hand variants, belonging to the product as originally planned, see Raasted 1981 999-1004. At the time I offered a number of possible explanations of this feature, without venturing any final answer. It looks as if time is now ready to resume these speculations which I started more than 15 years ago.

NOTE 16

One is his apparent predilection for changing the melodic field, from lower to higher. This may have been felt as a means to give more brilliance to the singing.

At times we find small changes which affect the musical accentuation of the text: Thus, in Example 4, the first of the Anabathmoi (No. 14a) ended in the older tradition – and in the three MSS of Group 3 - with a melody which corresponds to the accentuation κύριέ σοι κράζω. All four MSS of Group 2 have a melody which corresponds to κύ–ριε σοί κράζω. The opposite is the case in another of the Anabathmoi (No. 15a). The old tradition stresses ἵνα ὑμνω σε, in the entire Koukouzeles tradition we have, more correctly, ἵνα ὑμνῶ σε. I am sure that there is much more of that kind, once you begin to look for it!

Without taking my observations down, I have also noticed many cases where lineends are treated differently in the Koukouzelian and the non-Koukouzelian MSS. The main point is whether to rest at line ends or to connect with the following by means of some "leading-on" treatment of the last syllable of the line. This detail is perhaps most easily studied in Amargianakis' edition of the Deuteros Stichera in Sinai 1230 (see Armargianakis 1977), one of the Group 3 MSS, that has very many red musical variants – first-hand, of course – that indicate alternative ways of connecting two lines.

The Interpretation of the Old Sticherarion

George Amargianakis

NOTE 1
From the two-and-a-half-year period during which I lived and worked in Copenhagen I always preserve the very best of memories; on the occasion of the present Symposium I grasp the opportunity of once more expressing my gratitude to my supervisor professor Dr. Raasted, for all that I owe him, and also to the University of Copenhagen for their help in bringing a difficult task to a happy end.

I

Twenty years have already passed since I went to Copenhagen for doctoral studies in Byzantine music. With professor Jørgen Raasted as supervisor, I wrote my doctoral dissertation, titled "An Analysis of Stichera in the Deuteros Modes", subtitled "The Stichera Idiomela for the Month of September in the Modes Deuteros, Plagal Deuteros and Nenano, Transcribed from the Manuscript Sinai 1230 (A.D. 1365)", published in the *Cahiers de l'Institut du Moyen-âge Grec et Latin*, University of Copenhagen 1977, vols. 22-23[1].

As this paper is directly linked to my dissertation, I will make a brief reference to the method then followed, giving you some very general information which, I believe, will facilitate the understanding of what lies ahead.

Many researchers, older and contemporary, had noted that Byzantine melodies consist of small musical phrases (formulae), which, combined in various ways, form unities, half-units and units, corresponding to those of the poetic text they cover.

But exactly what is a formula? It is a brief musical phrase which, depending on its kind, shows up in a great or limited number of incidences in the melodies of a mode or a group of related modes. The same formula, in accordance with the number and accent pattern of the syllables of the poetic text it covers, or even the way it is connected to the preceding or following formula, may appear as a variation, without altering its basic melodic nucleus. Every formula, according to its kind (beginning, medial, cadential), lies at a specifically defined position in the text.

From the combination of two or more formulae, longer musical phrases are derived and, from these, whole melodies. One is then to infer that the composition of Byzantine melodies did not take place note-to-note, but rather formula-to-formula. There is no doubt that this original and particular fashion of composing, inherited by us in our days through an uninterrupted oral and written tradition, was based on strict musical rules which, however, were never written down. Retrieval of those unwritten rules, as shown in my research, is of course difficult but in no way unattainable. Fortunately, a large number of melodies of the kind has survived, and it is by studying them that the matter can be resolved.

My work, as a first step in that direction, could not possibly aim at an overall study of the phenomenon through time, due to reasonable limitations. It was confined within the period between 1100 and 1450, during which the sophisticated notational system known as 'Round Notation' or 'Middle Byzantine Notation' was in use, and it is based on the musicological analysis of a limited number of sticheraric melodies of the month of September, in the modes Deuteros, Plagal Deuteros and *Nenano*, all classified in later times in the chromatic modes group. The material of this research (56 melodies in all) was transcribed from a manuscript typical of the mentioned period, Sinai 1230 (Trapezunt A.D. 1365), while a provisional use was made of other manuscripts, earlier and later. The basic objective of my research was understanding the principles underlying the composition of Byzantine sticheraric melodies of the chromatic genus during the period 1100-1450.

The study was split in two parts, published in volumes 22 and 23 of Cahiers de l'Institut du Moyen-âge Grec et Latin" respectively. The First Part deals with the analytical presentation of the subject, while the Second comprises the melodies analysed and the special tables set up on the basis of the evidence collected.

To be more specific, from the 111 melodies of the month of September, only the ones in a chromatic genus were transcribed, 56 in all. Their enumeration corresponds to the serial number of the whole set of the September melodies, meaning that the missing numbers belong to melodies of other modes. Each melody was divided up into musical lines, also vertically numbered; thus, e.g., reference 3,10 signifies: melody No. 3, line 10. Reading the neumes and transcribing the melody have been carried out in an alphabetical system (A, B, C, D, E, F, G, a, b, c, d, ...) = (La, Si, Do, Re, Mi, Fa, Sol, la, si, do, re, ...).

By careful and meticulous analysis of the 56 melodies, 72 formulae were isolated and numbered. Variations of one and the same formula, due to the number and accent pattern of syllables, were noted with capital letters of the Greek alphabet, while small letters signify alterations of a formula for the sake of connection with adjacent ones. Thus e.g. the symbol 2A γ is to mean: formula number 2, variation A, case γ. The symbol for each formula was written above the section of the melody that it corresponds to. Table 1 renders melody No. 17 with the relevant symbols above the formulae.

Following that, special tables were set up for each of the 72 formulae, with precise references to the melodies (see Table 2 for melody 9 with the specific references). Finally, there were tables with the sole arithmetical symbols of the formulae, where signatures, musical and grammatical punctuation, cadential types, unities, half-units and units are also noted. These tables, besides giving an overall view of each melody, also assist in the examination of more specialised topics. Table 3 shows melodies 3 to 16 solely accompanied by their arithmetical symbols.

There followed an analytical description: a) of the formulae, which were divided into "beginning", "medial" and "cadential" ones; b) of cadences, divided into "real" and "connective" ones, with partial subdivisions according to their position at the end of unities, half-units or units; c) of signatures, divided into "beginning" and "medial" ones; d) of thematismos, divided into «ἔσω», «ἔξω» and «θες καὶ ἀπόθες»; e) of the musical punctuation in association with the grammatical punctuation; f) the ambitus; and g) the musical scales.

I shall not go into details here due to the limit of space available. However, I would like to summarize the results of this whole study as follows:

1. It asserts the remark that the composition of Byzantine sticheraric melodies is based on the employment of musical phrases (formulae) specific to each mode or group of modes; these formulae, connected to one another in various fashions, form unities, half-units and units corresponding to those of the poetic text.

2. From the description of the 72 formulae belonging to chromatic modes, as well as the examination of signatures, musical and grammatical punctuation and cadences, it is inferred that the melodist, in his effort to set the hymns to melody, would not act mechanically; he would follow upon the poetic text syllable by syllable and especially with regard to its 'stichurgy', its syntactical and metrical structure and he would select and combine such formulae as to literally interpret the poetic text and assist in the most effective illumination of the text's content and signification.

3. The existence of the chromatic genus also in the middle-Byzantine period is proved beyond reasonable doubt by unshakable evidence.
4. New terminology and abbreviating symbols are established for annotating idioms of the melos, and a tested method of melodic analysis is suggested, allowing the drawing of safe conclusions in a short time.
5. The musical material, as analysed, systematised and published in meticulously detailed tables, offers researchers a secure and multiply useful basis for further research in Byzantine music.

II

The entire venture has been, for me at least, exciting, and the conclusions very valuable. And yet I had the feeling that this was nothing but the first step, opening new roads for further research. This is why I never stopped delving into the matter and trying to go in depth in understanding the mechanisms of Byzantine melodic composition as much as possible. It was always my fervent desire to find even just one melody of the ones I had analysed, transcribed in the Chrysanthine period, so that I could discover how the formulae I described function within the new method.

In 1987, as a member of the Institute of Mediterranean Studies, seated in Rethymnon, Crete, in the frame of a wider research program on Greek music (ancient, Byzantine and folk music), I undertook the microphotography of the Byzantine Music Manuscripts of the Greek National Library (EBE). One of the first manuscripts photographed was MS No. 707 of the Metochion Panagiou Taphou (ΜΠΤ), containing the melodies of the Old Sticherarion transcribed by Chourmouzios Chartophylax. My joy was beyond words; at last I had found what I had been hoping for.

At once I started transcribing the melodies with the exact method I had employed in my dissertation, while simultaneously trying to locate and identify the various formulae and their interpretations. From the very first moment it was clear that there was an almost absolute identity as to the formulae; in other words, Chourmouzios had transcribed the known Old Sticherarion in precision.

Table 4 displays melody No. 50 from MS 1230 Sinai and Table 5 shows the transcription of the same melody from MS EBE 707 ΜΠΤ. A mere look at the two melodies makes it clear that the former constitutes a stenographic rendition of the latter.

When I went into a more detailed study, the first difficulties started cropping up. The first and most serious of them has to do with the tonal basis of the modes. In the Old Sticherarion, regardless of intervals for the time being, all three modes exhibit the same scale, with a basic pentachord E-b: dominant notes on E, G, b, a; E is the tonal basis.

.....C	D	E	F	G	a	b	c	d.....
.....Do	Re	Mi	Fa	Sol	la	si	do	re....
.....Νη	Πα	Βου	Γα	Δι	κε	ζω	νη	πα...

In the Chourmouzios transcriptions, the melodies of the Deuteros mode are transported a third lower, i.e. to C,

Thus the serious matter is in which of the three scales the melodies ought to be read; this becomes more serious if we are to take into account that all formulae, at

25

.....C	D♭	E	F	G	a♭	b	c	d.....
.....Do	Re♭	Mi	Fa	Sol	la♭	si	do	re....
.....Νη	Πα♭	Βου	Γα	Δι	κε♭	ζω	νη	πα....

while those of Plagal Deuteros and Nenano to D,

....C	D	E♭	F♯	G	a	b♭	c♯	d
.....Do	Re	Mi♭	Fa♯	Sol	la	si♭	do♯	re
.....Νη	Πα	Βου♭Γα♯	Δι	κε	ζω♭	νη♯	πα

least as would appear at first sight, are common to all three modes. A compromising solution would be to transport all melodies to the scale of Deuteros in view of the fact that, when the Deuteros mode, even in today's practice, turns Plagal, it uses C (=Do=Νη) as tonic. But in this case, which would appear to be the most practical, all older stenographic formulae ought to be transported a third lower as well. As this matter requires further research and exchange of views with other specialists, I left it aside and I started studying the analysis of the signs *per se*.

However, also another serious problem arose. Each analysed formula consists of partial segments, i.e. shorter sub-formulae, which we shall subsequently call 'elements'. For example the analysis of formula 1Aα, in case 84,9, is as follows:

If we take into account that the above formula, consisting of 7 elements with partial variations, appears 178 times, it

Example 1
Oktoechos, Protos, endings in "marginal" repertory: Distribution

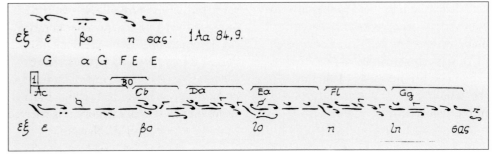

becomes evident that for each formula, and especially the most usual ones, a huge amount of work is in call. I would not be exaggerating if I were to say that each one of these formulae requires an amount of work equivalent to that of my entire doctoral dissertation. This can become more manifest by observing Table 6 of formula 1, where one can see the analysis of 7 elements, notated by Latin capitals: A, B, C, D, E, F, G, ..., as well as their variations, notated by small Latin letters: a, b, c, d, ...

Despite these difficulties, the work was continued and completed for nearly all formulae in this fashion:

In the initial phase, for each formula there was carried out a process of spotting and writing down of all cases in the order in which they appear in the tables of my dissertation (see Table 7 for formula 8 as is in my dissertation and Table 8 with the corresponding analyses).

Thereupon the partial elements of each formula were traced and notated, as already mentioned, in Latin capitals, with their variations under small Latin letters. The Latin alphabet was used in order to avoid confusion between the symbols of stenographic types and those of analysed formulae. But even at this stage a practical problem came up, i.e. whether the '-interpreted' formulae should be classified according to their order of appearance in the tables of the dissertation or whether similar cases should be set apart and arranged in groups. The former classification helps one observe the cases in succession and locate them easily; the latter has the advantage of a bird's-eye-view of the cases, but it is harder to spot each individual case. It is my feeling that the latter classification is preferable, under the condition that a way of facilitating the locating of cases is found. In Table 9 one can observe the partial elements of formula 8, while Tables 10a–10f show all cases in their order of appearance in the table of the dissertation, fully analysed. Some cases needing further research are missing from this table, because it seems that the MS transcribed by Chourmouzios has a different formula. Table 11 exhibits formula No. 3 in its original form and the partial elements of the analysis, while Tables 12a–12b show all the cases of the same formula, grouped into categories.

For more specific observations, two extra tables were set up for each formula. The first notes the partial elements of each formula with their symbols, accompanied by the frequency of their incidence. Thus one can have access to the basic elements of each formula and its variations (see Table 13). The second table exhibits anew the symbols of elements in pairs, as for example Aa-Ba, Ba-Ca, Ca-Da etc., as to facilitate the observation of the most basic combinations (see Table 14).

It is in my purposes to add one last table which, based on the preceding ones, will list the most numerous and most important forms of each formula. This last table will constitute a valuable help for a *grosso modo* interpretation of an old melody.

Up to this point the research has proceeded satisfactorily as regards its first part, i.e. the transcription of melodies, the identification of formulae and the designing of the various tables with their references. After this painstaking procedure there will follow a detailed study, whence, as it is expected, more and safer data will arise for the understanding of a formula as such in its stenographic form, but also of the global interpreting mechanism. I did notice, for example, that some formulae end with certain additional signs, used as a connecting bridge with the subsequent formula. In the course of my dissertation I sometimes took these signs as part of the formula, while in other cases as separate formulae. A close examination of the interpretations reveals that both of these approaches are valid, except that one ought to define precisely when the one and when the other is true. This means that in several cases the tables of my dissertation call for revision. A typical example is to be found in Table 10, where, whenever the formula ends on a (=la) rather than on G (=sol), there follows the characteristic formula Nenano, also familiar from more recent sources. In the perspective of its inclusion in a special category, it is referred to in the table simply as 'Nenano'.

So far, my research has led me to form a first impression, and I shall mention this with much reservation, as more specialised research in formulae of other modes is needed as well; each formula is not a succession of signs individually interpretable, but a *corpus* of signs that can appear in this or that form, purely for reasons of correctness of musical spelling. This is manifest in the following example, where a formula with differing signs is interpreted in the same way.

Example 2a and 2b

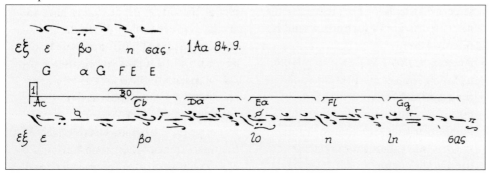

It was also observed that a formula with an identical arrangement of signs can sometimes be interpreted in a slightly divergent way, as it is clear from the following example, where, in the second case, we have a more extended interpretation, due to the repetition of certain syllables.

Example 3a

I have tried, within the limited space available, as concisely as possible to present the method I employed for my study of the interpretations. Yet I welcome any suggestion for the improvement of the method with great interest.

Finally, I would like to mention some general conclusions that are derived from the course of my work so far.

1. The stenographic character of the old notation is ascertained.
2. The examination of the whole interpreting mechanism also assures that

the modes concerned were indeed chromatic.

3. The comparative study carried out reveals that the splitting up of melodies into formulae, that took form in my dissertation, reflects the truth; however, many cases in need of revision were spotted.
4. In many cases discrepancies were found between the 1230 Sinai MS and the transcription. This means that Chourmouzios transcribed from a different MS; I have been trying to find

Example 3b

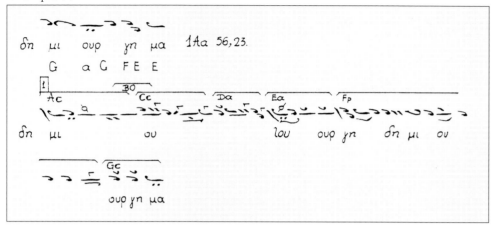

which MS that was. The Psachos library contains a MS of the Old Sticherarion in which it is stated that it is the MS used by Gregorios Protopsaltes for his transcriptions. It could conceivably be the same one; unfortunately though I have not had access to it yet.

5. It is evident from the study of the tables that for each formula there are various possible interpretations. This cannot be stressed enough, because a selective assembly of evidence for the interpretation of a formula would be plainly wrong.

6. All that has been said in this presentation concerns exclusively melodies of the Old Sticherarion and more specifically melodies in the chromatic genus. If we wish to achieve a full view of the global interpretation of the Old Sticherarion, we must have many other studies like my dissertation devoted to melodies of the other modes. I firmly believe that this same method, which I am advocating here, can also be successfully applied to the other kinds of Byzantine *melos*; but one has to wait to see this in practice.

I would like to conclude with a *simile*, touching upon an ancient myth from my island of origin, Crete. It is the legend of Theseus who, with the assistance of Ariadne, killed the Minotaur. Thus, just like the Minotaur, I do imagine the stenography of Byzantine music. Many have so far tried to get to the Minotaur, but without success. The Byzantine Minotaur lives on and torments us because, as you saw by what you heard, he is huge and monstrously strong. The method I presented yields, I think, Ariadne's thread for bringing the Minotaur within reach. But the final confrontation with him will require a coordinated, systematic and collective effort.

Table 1

#	Labels	Greek text	Pitches
1	8ΘB · 11ΓB · 15BB · 8Za	Ο τε τω πα θει σου κυ ρι ε	b b ba Gab bc α b Gα α
2	7Aa · 16Θa · 1Eη · 10BB	την αι κου με νην ε στε ρε ω σας·	α α bc GF EF G bG αG FE EFD
3	11Γa · 15Δa · 8Γε	το τε και οι α σθε νουν τες	Gαb b bc b α bα Gαb α
4	7AB · 16Iε · 1Ea	πε ρι ε ζω σαν το δυ να μιν·	α α bc GE G bG αG FE E
5	52EB · 16Λa · 16Δε · 4EB	γυ ναι κες πη φρι σαν το	α αG EF G G F EFGFG
6	10Δa · 2HB	κα τα του πι κρου τυ ραν νου·	EF D G cα b α G G
7	9AB · 34Aγ	και την πι ταν της μη τρος	G α bc b α G α
8	7Aa · 16Ξ B · 6Γγ	α να κα λι σα με ναι	α bc G E F E D
9	8Ha · 9Aa · 7AB · 16Iε · 1Ea	πα λιν ευ τη τρυ φη του πα ρα δει σου γε γο να σιν·	α bα G G G α bc b α bc GE G bG αGFE E
10	45a · 13EΔ · 34ΓΔ · 13EΔ · 34Γγ	εις δο ξαν σου ται γευ τη θεν τος εκ γυ ναι κος·	b cde d d c bα G α d d c bα Gα b
11	12ΓΔ · 16ΘB · 1Γa	και ομ σαν τος το γε νος των αν θρω πων:-	G b Gα α GF EFG α GF E E

Table 2

A	α	και G	υ a	πο bc	στα b	σις a	Δ	α	ων bc	κοι b	νω νους a
	β					a a a		β	βc	b	a a a
	γ			bc	b	a a a		γ	G bc	b	a a a
	δ	G	a	bc	bG	a		δ	bc	b	a a a
								ε	bc	b G	a
B	α	το G	αι bc	μα b	εξ εχεας		E	α	και G	αι b	ο δοι a
	β				a a a			β			a
	γ		bc	b	a a a			γ			a a
	δ	a	bc	b	a			δ			a a
								ε			a a a
								ζ			a
Γ	α	θε G	ο a	το b	χου a		Z	α	λει ψα Ga	νων b c	σου a
	β				a a			β	Ga	b	a a
	γ				a a			γ	Ga	b	a a
	δ				a a a			δ	Ga	b	a
	ε				a a a			ε	Ga	b	a a
	ζ				a a a			ζ	Ga	b	a a
	η				a a a			η	Ga	b	a a
	θ			bcb	a a a						
	ι	G	a	b c b	b a						

31

Table 2 (continued)

A´α´ 3,5.3,7.3,14.4,4.12,10.13,9.14,9.16,2.17,9.23,9.29,16.33,13.
36,6.37,10.37,13/14.44,8.49,4.56,12.56,16.68,8.68,17.81,9.81,16.
81,17.88,22.90,6.91,4.91,19.91,21.92,5.104,3.110,3.
  β´ 17,7.22,10.24,3.65,8.104,2.110,7.
  γ´ 4,9.11,10.16,6.68,12.78,15.97,3.103,11.
  δ´ 14,5.27,9.54,3.

B´α´ 21,6.23,6.24,5.28,4.29,6.54,8.54,21.54,26.91,3.91,20.92,8.97,7.
110,10.
  β´ 55,3.55,6.
  γ´ 28,8.66,11.92,7.
  δ´ 27,3.

Γ´α´ 4,10.9,4.11,2.21,12.21,15.24,13.29,4.29,7.51,9.54,16.54,27.56,8.
79,5.81,1.84,12.84,22.90,3.90,10.95,13.97,15.102,26.106,16.
  β´ 104,5.
  γ´ 90,12.95,15.
  δ´ 24,20.33,7.33,8.79,13.102,20.
  ε´ 3,10.18,3.18,9.22,6.29,12.29,17.38,5.44,10.
  ζ´ 50,6.81,5.84,26.
  η´ 11,13.28,3.55,13.55,14.57,7.66,8.72,7.78,9.88,18.95,11.
  θ´ 34,5.
  ι´ 102,2.

Δ´α´ 18,12.
  β´ 95,6.
  γ´ 48,7.56,22.68,15.84,16.91,8.103,16.
  δ´ 65,3.
  ε´ 14,11.91,14.97,11.

E´α´ 3,3.13,2.13,5.22,9.34,14.36,2.54,2.54,25.   79,7.79,15.84,5.
91,15.92,3.106,8.
  β´ 110,9.
  γ´ 102,12.
  δ´ 18,8.34,2.37,12.51,4.66,5.67,4.69,6.69,8.
  ε´ 35,17.67,2.88,3.
  ζ´ 23,3.54,22.

Z´α´ 13,1.104,1.
  β´ 4,3.56,4.
  γ´ 33,16.35,9.51,5.56,7.72,2.84,15.95,2.95,12.
  δ´ 56,4.57,7.66,8.104,5.
  ε´ 57,5.
  ζ´ 54,10.83,5.103,12.
  η´ 14,1.24,15.38,2.

Table 3

3

1 ÿ	12Λα-11Bδ	.ClC b ,
2	14Λγ-8Eβ	.CB G ,
3 ÿ	9Eα-7Λα-16θα-1Eβ-4Eα	.ClΛ EG·
4	10Δα-2θβ-33Λ	.CB G ,
5 ÿ	9Λα-7Λβ-16Iα-1Eε	.ClΛ Eᶠ ,
6	-10Λα-11Λα	CC b
	15Bβ-8Bβ	.CB G ·
7 ÿ	9Λα-8Γζ-	ClC Gᵃ
8	-7Bα-16θα-1Eη-10Bβ-	.ClΛ ED,
9 ÿ	-11Bα-15Bδ-8Bγ	.CB G ,
10 ÿ	9Γε-8Γε	ClC Gᵃ,
11	3Λ-1Λβ-10Γβ-	.ClΛ E ·
12	-12Γδ-	ClC Gᵃ
	-14θ-13Λγ	.ClB b
13	34Λα-11Bζ-15Λβ-2Λβ	.CB G .
14 ÿ	9Λα-8Γζ	.ClC Gᵃ·
15	7Λα-16Kα-1Eα	:-CA E .

9

1 ÿ	16Δβ-27Λα	.CC D
2	17Λι-7Λα-16IIγ-1Δα	.CA E ,
3 ÿ	16Λβ-17Zα-17Γα-8Bβ	.CB G
4	9Γα-7Γ-16Mβ	.CA E ,
5 ÿ	16IIβ-17Zα-17Γγ-18Λα	.CB G ,
6 ÿ	52B-21-16IIα-	
7	17IIγ-6Λγ	.CB D ,
8 ÿ	17Λε-10Zγ-17Eδ	ClC Ga ,
9	7Λα-16Kα-1Eα	:-CA E .

4

1 ÿ	11E-15Δγ-29Λγ	.CB b ,
2 ÿ	15Λγ-13Eβ-30Bα	.ClB bᵃ,
3	9Zβ-12Eβ	.CC G
4	9Λα-7Λβ-16Iα	(.)
5	1Eα	.CA E ,
6	26Λ-17Δα-7Γ-16Ξα-4Eγ	.ClB Eᴳ
7	10Λα-12Γα	
8	2IIα	.CB G ,
9 ÿ	9Λγ-7Λα-16Zε	.CC Eᵃ,
10	20-9Γα	CC a ,
11	7Λβ-16Iα	
12	1Eα	:-CA F .

11

1 ÿ	8θα-11Bδ-30Λ	.ClC bᵃ
2	9Γα-7Λα-16Zα-17θα	,CC a ,
3	7Λα-16θα-1Zβ	.CA E ,
4 δ	72-14Zβ-13Eγ	.ClB b
5	34Λα-11Bζ-15Bγ-8Bγ	.CB G ,
6 ÿ	14Λ-6Γγ	.CC D
7	17Bα-1Λα	.CA E ,
8 ÿ	16Δα(16Δγ)-10Λα-11Bα	CC b
9	13Bβ-2Λβ	.CB G ·
10 ÿ	9Λγ-7Γ-16Ξα-4Eγ	.ClB Eᴳ
11	10Λα-12B-4Γβ	.CB b ,
12 ÿ	13Bβ-2Λβ	.CB G
13 ÿ	9Γη-53Λγ-	,
14	3B-1Λα	:-CA E .

Table 3 (continued)

12

1 ÿ	12Γα-15Βε	CC	α
2	22Λ-15Βε	CC	α ,
3	16θβ-1ΛΒ	. CA	E ,
4 ĥÿ	17ΙΙβ-2Ιβ	ClC	Gα
5	3Λ-1Λα	. CA	E ·
6 ĥÿ	10ΕΒ-17Λδ-1Λη-10Βδ-	ClC	ED
7	2Εα	. CB	G ,
8 ÿ	3Γ-19ΚΒ-1ΕΒ	. CA	E ,
9 ĥÿ	17Λα-33Λ-2Λα	. CB	G ,
10	9Λα-36α-19-4Βδ	. ClC	α ·
11	8θγ-12Εδ	, ClC	G¹
12	7Λα-16θα-1Εα	:-CA	E .

14

1 ÿ	8θα-12Εζ-9Ζη	CC	α ,
2	36α-52Εδ-16Λα-1Γα	. CA	E ,
3	7Βδ-10Ζβ-11Γα	CC	b ,
4	23-15Βη-2Λα	. CB	G ·
5 ÿ	9Λδ-7Βα-16Ζα-6Γβ-17Λη	CC	α
6	7Γ-16Με	. CA	E ·
7	15Βε-2β-10Ζβ-4Λα	. CB	b ,
8 ĥÿ	26Β-17Γγ-18ΛΒ	. CB	G ,
9 ÿ	9Λα-8Βα-11ΓΒ	CC	b
10	15Βγ-8Βγ	. CB	G ·
11 ÿ	9Λε	CC	α
12	7Λα-16θα-1Ζα	:-CA	E .

13

1 ÿ	34Βγ-9Ζα-8Λα	. CB	G ,
2 ÿ	9Εα-8Γζ	, ClC	Gα ,
3	3Λ-1Λα	. CA	E ·
4 ĥÿ	10Εα-12Λα-30ΒΒ	ClC	bα
5	9Εα-8Γζ	, ClC	Gα ,
6	3Λ-1ΛΒ	. CA	E .
7 δ	13Εα-13Βα	CC	b
8	23-15ΒΒ-8Βγ	. CB	G ,
9 ÿ	9Λα-36α-19-4Βδ	. ClC	α ,
10	8θγ-12Εδ	ClC	Gα
11	7Λα-16θα-1Εα	:-CA	E .

16

1 ĥÿ	7Λγ-16Ξζ-10ΒΒ-2Βα	. CB	G
2 ÿ	9Λα-8Βα-24Βα	ClC	Gα ,
3	16θΒ-1Λδ-	. CIA	EF ·
4	-10Λα-4ΛΒ	. CB	b
5	13Εα-13Γ-2Λα	. CB	G ,
6 ÿ	9Λγ-3Ε-16Ιβ-1ΕΒ	· CA	E ,
7 ĥÿ	5Λα	CC	D ,
8	17Λα-18ΒΒ	. CB	G
9 ÿ	12Γγ	ClC	Gα
10	-7Βα-16Κα-1Εα	:-CA	E .

34

Table 4

M.M.B. Τι. I, Sept. No. 50
Sinai 1230, 13c.

ἀνατολίου

1. λ̣ π̈ ÿ — 25B — 27Aβ
Την μνη μην των εχ και νι ων
E FG F G E G α D

2. — 6Aα — 17Bα — 1Aζ — 10Bβ
ε πι τε λουν τες κυ ρι ε·
E FE D EF G α G FE EFD

3. — 4Bα
6ε·
G α c b α

4. — 28 — 16Bα
τον του α γι α σμου δο τη ρα
α α α α α α FG GF E

5. — 6Γα — 17Aα — 18Aα
δο ξα ζον τες δε ο με θα·
E F E D EF α G G

6. ÿ — 9ΓΖ — 34Bβ
α γι α εθη ναι η μων
G G α b α Gα α

7. — 53Aθ — 2Δα
τα αι εθη τη ρι α των ψυ χων·
G G G α cα b α G G

8. ÿ — 7Γ — 16Δβ — 6Γα
τη πρε σβει α των εν δο ξων α θλο φο ρων
G α bc G E E G F E E F E

9. — 17Aη — 1Hα
α γα θε παν το ων να με:—
D EF α α bG α G FE E

Table 5

E.B.E. 707, 102r

Ηχος πλ πα

1 Τη πν μνη μη Ιη πν των ε εχαι νι ιι ων ς

2 ε πι τε λου ουν τε ες κυ ω

ρι κυ ρι ε

3 σε ς με με

4 τον του α γι α εμου δο τη ρα

5 δο ξα ζο δο ξα ζο ον τες σε ο

με δε ο με θα ς

6 α γι α εθη ναι η μω ωγ δο

7 τα αι εθη τη ρι α τω ων ψυ χω ων

8 τη πρε σβει α ια των ε εν δο

ξων α θλο φο ρω ων

9 α γα θε ιε παν το δυ

ω να παν το δυ να με

Table 6

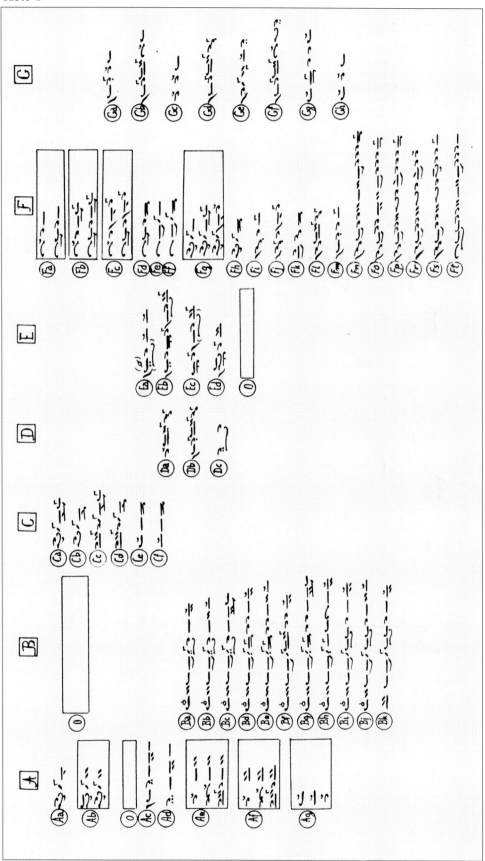

Table 7
Formula No. 8

Α α		ϑη	χη
	a	ba	G
β			G

Left table:

Α α	a	ϑη ba	χη G / G	
β				
Β α	μα a	χα ba	ρι G	ου
β				G
γ				G
Γ α	ηγλα a	ϊ ba	σμε Ga	νης a
β				a
γ				a
δ			Ga	a a
ε			Gab	a
ζ				a
Δ α	a	εν ba	γυ G / G	ναιξυ
β		aba	G	
γ		aba	G	G

Right table:

Ε α		a	ε b	χων a	προς G
β					G
γ		a	b	a	G
Ζ α		a	χυ b	ρι Ga	ε a
β		a	b	G	
γ		a	b	G	
δ				Ga	a
ε				G	a
ζ		Ga	b	G	
Η α			πα aba	λυ G	
β	τυ G	χου a	σα aba	G	
θ α		εχ b	ρι b	ζης a	α γαϑης G
β	ο	τε b	τψ b a	πα G	ϑει
γ		μεϑ b	ων b	ι G	χε τευε

Table 8

	Greek syllables	
Aα 13,1	σου θη ζη κη	β
104,1	πα αρ θε ζε νε	β
Aβ 29,7	της α ειδιου	
29,12	εν α σφαλη	
91,4	του ε πικρου	
14,9	του μα κα ρι ου	
16,2	των λει ψα νων	
54,2	ευ λο με νου	
81,16	ταις ψυ χαις	

Table 9
Formula No. 8

Table 10a
Formula No. 8

#			Λa	Bf	O	Da	Eb			
1	Λα	13,1.							β·ϛ	
			σου	θή		Iη	χη			K
			Λb	Bg	O	Da	Eb			
2	Λα	104,1.							β·ϛ	
			παρ	θέ		Iε	νε			K
			O	Bd	Ch	O	O			
3	Λβ	29,7.								
			—	της	α·			ειδίον		A
			O	Bd	Ci	O	O			
4	Λβ	29,12.								
			—	εν	α·			σφαλή		A
			O	Bd	Ch	O	O			
5	Λβ	91,4.								
			—	του	ε·			πικρου		A
			Λc	Ba	Ci	O	O			
6	Βα	14,9.								
		του	μά	χα	ρι·			ου		E
			Λf	Ba	Ci	O	O			
7	Βα	16,2.								
			των	λει	ψά·			νων		E
			Λf	Ba	Ci	O	O			
8	Βα	54,2.								
		ευ-	λο	γη	μέ·			νον		E
			Λf	Ba	Ch	O	O			
9	Βα	81,16.								
			ταις	ψυ	χαις			ημων		E
			Λd	Ba	Ci	O	O			
10	Βα	84,16.								
			τους	φιλ	τά·			τους		E
			Λd	Ba	Ci	O	O			
11	Βα	91,3.								
			χατ	ε	προ			νησας		E
			Λd	Ba	Ci	O	O			
12	Βα	91,19.								
			ι	χέ	τευ·			ουσα		E
			Λd	Ba	Ch	O	O			
13	Βα	97,7.								
			ω	ραι	ω·			σασα		E
			Λe	Ba	Ca	Da	Eb			
14	Ββ	3,6.							β·ϛ	
		χαι	συν	εϱ	γει	Iει	α			K
			Λg	Bb	Cb	Da	Ea			
15	Ββ	9,3.							Γ·ϛ	
		χαι	α	ο	ρά·	Iα	των			K
			Λe	Ba	Ca	Da	Eb			
16	Ββ	21,14.							Γ·ϛ	
		αεισέ-	βα	στον	μνή	Iη	μην			K
			Λe	Ba	Ca	Da	Eb			
17	Ββ	22,8.							Γ·ϛ	
		ι-	ε	ϱο	μά·	Iα-ϱ	τυς			K
			Λk	Bh	Cc	Da	Ea			
18	Ββ	24,2.							β·ϛ	
		αγι-	ων	ει	σέ	Iε	διϛ			K

41

Table 10b
Formula No. 8 (continued)

			Ah	Bb	Cb	Da	Eb		
19	Bβ	33.12.	ζω Δε	η Bc	φό Cb	Ιο Da	ϱον Εα		K
20	Bβ	44.9.	ιε- ϱουϱ Δε	γου Ba	μέ Ca	ιε Da	νες Εα	β	K
21	Bβ	44.15.	αχϱάν- τους Αε	θυ Bc	σί Cb	li Da	αις Εα	β	K
22	Bβ	72.6.	χα Αε	τα Bc	λϵι Cb	Ιϵι Da	νας Εα		K
23	Bβ	72.11.	χα Αε	τή Bc	σχυ Cb	Ιυ Da	νας Εα		K
24	Bβ	81.4.	τους Αϱ	στε Bc	φά Cb	Ια Da	νους Eb		K
25	Bβ	88.2.	σήμε- ϱον Αε	νη Ba	δύ Ca	Ιυ Da	ος Εα		K
26	Bβ	88.17.	μεί- ζων Αε	υ Bc	πά Cb	Ια-ϱ Da	γων Ec		K
27	Bβ	88.19.	πί- στει Αf	τι Bc	μό Cb	Ιο-ν Da	των Εα		K
28	Bβ	91.20.	τω Αε	Κυ Bb	ϱί Cb	li Da	ω Eb	β	K
29	Bγ	3.9.	εχά- λυ Αε	νας Bb	πλά Cb	Ια Da	σμα Eb	β	K
30	Bγ	11.5.	το σκυ- μα Αε	υ Bb	ψώ Cb	Ιω Da	σας Eb		K
31	Bγ	13.8.	παϱ Αc	οη Bb	σί Cb	li Da	αν Eb	β	K
32	Bγ	14.10.	έ- τυ Αε	χες Bb	τέ Cb	ιε Da	λους Eb	β	K
33	Bγ	24.18.	ο Αε	γεν Bb	νέ Cb	ιε Da	της Εα	β	K
34	Bγ	38.8.	Οι- χο Αε	νο Bc	μι Cb	li Da	ας Ed		K
35	Bγ	48.6.	Η Αd	σα Bc	ῑ Cb	li Da	ας Eb		K
36	Bγ	54.26.	Οι- χο	νο	μι	li	α	β	K

42

No.		Ref.	Prefix	Ah	Bb	Cb	Da	Eb		
19	Bβ	33.12.		ζω (Δε)	η (Βc)	φό (Cb)	ιο (Da)	ϱον (Εα)		K
20	Bβ	44.9.	ιε-	ϱουϱ (Δε)	γου (Βα)	μέ (Ca)	ιε (Da)	νες (Εα)		K
21	Bβ	44.15.	αχϱάν-	τους (Δε)	θυ (Βc)	σί (Cb)	ιι (Da)	αις (Εα)		K
22	Bβ	72.6.		χα (Δε)	τα (Βc)	λεί (Cb)	ιει (Da)	ψας (Εα)		K
23	Bβ	72.11.		χα (Δε)	τή (Βc)	σχυ (Cb)	ιυ (Da)	νας (Εα)		K
24	Bβ	81.4.		τους (Αg)	στε (Βc)	φά (Cb)	ια (Da)	νους (Εb)		K
25	Bβ	88.2.	σήμε-	ϱον (Δε)	νη (Βα)	δύ (Ca)	ιυ (Da)	ος (Εα)		K
26	Bβ	88.17.	μεί-	ζων (Δε)	υ (Βc)	πά (Cb)	ια-ϱ (Da)	χων (Εc)		K
27	Bβ	88.19.	πί-	στει (Αf)	τι (Βc)	μό (Cb)	ιο-ν (Da)	των (Εα)		K
28	Bβ	91.20.		τω (Δε)	Κυ (Βb)	ϱί (Cb)	ιι (Da)	ω (Εb)		K
29	Bγ	3.9.	εχά-	λυ (Δε)	νας (Βb)	πλά (Cb)	ια (Da)	σμα (Εb)		K
30	Bγ	11.5.	το σώ-	μα (Δε)	υ (Βb)	ψώ (Cb)	ιο (Da)	σας (Εb)		K
31	Bγ	13.8.		παϱ (Δε)	ϱη (Βb)	σί (Cb)	ιι (Da)	αν (Εb)		K
32	Bγ	14.10.	έ-	τυ (Δε)	χες (Βb)	τέ (Cb)	ιε (Da)	λους (Εb)		K
33	Bγ	24.18.		ο (Δε)	γεν (Βb)	νέ (Cb)	ιε (Da)	της (Εα)		K
34	Bγ	38.8.	Οι-	χο (Δε)	νο (Βc)	μι (Cb)	ιι (Da)	ας (Εd)		K
35	Bγ	48.6.		Η (Αd)	σα (Βc)	ϊ (Cb)	ιι (Da)	ας (Εb)		K
36	Bγ	54.26.	οι-	χο (Δε)	νο (Βc)	μι (Cb)	ιι (Da)	α		K

#	Ms.		Af	Ba	Ck	0	0		K
55	ΓΒ	84,5.							
		χρημά-	των	και	παί	Νεναινω		δων	Κ
			Λh	Ba	Ck	0	0		
56	ΓΒ	102,3.							
		ορ-	θο	δο	ξί	Νεναινω		ας	Κ
			Λe	Ba	Ck	0	0		
57	ΓΒ	102,30.							
		θέμε-	θλος	ν	πάρ	Νεναινω		χων	Κ
			Af	Ba	Ck	0	0		
58	Γγ	22,9.							
		πρεσβεύ-	ων	α	παύ	Νεναινω		στως	Κ
			Af	Ba	Ck	0	0		
59	Γγ	56,22.							
			των	χει	ρών	Νεναινω		σου	Κ
			Af	Ba	Ca	Da	Eb		
60	Γδ	37,10.							
			με	τά	τό	Ιο	χον		Κ
			Λg	Ba	Ck	0	0		
61	Γε	3,10.							
		εξ	α	πει	ράν	Νεναινω		δρου	Κ
			Λd	Ba	Ck	0	0		
62	Γε	17,3.							
			α	σθε	νούν	Νεναινω		τες	Κ
			Λe	Ba	Ck	0	0		
63	Γε	35,5.							
		γε	νη	θέν	Νεναινω		των	Κ	
			Af	Ba	Ck	0	0		
64	Γε	37,5.							
		έ-	πνευ	σαν	αύ	Νεναινω		ραι	Κ
			Af	Ba	Ci	0	0		
65	Γε	102,14.							
			με	τά	ταύ	Νεναινω		τα	Κ
			Λd	Ba	Ck	0	0		
66	Γζ	3,7.							
			ε	ξου	σί	Νεναινω		α	Κ
			Af	Ba	Ci	0	0		
67	Γζ	3,14.							
			σοι	βο	ώ	Νεναινω		μεν	Κ
			Af	Ba	Ci	0	0		
68	Γζ	13,2.							
		πανευ-	φη	με	πά	Νεναινω		τερ	Κ
			Λd	Ba	Ck	0	0		
69	Γζ	13,5.							
		αγγέ-	λοις	συ	νού	Νεναινω		σα	Κ
			Af	Ba	Ci	0	0		
70	Γζ	51,9.							
		εσχά-	των	α	τρέ	Νεναινω		πτως	Κ
			Af	Ba	Ci	0	0		
71	Γζ	90,3.							
		πρωτομάρ-	τυ	ρα	θέ	Νεναινω		χλαν	Κ
			Λd	Ba	Ci	0	0		
72	Γζ	92,12.							
		από-	στο	λε	θέ	Νεναινω		χλα	Κ

Table 10e
Formula No. 8 (continued)

			Λh	Ba	Ci	0	0		
73	Iζ	102,8.							K
			χαι / Λf	παρ / Ba	θέ / Ck	Νεναινω 0	νον 0		
74	Iζ	102,26.							K
			της 0	α / Bj	γά / Ch	Νεναινω 0	πης 0		
75	Δα	35,9.							E
		τε-	— / Λf	χθεί / Ba	σα / Ch	0	μπτρός 0		
76	Δα	95,12.							A
		Χρι-	στού 0	εν / Bi	γι- / Cd	Da	ναιξί Eb		
77	Εα	21,11.							E
		παρρησίαν	— 0	έ / Bk	χω / Cd	ω-ν / Da	προς αυτόν Eb		
78	Εα	44,2.							K
		να-	— 0	ού / Bi	τη / Ce	Ιη-ς / Da	α ναστάσεως Ee		
79	Εα	103,9.							K
		μεθι-	— 0	στά / Bi	με / Cd	Ιε / Da	νον Eb		
80	Εβ	3,2.							K
		τα	— 0	έρ / Bi	γα / Cd	Ια / Da	σου Eb		
81	Εβ	92,2.							K
		παντοδυνάμω	— 0	νεύ / Bd	μα / Ck	Ια 0	τι 0		
82	Ζα	17,1.							K
			— 0	κύ / Bd	ρι / Cn	Νεναινω 0	ε 0		
83	Ζα	28,4.							K
		μοι	— 0	λέ / Bd	γον / Ck	Νεναινω 0	τες 0		
84	Ζα	68,12.							K
		χατα-	— 0	πτώ / Be	σε / Co	Νεναινω 0	ως 0		
85	Ζγ	83,3.							K
		α	0	λή / Bd	χτως / Cp	0	0		
86	Ζγ	95,6.							K
		Θάμυριν	— / Aj	έ / Bd	φυ- / Cm	0	γες 0		
87	Ζγ	102,12.							K
		έ-	φη / Al	σε / Bd	του / Cp	Νεναινω 0	λόγου 0		
88	Ζδ	21,6.							K
		εξ / Al	έ / Bd	χε / Ck	Νεναινω 0	0		
89	Ζδ	78,15.							K
		παν 0	εύ / Bd	φη / Ck	Νεναινω 0	0		
90	Ζε	24,20.							K
		εχτενώς	—	πρέ / Bd	σβευ	Νεναινω			

45

No			Al	Bd	Ck	0	0		
91	Ζε	84.12.	χυρί- / ω / Al	έ / Bε	δω / Cn	Νενανω / 0	0		K
92	Ζε	97.3.	ε- / χοη / Al	μά / Bd	τη / Ck	Νενανω / 0	0		K
93	Ζε	106.16.	ι / Λi	χέ / Bm	τευ / Ch	Νενινω / 0	0		
94	Ζζ	38.10.	εχ / Αn	της / Bi	φθο / Cd	Da	φάς / Eb	φθοράς	E
95	Θα	14.1.	Η / Αn	γά / Bi	πη / Cf	Ιη / Db	σας / Ef		Λ
97	Θα	11.1.	Εχ / 0	φι / Bi	ζης εχ / Cd	φι ζης / Da	α / Ea	γαθης	Λ
96	Θα	54.12.	— / 0	αι / Bi	μι / Cg	Ια / Dc	τι / Ef		Κr.
98	Θα	55.1.	— / Αo	Θει / Bl	ος / Cd	Θει ος / Da	Θη / Eb	σαυρός	K
99	Θα	81.1.	Ο / Αq	δεύ / Bd	τε / Ci	Ιε / 0	φος / 0		E
100	Θβ	24.1.	Ως χα / Θα— / Aj	— / Bn	φός / Ci	0	0		Λ
102	Θβ	17.1.	ό- / τε / Λi	τω / Bo	πά- / Ci	0	0	θει σου	Λ
101	Θβ	102.1.	Τον / Αp	τι / Ba	όν / 0	0	0		E
103	Θγ	12.11.	μεθ' / Αm	ων / Ba	ι- / 0	0	0	χέτευε	Λ
104	Θγ	13.10.	Χρι / στόν	ι-				χέτευε	Λ

Table 11
Formula No. 3

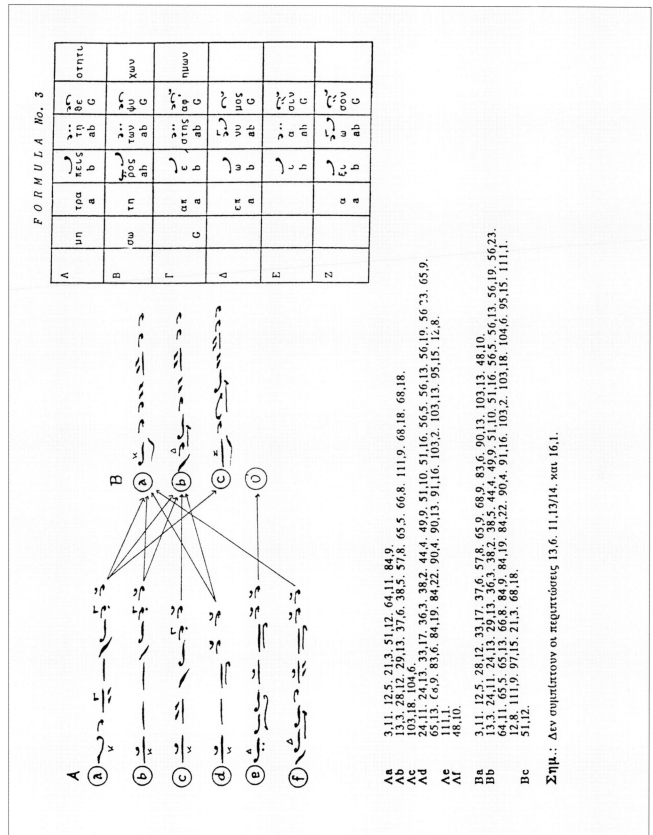

47

				Aa	Ba	
A	3,11.	Aa	Ba	μή τρα- πείς	τη	θεότητι
A	12,5.	Aa	Ba	ρά	πων	μακάριε
			Aa		Bb	
A	64,11.	Aa	Bɔ	δ αί	μο	νες έφριξαν
A	84,9.	Aa	Bb	του Ι- ώ β	εξ	εβόησας
E	21,3.	Aa	Bb	εχρη- μ ά	τη	σας
			Aa		Bc	
A	51,12.	Aa	Bc	αν- μνού	μεν	σε
			Ab		Ba	
A	28,12.	Ab	Ba	π ά	α	την είσοδον
A	37,6.	Ab	Ba	σωτη- ρί	ας	προάγγελος.
A	57,8.	Ab	Ba	προσκυ- ν ώ	χαι	δοξάζω
			Ab		Bb	
A	13,3.	Ab	Bb	πη- γ ά	ζει	ιάματα
A	29,13.	Ab	Bb	ζω- ή	εισ	οικίζεται
A	38,5.	Ab	Bb	χαι χτί	στει	Χριστώ
A	65,5.	Ab	Bb	Χρι στέ	ο	θεός
A	66,8.	Ab	Bb	πλού	σι	ον έλεος
			Ac			
A	103,18	Ac	Bb	τι μ ών	τας	την μνήμην
A	104,6.	Ac	Bb	ότι σού	ε	σμέν
			Ab		Bb	
Γ	111,9.	Ab	Bb	εχ της ά	νω	δόξης
Δ	97,15.	Ab	Bb	επ- ώ	νυ	μος
Ζ	68,18.	Ab	Bb	α- ξί	ω	σον
			Ad		Ba	
A	33,17.	Ad	Ba	χ ύ	ρι	ε δόξα σοι
A	65,9.	Ad	Ba	συντρι- β έν	των	τα χέρατα
A	68,9.	Ad	Ba	χαταγ- γ έλ	λει	ανύψωσιν
A	83,6.	Ad	Ba	τρι	ά	δα άχτιστον
A	90,13.	Ad	Ba	τε- λούν	τας	την μνήμην
A	103,13	Ad	Ba	δευ	τέ	ραν έλευσιν

			Ad		Bb	
A 24,11.	Ad	Bb		δι- ό	και	πεφόνευσαι
A 24,13.	Ad	Bb	σωτήριον	β ά	πτι	σμα
A 36,3.	Ad	Bb		θ ε ί	α	προέρχεται
A 38,2.	Ad	Bb	Άννα	τ ί	χτει	θεόπαιδα
A 44,4.	Ad	Bb	σέ δο-	ξ ά	ζο	μεν
A 49,9.	Ad	Bb		παι	δα	γωγήσωμεν
A 51,10.	Ad	Bb	γε-	ν ό	με	νος
A 51,16.	Ad	Bb	βασι-	λεύς	η	μών
A 56,5.	Ad	Bb	προε-	δ ή	λω	σε
A 56,13.	Ad	Bb	την παν-	ν ώ	λε	θρον
A 56,19.	Ad	Bb	βο-	ώ ν	τες	προσφέρομεν
A 56,23.	Ad	Bb	οο-	φ ό ν	δη	μιούργημα
A 65,13.	Ad	Bb	εν τοις	ἑ ρ	γοις	σου
A 84,19.	Ad	Bb		προ	μη	θευσάμενος
A 84,22.	Ad	Bb	μακάριον	τ έ	λος	υπέμεινας
A ς.,4.	Ad	Bb	εν	ύ	μνοις	τιμήσωμεν
A 91,16.	Ad	Bb	του α-	γ ί	ου	βαπτίσματος
A 103,2.	Ad	Bb	θεολο-	γ ί	ας	την σάλπιγγα
Γ 12,8.	Ad	Bb	ουχ α-	π έ	στης	αφ᾽ ημών
B 95,15.	Ad	Bb	λιτρώ-	σαι	ταις	πρεσβείαις σου

			Ae			
B 111,1.	Ae	Bb	γνό-	φον	του	αφράστου

			Af		Ba	
B 48,10.	Af	Ba	λαμβανού-	σας	β ά	σιμον

		;		;	
A 13,6.		α-	ξ ί	ως	αγάλλεται
B 11,13.		σωτή-	ρος	των	ψυχών ημών
E 16,6.		την	ί	α	σιν

Table 13
Formula No. 8

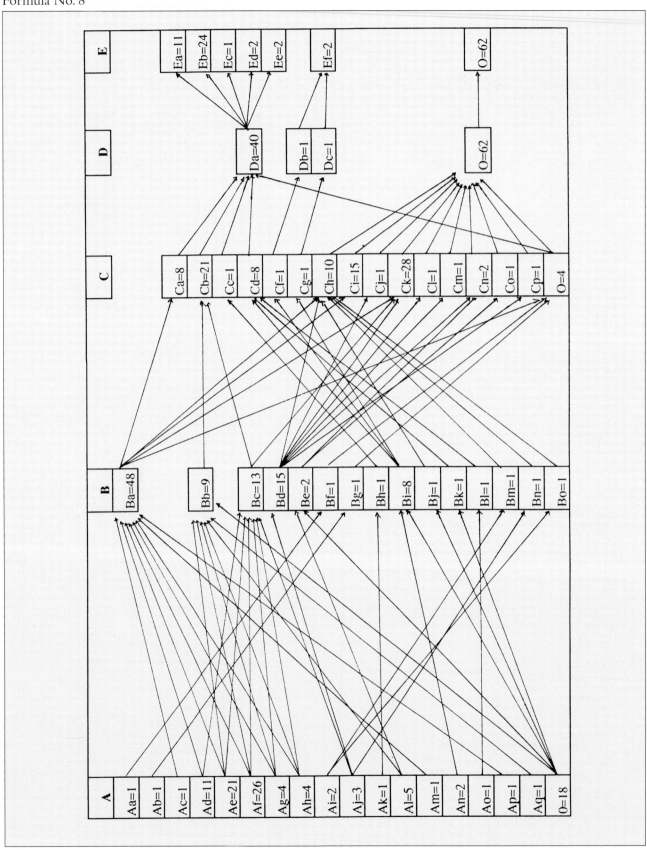

Table 14
Formula No. 8

A	—	B		
0	—	Bd	=	9
0	—	Be	=	1
0	—	Bi	=	6
0	—	Bj	=	1
0	—	Bk	=	1
Aa	—	Bf	=	1
Ab	—	Bg	=	1
Ac	—	Ba	=	1
Ad	—	Ba	=	10
Ad	—	Bc	=	1
Ae	—	Ba	=	8
Ae	—	Bb	=	6
Ae	—	Bc	=	7
Af	—	Ba	=	24
Af	—	Bb	=	1
Af	—	Bc	=	1
Ag	—	Ba	=	1
Ag	—	Bb	=	1
Ag	—	Bc	=	2
Ah	—	Ba	=	2
Ah	—	Bb	=	1
Ah	—	Bc	=	1
Ai	—	Bm	=	1
Ai	—	Bo	=	1
Aj	—	Bc	=	1
Aj	—	Bd	=	1
Aj	—	Bn	=	1
Ak	—	Bh	=	1
Al	—	Bd	=	4
Al	—	Be	=	1
Am	—	Ba	=	1
An	—	Bi	=	2
Ao	—	Bl	=	1
Ap	—	Ba	=	1
Aq	—	Bd	=	1
Σύνολο				104

B	—	C		
Ba	—	0	=	2
Ba	—	Ca	=	8
Ba	—	Ch	=	3
Ba	—	Ci	=	15
Ba	—	Ck	=	20
Bb	—	Cb	=	9
Bc	—	Cb	=	12
Bc	—	Ck	=	1
Bd	—	Ch	=	3
Bd	—	Cj	=	1
Bd	—	Ck	=	7
Bd	—	Cl	=	1
Bd	—	Cm	=	1
Bd	—	Cn	=	1
Bd	—	Cp	=	1
Be	—	Cn	=	1
Be	—	Co	=	1
Bf	—	0	=	1
Bg	—	0	=	1
Bh	—	Cc	=	1
Bi	—	Cd	=	6
Bi	—	Cf	=	1
Bi	—	Cg	=	1
Bj	—	Ch	=	1
Bk	—	Cd	=	1
Bl	—	Cd	=	1
Bm	—	Ch	=	1
Bn	—	Ch	=	1
Bo	—	Ch	=	1
Σύνολο				104

C	—	D		
0	—	0	=	2
0	—	Da	=	2
Ca	—	Da	=	8
Cb	—	Da	=	21
Cc	—	Da	=	1
Cd	—	Da	=	8
Cf	—	Db	=	1
Cg	—	Dc	=	1
Ch	—	0	=	10
Ci	—	0	=	15
Cj	—	0	=	1
Ck	—	0	=	28
Cl	—	0	=	1
Cm	—	0	=	1
Cn	—	0	=	2
Co	—	0	=	1
Cp	—	0	=	1
Σύνολο				104

D	—	E		
0	—	0	=	62
Da	—	Ea	=	11
Da	—	Eb	=	24
Da	—	Ec	=	1
Da	—	Ed	=	2
Da	—	Ee	=	2
Db	—	Ef	=	1
Dc	—	Ef	=	1
Σύνολο				104

The musical notation of the Sticherarion MS Vat. Barb. gr. 483[1]

Ioannis Papathanassiou

The manuscript Vat. Barb. gr. 483[2] is a parchment sticherarion of the 12th century, measuring 260 x 190 mm and consisting of 136 folios. Because of the bad state of the parchment, the ruling can only be detected with difficulty and is only visible on some folios. Ruling systems Leroy 9 and 12 and types Leroy 44B1 and 20C1 are represented in the manuscript[3]. Both the text and the musical signs are written with sepia-coloured ink. Its repertory[4], mutilated and deficient[5], includes stichera idiomela for the months November to April and a part of the Triodion. It can reasonably be presumed that the codex originally contained the Pentekostarion as well, and perhaps also the Oktoechos. The manuscript is written in a script (see tables 1 – 6) derived from the type witnessed in chancellery documents from the Calabrian-Sicilian area between the 12th and 13th centuries, and it can with all probability be dated to the last quarter of the 12th century. A script very similar to that of the Barberinian codex is found, for example, in the subscription of Mess. gr. 98 (c. 1184?)[6] and in the document Par. suppl. gr. 1315, 7 (c. 1195)[7]. In the script of both Mess. gr. 98 and Vat. Barb. gr. 483, many common elements occur, as for example the ligature *epsilon-iota, alpha-iota*, the linked *sigma-tau*, as well as some letters: *beta* in the heart shaped uncial form, the minuscule *ny*, the minuscule *eta* -in ligature- with doubled vertical stroke, *kappa, omega, iota*, uncial *delta*, the uncial *pi* in which the horizontal stroke is extended beyond the body of the letter and is joined to the following one. In spite of the different characteristics pertaining to the two types of writing (the documentary one of Par. Suppl. gr. 1315,7 and that of the Barberinian which is adapted for book use), one recognizes the same elements emerging from the comparison of Vat. Barb. gr. 483 with Mess. gr. 98 (and in addition the minuscule theta in ligature).

It is interesting, however, to note the bilingual annotation appearing on fols. 105v-106r, the work of a deacon named Ἰωάννης from Sinopoli (Southern Italy-Calabria), reporting a formula which is typical of documentary testimonial subscriptions: Ego Joannes [...] de Sinopoli[s] [testis sum] / Ἐγὼ διάκονος Ἰωάννης [ς εντρας] στέργω καὶ μαρτυρῶ. Such an annotation testifies to the circulation of the codex in the Calabrian-Sicilian region in a later period.

The notation of Vat. Barb. gr. 483 immediately reveals a very different aspect compared to that of more recent manuscripts in Middle Byzantine notation; the notation is written with the same instrument as was used for the text of the chants and, consequently, it carries the same subtle traits.

The middle Byzantine notation follows the vein of the Paleobyzantine Coislin type notation (the Chartres notation had not yet fallen into disuse in the 12th century but it had certainly been relegated to a secondary position). The Coislin notation reached its own maturity and was stabilized in the fundamental arrangement which would be maintained in the Middle Byzantine notation itself, by means of the passage from the third to the fourth stage according to the classification by Constantin Floros[8]. With regard to the paleobyzantine notations, we will follow the divisions proposed by Floros of Coislin in six stages and of the Chartres in four stages because it allows us to speak more precisely about the semiographic evolution. The Coislin stage IV in fact is characterized by the appearance of the *ison* and of the *oligon* and the ensuing specialization of the *apostrophos* as a descending sign; Moreover, the *hypotaxis* appears for the first time in a framework of the Coislin IV notation. The "long" neumes (i. e. those including a *diple* sign: *diple*, kratema, *xeron klasma* etc), the *bareia* and the *apoderma*, however, continue to lack indications as to the direction of the melodic movement. It is precisely the presence of diastematic signs (originally sporadic, then more frequent until it, finally, became constant) specifying the melodic figure of the "long" neumes, of the *bareia* and of the *apoderma* along with the analytical notation of the *thematismos*, the new writing of the *kratema* and of the *xeron klasma*, and the appearance of neumes on the initial *martyriai* of the sticheraic chants, that distinguish the Coislin V and VI stages. The Coislin notation thus ends up just one step before the Middle Byzantine notation takes over, a notation in which, when the evolution outlined above was over, the diastematic value of interval signs had become definitive.

The passage from Coislin VI to Middle Byzantine notation is demonstrated by the manuscript Athos Iviron 470[9]; According to Floros, its notation reveals a great many elements from Paleobyzantine notation Coislin VI, as for example, the abbreviated notation of the *kylisma* and *syrma*[10] and the semi-abbreviated notation of the *bareia*. In addition the *hypotaxis*, of both Early and Middle Byzantine types, indicates that it is closely related to ancient notations.

The musical notation of Vat. Barb. gr. 483 can be defined as a fully developed Middle Byzantine notation in spite of some elements which still bear vestiges of the Coislin notation stage VI. Such elements are the *thematismos*, the *thema haploun*, the *kylisma*, the *xeron klasma*, the *apoderma*, the type of *hypotaxis* as well as the figurations *dyo, anastama* and *anatrichisma*.

– The evolutionary process of *thematismos* consists of the passing from abbreviated notation, as such by the Coislin I – IV stages (fig. 1. 1) to its more analytical form of stages V (fig. 1. 2) and VI (fig. 1. 3). The fourth real sounded tone of this neumatic figuration appears only in Middle Byzantine notation (fig. 1. 4), frequently without the letter theta.. The manuscript Vat. Barb. gr. 483 reveals both the Coislin VI figuration and the Middle Byzantine one, in contrast to MS Sin. gr. 1218[11] and Vind. Theol. gr. 181 which present the Middle Byzantine form alone.

– The *thema haploun* was originally a fully abbreviated sign (fig. 1. 5-6). In more recent Coislin notations, an *apostrophos* is sometimes added, especially in the *thema haploun* with *katabasma* (fig. 1. 7). In the 13th century this figuration appears, for example in MS Vind. Theol. gr. 181, in the following form without the theta (fig. 1. 8), while in Vat. Barb. gr. 483 the same form appears (fig. 1. 9) as also occurs in Athos Iviron 470 and in Sin. gr. 1218.

– As far as the *hypotaxis* is concerned, three stages can be distinguished in its evolution: a first in the Chartres notations (fig. 1. 10), a second in the Coislin notations (fig. 1. 11) and a third occurring in Middle Byzantine notation (fig. 1. 12). The third stage is found throughout the Vat. Barb. gr. 483 while in Athos Iviron 470 the second one is also present, although the *hypotaxis* of petasthe and *oxeia* with *kentemata* in Vat. Barb. gr. 483 occurs according to the more ancient system (fig. 1. 13) which is also used in Sin. gr. 1218. In Vind. Theol. gr. 181 the Middle Byzantine form is found (fig. 1. 14)[12].

– The *apoderma* occurs in Coislin I - IV notations in its simple arched form

Fig. 1

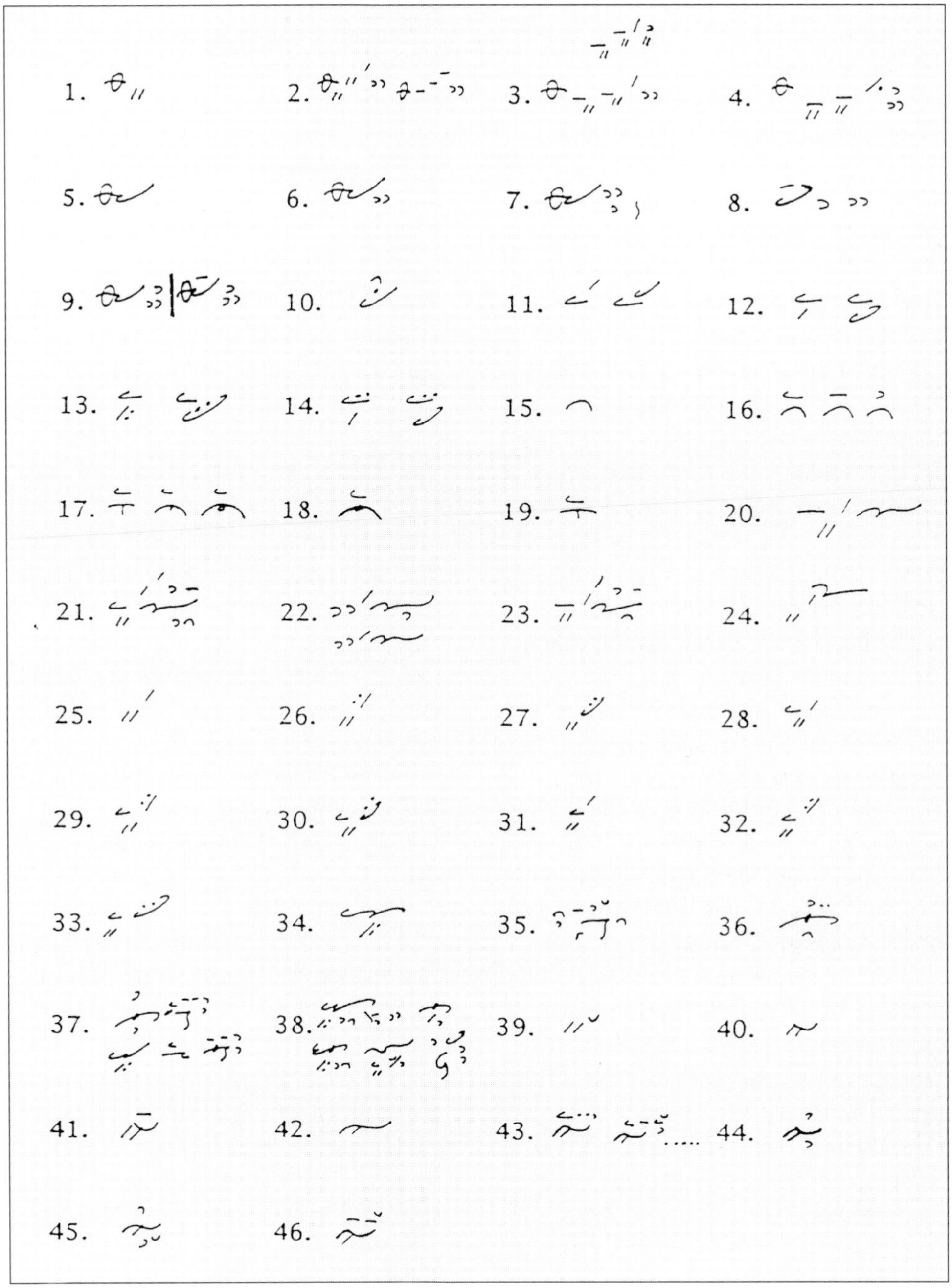

(fig. 1. 15). Subsequently, a neume for the diastematic specification is added in Coislin V-VI (fig. 1. 16). The latter is used in Vat. Barb. gr. 483 as well as in the Sin. gr. 1218[13] instead of the form (fig. 1. 17) which is seen in later manuscripts in Middle Byzantine notation as, for example, in Vind. Theol. gr. 181 (fig. 1. 19).

– The *kylisma* sign does not appear in the more ancient Coislin notations. In Coislin VI the sign occurs in the following abbreviated form (fig. 1. 20). In Vat. Barb. gr. 483 the Middle Byzantine form appears more frequently (fig. 1. 21) but at times the Coislin VI abbreviated form is found (fig. 1. 22). The analytical, and in some cases abbreviated, form is also used in Sin. gr. 1218 (fig. 1. 23, 24) while Vind. Theol. gr. 181 invariably presents the analytical form of the figuration.

– In Coislin notation, stages I-V, the *dyo, anatrichisma* and *anastama* figurations appear as follows (fig. 1. 25-26-27). In Coislin VI the diastematic value of the neumes is specified, moved to the left of the *diple* (fig. 1. 28-29-30). Finally, in Middle Byzantine notation, they appear in the following forms (fig. 1. 31-32-33). Vat. Barb. gr. 483 and Sin. gr. 1218 present the forms of Coislin VI, apparently with precise diastematic values. In contrast, the use of Middle Byzantine forms is constant in Vind. Theol. gr. 181.

– In Vat. Barb. gr. 483 the use of *megala semadia* is sporadic; one finds the Middle Byzantine *parakletike*[14] (fig. 1. 34), the *homalon*[15] (fig. 1. 35) and rarely, the *antikenoma* (fig. 1. 36). Such a sporadic use of *megala semadia* appears also in Sin. gr. 1218 (fig. 1. 37) while these are found constantly in Vind. Theol. gr. 181 (fig. 1. 38).

– A further element can be identified in the use of the *xeron* klasma and, particularly, of the diastematic signs accompanying it. In Coislin I-IV notations it appears with the two elements detached (fig. 1. 39); in Coislin V the two elements are joined (fig. 1. 40) and in Coislin VI the diastematic interval is specified (fig. 1. 41). In Middle Byzantine notations, it appears in the form (fig. 1. 42) – obviously accompanied by the necessary diastematic values. In Vat. Barb. gr. 483 it occurs in the following form (fig. 1. 43). Moreover, in Vat. Barb. gr. 483 as well as in Sin. gr. 1218[16] and Iviron 470 the second note of a *xeron klasma* of two notes is never accompanied by the *klasma* (fig. 1. 44) as is the case, instead, in more recent notations as for example in Vind. Theol. gr. 181 (fig. 1. 45).

It would therefore be reasonable to assume, analyzing the neumatic forms of our sticherarion Vat. Barb. gr. 483, that its notation (between that of Sin. gr. 1218 and of Vind. Theol. gr. 181) testifies to the use of a very advanced musical notation in a peripheral region of the Byzantine Empire in the last quarter of the 12th century. Innovations introduced in the capital would certainly reach peripheral regions with a varying degree of delay, and, consequently, more than one semiographic stage was probably used at the same time within the Empire. It is interesting to note the case of Saba 83[17], written in the second half of the 12th century while the notation employed the Coislin II-III (modernized at a later period, which, I think, can not be later than the first half of the 13th century). It can be assumed that the copyist used a manuscript with an archaic notation as his model. In this case, why did the copyist choose to use a codex whose notation was no longer in use at the end of the 12th century as a model for a book destined to be used for learning the melodies? I think that the act of choosing a much more ancient notational stage compared to the date of writing of the codex, would be an indication of the use of more semiographic stages even within the same geographic zone[18].

An example[19] testifying to the use of a different semiographic stage in two different regions with an interval of 71 years between them occurs in manuscripts St. Petersburg GPB 789 and Sin. gr. 754[20]. The St. Petersburg codex, written on Mount Athos in 1106, shows a more developed Coislin notation in comparison to that of the provincial Sinaitic codex completed in 1177 (Coislin V)[21]; However, the notation of St. Petersburg GPB 789 deserves a more detailed examination.

Based on the musical notation of the so-called "menaia Carbonesi" (Crypt. Δ. α. XIII-XVII + fragments on Vallicell. E 55 and R 32)[22], Oliver Strunk suggested that the Coislin notation in its primitive form was introduced in Southern Italy around the year 1000[23]. Consequently, we can suppose that this stage of notation already was used in the zone of Constantinople in the second half of the 10th century.

Alberto Doda, based on the MS Vat. gr. 2018, has demonstrated how it would have been possible to use a more advanced Coislin stage (IV/V) in a central part of the Empire in the first half of the 11th century. According to Doda, the passage from Coislin III to Coislin IV could have taken place in the beginning of the 11th century[24].

In the 12th century, during which it is generally agreed that the passage from Coislin VI to the Middle Byzantine notation occurred[25], also the following dated codices were written: the above mentioned Sin. gr. 1218, written by Nikephoros in 1177 is a provincial codex and one of the most ancient manuscripts in Middle Byzantine notation with vestiges[26] of Coislin VI. Patmos 218[27] is written in Coislin notation, stages V-VI (1166). On the other hand the Patmos 221 dated to 1168-1179 [1161-80][28], bearing a subscription by Nikephoros (perhaps identical with the scribe of Sin. gr. 1218) and probably written in Bithynia[29], presents a Middle Byzantine notation with some Coislin elements.

Starting from the fact that innovations from the capital reach the peripheral zones with some delay and considering the remarkable evolutionary stage revealed in the notation of Vat. Barb. gr. 483, written in the last quarter of 12th century in Southern Italy, one is led to the hypothesis that the passage from the last Coislin stage to Middle Byzantine notation could have begun during the first half of the 12th century. The musical notation and obviously the music it transmits is like an organism in constant evolution. Whereas in our days' innovations are transmitted within a narrow span of time, it took in the Middle Ages a while for any evolution to penetrate and become part of the mental baggage of common man and scholar alike, and it needed to mature over a much longer period. However, allowing for some reservations as to the hypothesis being presented here, and considering the possibility that an innovation (in this case the introduction of an advanced notational stage) was transmitted for some reason within the briefest possible period of time, we are led to focus our attention on the phenomenon of its prompt propagation to the peripheral zones of the empire.

This remains a working hypothesis and we will be able to speak more confidently only if dated musical manuscripts from the first half of the 12th century originating in the Constantinopolitan area and provided with Middle Byzantine notation are discovered, and if new paleographic studies allow us to use more refined criteria in the dating of Byzantine musical manuscripts; consequently, the dates of many previously noted and studied codices may have to be reconsidered.

Bibliography

Biezen, J. v., 1968
The Middle Byzantine Kanon-Notation of Manuscript H, Bilthoven.

Canart, P. and Leroy, J. 1977
Les manuscrits en style di Reggio. 'Etude paleografique et codicologique, in La paleographie grecque et byzantine, (Colloques internationaux du Centre Nationale de la Recherche Scientifique, 559), Paris, 241-261.

Doda, A. 1989
Note codicologiche, paleografiche e paleografico - musicali su uno sticherarion dell'XI secolo, in Jahrbuch der Österreichischen Byzantinistik, 39 (1989), 217-239.

Doda, A. 1991
Osservazioni sulla scrittura e sulla notazione musicale dei menaia "Carbonesi", in Scrittura e Civiltà, 15 (1991), 185-204.

Floros, C. 1970
Universale Neumenkunde, Vols. I-III, Kassel.

Foti, M.B. 1989
Il monastero del S.mo Salvatore in lingua phari, Proposte scrittorie e coscienza culturale, Messina.

Guillou, A. 1963
Les actes Grecs de S. Maria di Messina, Enquête sur les populations grecques d'Italie du Sud et de Sicile (XI -XIV s.), Cartes et Planches, Palermo 1963.

Harlfinger, D., Reinsch, D.R., Sonderkamp, J.A.M., and Prato, G. 1983
Specimina Sinaitica. Die datierten griechischen Handschriften des Katharinen-Klosters auf dem Berge Sinai, 9. bis 12. Jahrhundert, Berlin.

Høeg, C. 1938
Hirmologium Athoum, (Monumenta Musicae Byzantinae, série principale, vol. II), Copenhagen.

Høeg, C., Tillyard, H.J.W, and Wellesz, E. 1935
Sticherarium. Codex Vindoboniensis Theol. gr. 181, (Monumenta Musicae Byzantinae, vol. I), Copenhagen.

Kominis, A. 1968
Facsimiles of Dated Patmian Codices, Athens.

Lake, K. and S. 1934-35
Dated Greek Minuscule Manuscripts to the Year 1200 (Monumenta Paleographica Vetera, First series), Boston.

Leroy, J. 1976
Les Types de réglure des manuscrits grecs, Paris 1976.

Leroy, J. 1977
La description codicologique des manuscrits grecs de parchemin, in La paleographie grecque et byzantine, (Colloques internationaux du Centre Nationale de la Recherche Scientifique, 559), Paris, 27-44.

Leroy, J. 1977
Quelques systèmes de réglure des manuscrits grecs, in Studia codicologica, 124, Berlin, 291-312.

Raasted, J. 1963
*A primitive paleobyzantine musical notation, in
Classica et Medievalia,* XXIII (1963), 302-
310.

Raasted, J. 1968
*Hirmologium Sabbaiticum, (Monumenta Music-
ae Byzantinae,* série principale vol. VIII),
Copenhague.

Stathis, G. Th. 1979
*Οἱ ἀναγραμματισμοὶ καὶ τὰ μαθή-
ματα τῆ ς βυζαντινῆ ς μελοποιῖας,*
(second ed. Athens 1992), Athens.

Strunk, O., 1965
*Specimina Notationum Antiquiorum, (Monu-
menta Musicae Byzantinae, pars suppletoria*
VII), Copenhagen.

Strunk, O., 1977 (Class.)
*The Classification and Development of the Ear-
ly Byzantine Notations, in Essays on Music in
the Byzantine world,* ed. Kenneth Levy, New
York 1977, 40-44. (Reprint of a paper read
in 1950)

Strunk, O., 1977 (Not.)
*The notation of the Chartres Fragment, in
Essays on Music in the Byzantine World,* ed.
Kenneth Levy, New York 1977, 68-111. (-
Reprint of an article from 1955)

Tardo, L. 1931
*I codici melurgici della Vaticana e il contributo
alla musica bizantina del monachismo Greco della magna Grecia, in Archivio storico per la Cala-
bria e la Lucania,* I (1931), 225-248.

Thodberg, C. 1966
*Der Byzantinische Alleluiarionzyklus, (Monu-
menta Musicae Byznantinae, subsidia VIII),*
Copenhagen.

Tillyard H. J. W. 1935
*Handbook of the Middle Byzantine Musical
Notation, (Monumenta Musicae Byzantinae,
subsidia* I), (second impression, Copenhagen
1970), Copenhagen.

Touliatos-Banker, D. 1987
*Check list of Byzantine Musical Manuscripts in
the Vatican Library, in Manuscripta,* 31 (1987),
22-27.

Troelsgård, C. 1995
*The rôle of paraklitiké in Palæobyzantine nota-
tions, in Palaeobyzantine Notations, A Recon-
sideration of the Source Material,* Hernen, 81-
117.

Wellesz, E. 1961
*A history of Byzantine music and Hymnogra-
phy,* (second ed.) Oxford.

Notes

NOTE 1

I would like to express my thanks to Jørgen Raasted, Alberto Doda and Christian Troelsgård for the helpful advice they offered me. All errors that remain are, of course, my own.

NOTE 2

Description of the codex in Tardo 1931 225-248, especially. 242. The codex appears also in Touliatos-Banker 1987 24.

NOTE 3

For the ruling systems and types see Leroy 1977, (Quelques systèmes...) 291-312 and Leroy 1977 (La description codicologique...).

NOTE 4

The repertory included in Vat. Barb. gr. 483 is very similar to that of Vindob. Theol. gr. 181, see Høeg, Tillyard, and Wellesz 1935. The Barberini manuscript, in comparison to the Vienna codex contains some additional stichera: Triodion: παρισταμένη τῷ σταυρῷ (staurotheotokion), ἡ ἄσπιλος καὶ πανάμωμος γεννήτρια (staurotheotokion), σήμερον ὁ δεσπότης καὶ Κύριος παρίσταται (Good Friday), ἐν τῷ δείπνῳ σου Χριστὲ ὁ Θεός (Good Friday). The Barberini codex, however, lacks the following stichera that the Vienna manuscript includes: πατρίδα γένος ὕπαρξιν (December 4th), ὄντως ἡ γλῶσσα σου (December 10th), μαρτυρικὴ χορεῖα εὐσεβείας πρόμαχος (December 10th), μνήμην ἐπιτελοῦμεν Δαβὶδ καὶ Ἰακώβου (Sunday after Christmas), ἱερέων μνήμην καὶ βασιλέων κράτος (Sunday after Christmas), αἷμα καὶ πῦρ καὶ ἀτμίδα καπνοῦ (Sunday after Christmas), σῶσαι βουλόμενος τὸν πλανηθέντα ἄνθρωπον (January 6th), φωνὴ Κυρίου ἐπὶ τῶν ὑδάτων (January 6th), δέχου Συμεών (February 2th), δεῦτε καὶ ἡμεῖς ἄσμασιν (February 2th), τὸν ὀχούμενον ἐν ἄσμασιν (February 2th), τὸν ἐκλάμψαντα πρὸ αἰώνων ἐκ πατρός (February 2th).

NOTE 5

In fact, the order of the folios and of the fascicles has been disturbed. The correct order of the folios is the following: [lacuna: the stichera for September, October and half of November (until the 14th) have been lost], fols 130-136, fols 1-31, [lacuna: the text is interrupted in the middle of Ἡρώδης ὁ παράνομος (December 29th) and begins again with οὐκ ἐπαισχύνθη ὁ πανάγαθος (first of January)], fols 32-71, [lacuna: the text is interrupted after the first line of ὁ λαμπρὸς ἀριστεὺς Γεώργιος (April 23th) and begins again with the last lines of ὡς ὁ ἄσωτος υἱός (Sunday of the Prodigal Son)], fols 72-76, [lacuna: the text is interrupted after the end of ὁ τοῦ Κυρίου σταυρός (Cheese Thursday) and begins with the last lines of οἴμοι ὁ Ἀδὰμ ἐν θρήνῳ κέκραγεν (Cheese Sunday)], fols 77-85, [lacuna: the text is interrupted after τὴν πνευματικὴν νηστείαν (Second Week in Lent, Monday morning) begins again with the second line of μετανοίας ὁ καιρός (Second Week in Lent, Monday morning)], fols 86-93, [lacuna: the text is interrupted after ἡ τὴν ἀγαθῶν πρόξενος (Fourth Week in Lent, Thursday morning) and begins with αὐτεξουσίως ἐξεδύθην τῇ πρώτῃ μου παραβάσει τῶν ἀρετῶν (Fifth Week in Lent, Thursday evening)], fols 94-129, [lacuna: the text is interrupted after the first line of διὰ τὸν φόβον τῶν ἰουδαίων (Good Friday)].

The numbering of the fascicles is placed in the Middle of the external margin of the first folio recto of the quaternions: fols 1-8, 9-16, 17-24, [lacuna], fols 32-39, 40-47, 48-55, 56-63, after which the fascicles are no longer numbered: fols 64-71, [lacuna], from fols 72-95 the reconstruction of the fascicles, due to the lacunae, is problematic. What follows is: fols 96-103, 104-111, 112-119, 120-127, 128-129 [lacuna], [lacuna] fols 130-136.

6 Reproductions of the MS. in Foti 1989, figure 27, see also Lake 1934-35, fasc. IX, figures 656 and 657. The type of writing of Vat. Barb. gr. 483 is also in some way con- nected to the Reggio style. In fact, the Messanese is written entirely in Reggio style, but its subscription is in a script very similar to that of the Barberinian manuscript. For the Reggio style, see Canart/-Leroy 1977 241-261.

NOTE 7

Reproduction of the document Par. Suppl. gr. 1315, 7 in Guillou 1963, pl. IX.

NOTE 8

See Floros 1970, Vol. I, 311-326.

NOTE 9

See Høeg 1938, van Biezen 1968, and Floros 1970, Vol. I, 326-327.

NOTE 10

The group of neumes accompanying the syrma according to Floros, found in the ms. Athos Iviron 470 fol. 72r and 73r, is strictly connected to the figuration of the choreuma that I have come across in later manuscripts as for example Athens EBE 2458 (1336) fol. 4r, Athens EBE 885 (14th/15th century) fol. 7v and Brussels IV 515 (18th century) fol. 6v. In all these cases the same neumes are found, and without exception the figuration includes xeron klasma. The neumatic line of the syrma in the above mentioned manuscripts is given with the combination of different interval signs, for example in the ms. Athens EBE 2458, fol. 3v. It is interesting to note, however, how the choreuma figuration of Iviron 470, is transmitted in the later tradition. See Floros 1970, Vol. I, 271 and 327, and Vol. III, 46-47.

NOTE 11

Reproductions of the manuscript in Harlfinger/Reinsch/ Sonderkamp/Prato 1983, figures 144-148.

NOTE 12

However, there are some very rare cases with the form (fig. 1. 13).

NOTE 13
In Sin. gr. 1218 the form (fig. 1. 18) also occurs, though rarely.

NOTE 14
For the use of the paraklitiké in the paleo-byzantine notations, see Troelsgård 1995.

NOTE 15
In the papadikai there is a great confusion concerning the figure of the chironomic signs homalon and tromikon, which are often accompanied by the same neumes and melodic line.

NOTE 16
Rarely I have come across the form (fig. 1. 46).

NOTE 17
See Raasted 1968.

NOTE 18
See Doda 1989 217-239, esp. p. 227 and note 30.

NOTE 19
See Doda 1989 227, note 31.

NOTE 20
Reproductions of the manuscript in Harlfinger/Reinsch/ Sonderkamp/Prato 1983, tables 136-143.

NOTE 21
In the manuscript are found more semiografic stages; for the archaic one, see Raasted 1963 302-310.

NOTE 22
See Doda 1991 185-204.

NOTE 23
See Strunk 1977 (Not.), 68-111, especially 109.

NOTE 24
See Doda 1989 226.

NOTE 25
Strunk 1965 and 1977 (Class.) 41 fixes the introduction of the "round notation" to the year 1175 or thereabouts. The date 1177 is accepted by Στάθης, van Biezen 1968 13 dates it to the periode between 1150 and 1200 while Wellesz 1961 262 accepts that the introduction of the round notation took place in the 12th century. On the contrary Tillyard 1935 14 considers the date 1100.

NOTE 26
They consist of imprecision in the notation of diastematic signs which do not always have a precise significance, see Floros 1970, Vol. I 328.

NOTE 27

See Floros 1970, Vol. I, 324-326.

NOTE 28

See Kominis 1968.

NOTE 29

See Thodberg 1966 21. Kominis 1968 proposed the years between 1161 and 1180.

Table 1

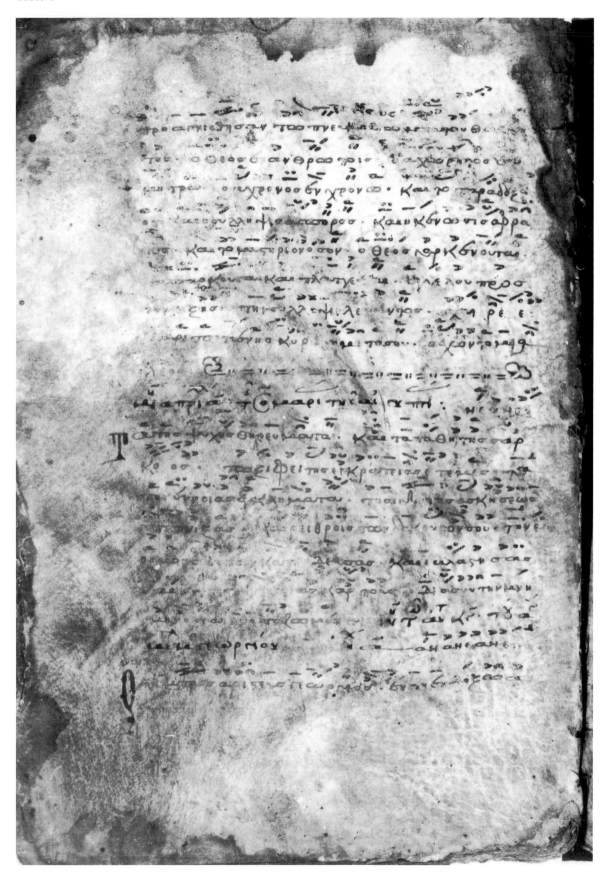

Table 2

Table 3

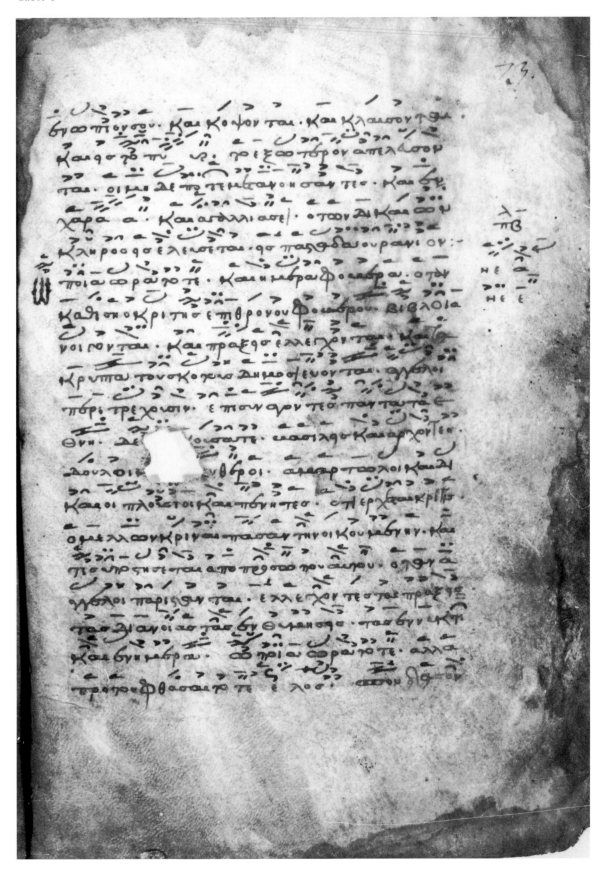

Table 4

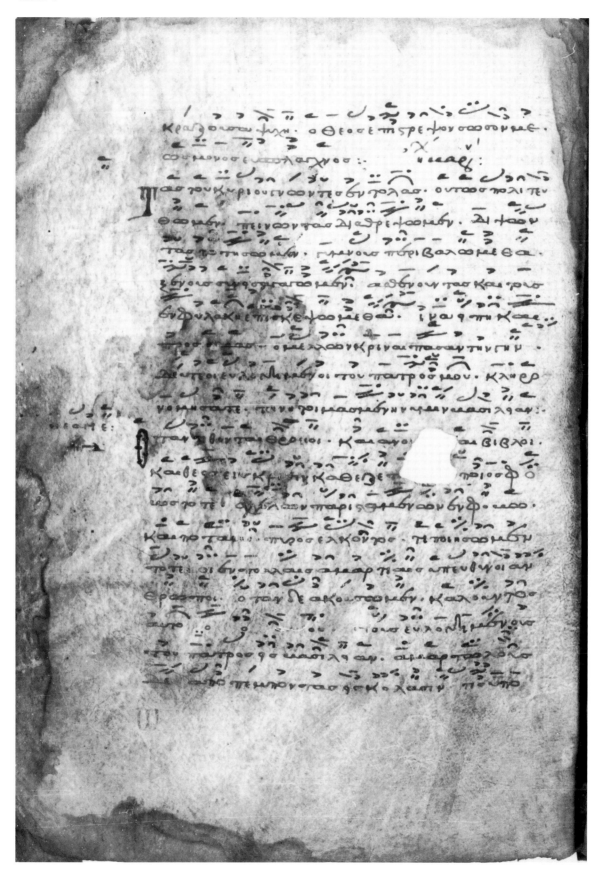

65

Table 5

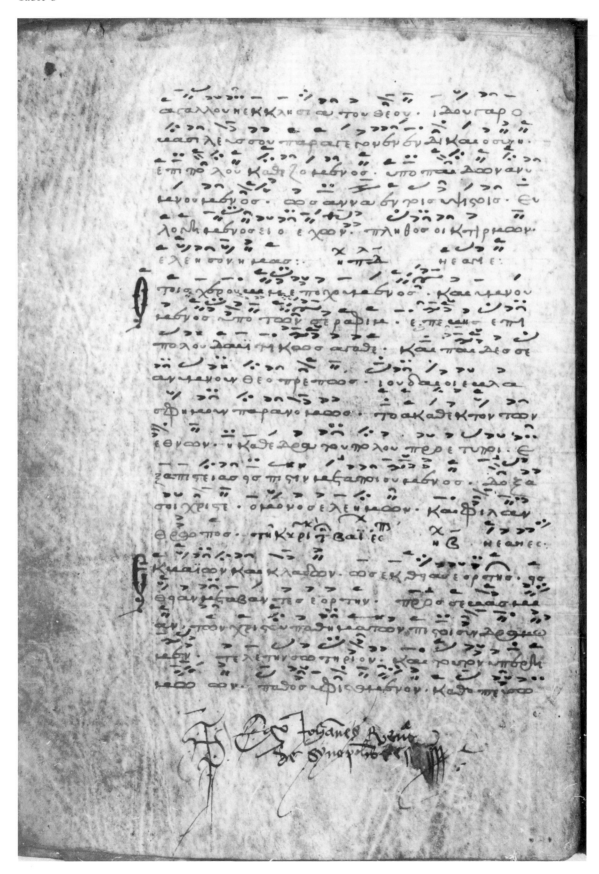

αγαλλουμεκκλησι αυτου θεου· ιδου γαρ ο
λαος λισουσου παραςτεου θυ θυ δικαιοσυν
επι πολου καθεχο λεθνοσ· υπο παιδοσ αν
λεχουλεθνοσ· σοσ αννα θυ πιοννησοιο· εν
λοκλι λεθνοσ ει ο εχου· πληθοσ οι κτηρεσ
εχεν σουν λεασ:· ηπ̄ʹ νεαμε:
Τοιαχορου εαλι ημ πολχαλεθνοσ· και αλου
λεθνοσ υπο τοσου σεραφι̅· επεσεν επι
πολου λαλιμ κοσ αγαθ̅· και παιδεοσε
αναεκου θεο πρεπασο· ιουδαιοι ελα
οφηλεου παρανοεασο· τοσ ακαθεκτον τοσ
εθνον· η καθε δεθ τουπολου περετυρι ε
ζωπιςειασ φο πι θν λεξαπου λεθνοσ· δοξα
σοι χριςτε· ο θεον ο ελεημσον· και φιλεν
θεθρπασ· τηκυρι τ̄ βαϊ εσ ηβʹ νεαμεσ:
Κλαιδουν και κλαδουν· σοσ εκ θλαισ εορτησ· θο
εθαν εθ αβαν πο εορτην· τπερ ο σεσαδοσσ
ρελκου εαλι πανμεαπου πι ποι ον δεδι
κελι τελετην σοσ σπηριον· και τουερ μποεμ
λεασο σος· πασοσ φιςσαλθλου· και θα πητοσ

℟ Johanes Læni
dr̄ φ̄ πορελ̄

Table 6

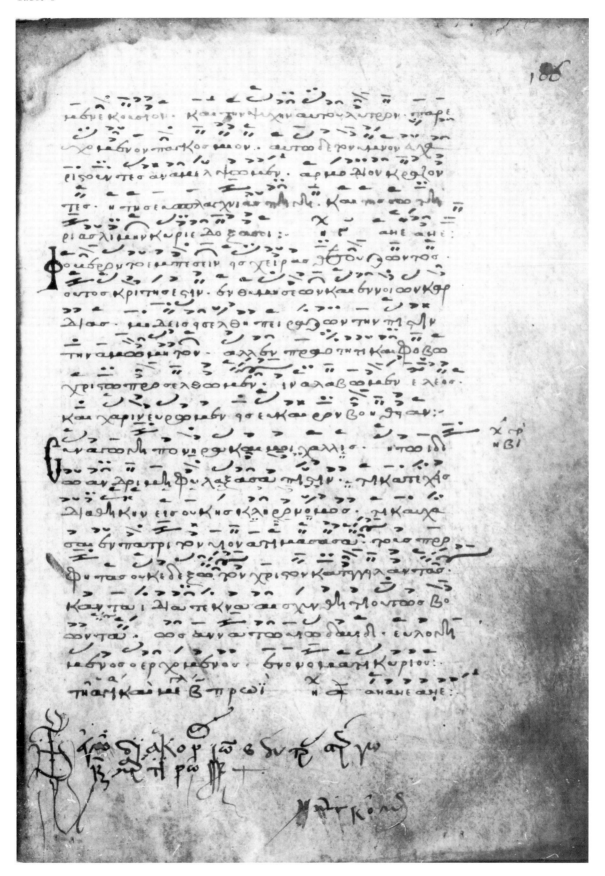

The Development of a Didactic Poem. Some remarks on the Ἴσον, ὀλίγον, ὀξεῖα by Ioannes Glykys.

Christian Troelsgård

When the discussion is about musical tradition and reform in general, didactic material often holds a central position. Such material may be determined as relating exclusively to traditional genres, or, through inclusion of innovative elements, as a vehicle of reform. Especially if we consider the late 13th and early 14th century Byzantine music, a period of intense activity, the question of continuity versus reform attracts great interest. As a way of approaching this topic, I will in this paper focus on the transmission of the ison-poem ascribed to Ioannes Glykys, the Protopsaltes, whose activities must be dated around the year 1300.

The Ἴσον, ὀλίγον, ὀξεῖα with ascription to Glykys is found in several MSS of the *anthologia*-type dating from the 14th cent. onwards, though it is easily outnumbered by the homonymic poem by his supposed pupil, Ioannes Koukouzeles. The Glykean ison-poem is normally placed in the first part of the manuscripts, in the conventional block of introductory and educational material, and it consists textually of a succession of neume-names, apparently accompanied by their musical realization, written with neumes. However, a closer look at the pieces ascribed to Glykys reveals that even if they share the incipit, some versions are shorter, some are longer, and the sequence of signs differs a great deal from one version to another. The tradition divides into three main types (here labelled A - C), each of which seems to represent an evolutionary stage of the poem.

Type A is a short list of nine cheironomic signs accompanied by their neumatic representation (see Ex. 1). Systematically these signs belong to different groups. The *ison, oligon, oxeia* and *petasthe* belong to the basic stock of interval-neumes, whereas the *kouphisma* is more rare. The remaining signs are *aphona* ("without interval value") and as such they belong to the rhythmical signs and to the group signs, the so-called *hypostaseis*. The neumation is composed to show the simple signs and some typical combinations. It is clear that type A was not intended for singing, being without a signature, and the individual signs being placed without any coherence[1]. It remains an exercise of *cheironomia*, i.e. an exercise of hand-movements, which were probably performed by the *protopsaltes* in order to conduct the choir. Since the cheironomy of the root sign is exactly the same as that of its combinations[2], the exercise might aim at the correlation of a specific hand movement with a corresponding notation. It may originally have been put together by I. Glykys because of its usefulness exclusively as such an exercise; no theoretical system whatsoever seems to lie behind the selection of signs included in the list. Nevertheless, this short version is rather frequently transmitted in the MSS. from the 14th cent. onwards and it seems to have maintained a position as an individual entity among the educational and theoretical material of Byzantine chant[3].

Type B consists of the same nine signs that we have seen in type A, still without *martyria*, but expanded with a list of intonations with differentiations and a selection of group-signs, *hypostaseis*, in each of

Ex. 1 (Type A)

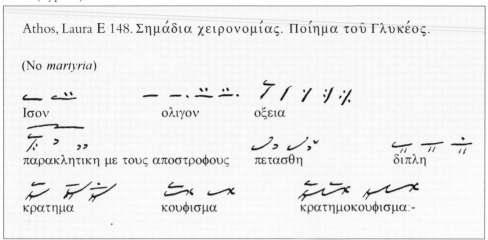

Athos, Laura E 148. Σημάδια χειρονομίας. Ποίημα τοῦ Γλυκέος.

(No *martyria*)

Ισον   ολιγον   οξεια

παρακλητικη με τους αποστροφους   πετασθη   δίπλη

κρατημα   κουφισμα   κρατημοκουφισμα:-

the eight modes (see Ex. 2)[4]. The appended part of type B has two lines of text. In the row below we find, with black ink, the name of the intonation or hypostasis in question – obviously not as a text to be sung, but only as a label – and between the "black" text and the neumes are, with red ink, placed the words of the *echemata* (αανανεανες, νεανες etc.), alternating with vocalises (the so-called asmatic syllables νε να χε etc.) and at least ten textual quotations from the sticherarion. This part of the piece, on the contrary, could have been intended for loud performance, as we do not find unconventional jumps between the final note of one figuration and the starting note of the next. The transitions between the modes might be exceptions, but generally the various intonations and signs are properly adapted to each other. Notice for example the πλάγιος πρῶτος ἔξω and the κρατημοϋπόρ-ροον, and the transition between the echema ἕτερος πλάγιος δευτέρου and the figure χαιρετισμός. However, type B has inherited the basically sche-matic character from its forerunner.

One member of this group, the MS. Kos-tamonitu 86[6], must be treated as a special case (here labelled B'). Example 3 shows the beginning of this version. Just like type B, it is furnished with a double text, but in this case it has been extended to cover the whole piece. In addition, the first group of cheironomic signs is slight-ly different, the oxeia and the *parakletike* have been put together as one figure, the *kratema* has disappeared and a new sign, *bareia*, is included as sign no. five. The version of Kostamonitu 86 suggests that the original list of cheironomic signs, more or less successfully, has been inte-grated in the eight modes structure of the *echemata-* /*hypostaseis*-list by means of double notation, double text and the addition of a *protos* signature. It looks as if a teacher or composer tried, in a second line of notation, to make singable what was originally just a list of signs and their combinations in a cheironomic exercise. Exactly in this portion of the ison-poem the layout did not come out very suc-cessful, – I have tried to show some of these odd features in my rendition of Example 3[7]. Actually, this observation supports the hypothesis that somebody through the addition of *echema*, double text and double notation has tried to integrate the now eight cheironomic signs in a version corresponding to type B. Additionally, we can with great cer-tainty contend that this adaption took place in the model of Kostamonitu 86, not in the manuscript itself. The evidence for this hypothesis is that the scribe cop-ied, erroneously, the extended and sing-able notation of the *kratemokouphisma* also for the upper line of notation, eventually

Ex. 2 (Type B)[5] (to be read column-wise)

Athens 885. Αἱ χειρονο[μίαι, ποίημα τοῦ Γλυκέος suppl.]

Ισον

ολιγον

οξεια

παρακλητικη

πετασθη

διπλη

κρατημα

κουφισμα

κρατημοκουφισμα

α- να- νε- α- νε-   ες
ηχος πρωτος τετραφωνος

α- να- νε- α- νες
ομοιος εξω

α- να- νε- α- νες
ο αυτος εσω

νε-   ε-   να
a   bcbG   b   a
κυλισμα

νε-   να
a   c b a G   b a   G F   ab a
πετασθοκαταβασμα ηγουν πελαστον

[♭]   νε- α- νες
ηχος δευτερος

νε- α- νες
ο αυτος εξω

νε-   να
G   a   bG a   G
αντικενοκυλισμα

νε-   νε-   ε
cb   c   a   ba   b   G
ετερον του ψαλτικου

leaving out the simple cheironomic notation of the sign known from types A and
B. Compared to the B-type, B' displays
some further differences: some extra
hypostaseis have been added, one of the
quotations from the sticherarion is shorter, and some extra have been inserted. In
the last figuration δαρτά, the schematic
way of presenting the material is
resumed. The *darta* of Kostamonitu 86
make up a long series of combinations
with *dyo kentemata* that could not possibly be sung. Also this shift in character
shows that type B' represents an interme-
diary stage in the development of the
ison-poem. It witnesses the process of
fusing together different elements of
musical exercises. In fact, we can almost
watch a *maïstor* at work, editing, composing and appending new material to his
compendium of Byzantine chant.

The complete sequence of signs in
type B' is:

νε- ε
G a cb a
θεματισμος εσω

νε- ε
G a dc b
ετερος εξω

α- να- νε
b abG a
επεγερμα

ση- με- ρον¹
G ab b
δαρτα

νε
bcba bcba bcba G
τρομικον*στρεπτον*εκτρεπτον

νε-
Ga G aF Ga G aF G
ομαλον

ση- με- ρον* χο- ρει - αν ε- πι-
bc b a ba Ga a G a
κρο- τη- σω- μεν²
ca b aG G
ορθιον μετα και αλλων σημαδιων

α- νε- α- νες
ηχος τριτος

α- νε- α- νες
ο αυτος εσω

α- νε- α- νες
ετερος εξω

α- νε- α- νες
ομοιος θες και αποθες

νε- ες
cb cd
σταυρος

νε- ες
ο αυτος

νε-
c d c b a
αναβασις και καταβασις

α- γι- α- α
ηχος τεταρτος

α- γι- α
ο αυτος εξω

α- γι- α
ετερος εσω

νε- χε- ε
dc d c b
αντικενωμα

νε-
d c d c ba b
συναγμα

νε-
e d c b a G b c d c d ε
τρομικοσυναγμα

νε- ε
d cb c
σεισμα

νε- ε
[e c]
πιασμα

α- νε- α- νες
ηχος πλαϊ πρωτου

α- νε- α- νες
ο αυτος

α- νε- α- νες
ετερος εξω

νε- ε
GFE GFE FE FED
κρατημοῦπορροον

χαι- ρε³
G F E FG FE FG FED
θεμα απλουν

χαι- ρε⁴
D F E D C CD FED
ουρανισμα

νε- α- νες
ηχος πλαϊ δευτερου

νε- α- νες
ο αυτος

νε- α- νες νε- να- νω
ετερος εξω φθορα

χαι- ρε τε⁵
a bcba b G a GF G aF G
χορευμα μετα και αλλων σημαδιων

ση- με- ρον⁶
EF DE E
συρμαν

ση- με- ρον⁷
FG DF E
δαρμος

νε- α- νε- ες
E FGF E CD G
ετερος πλαγιος δευτερου

χαι- ρε⁸
G F F Ga b a GF G EFED
χαιρετισμος

α- νες
ηχος βαρυς

α- νες
ο αυτος

α- νε- α- νες
F G D ED CF
αναστομα

νε- α- γι- ε
ηχος πλαϊ τεταρτου

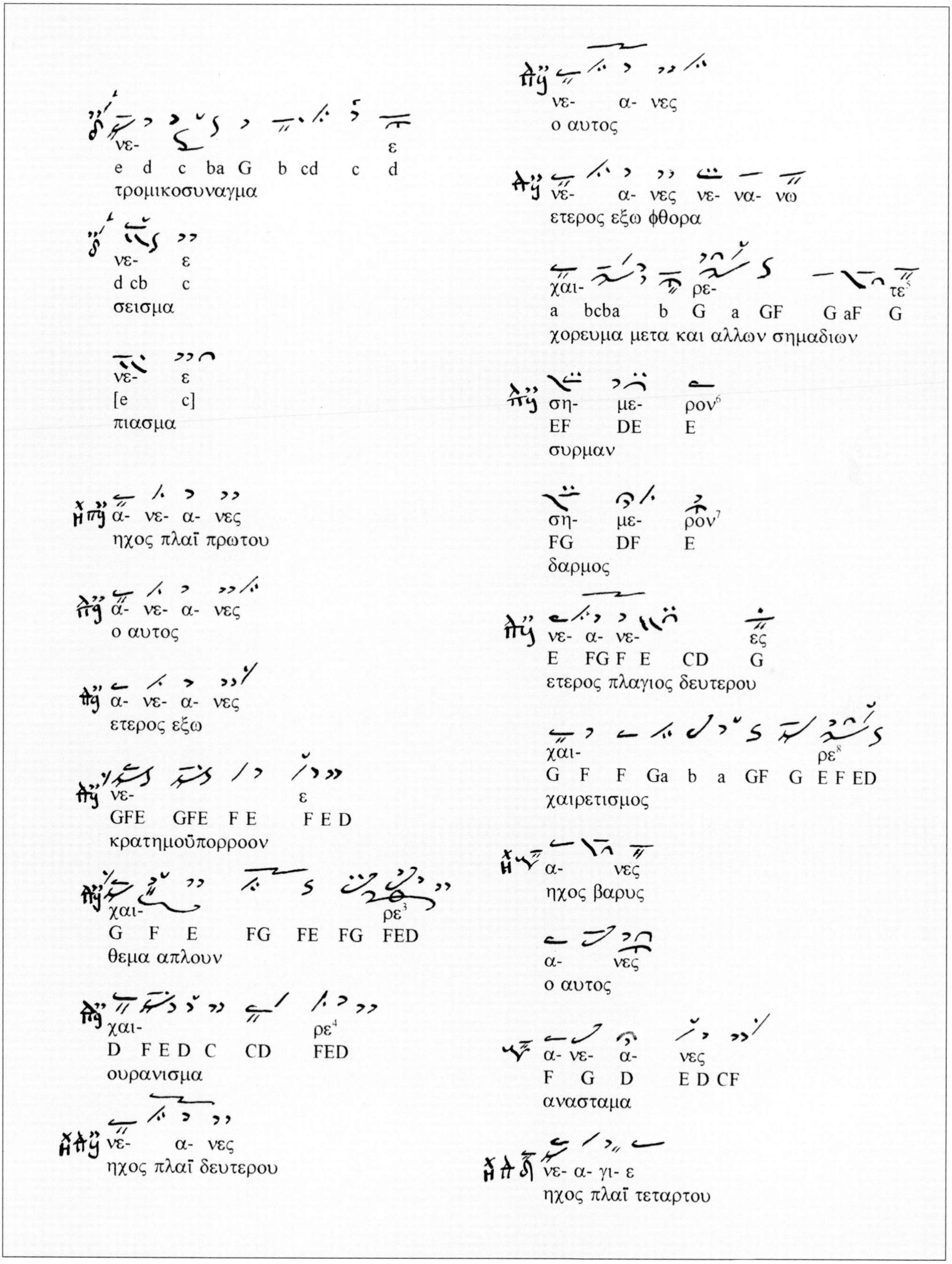

Ex. 2 (continued)

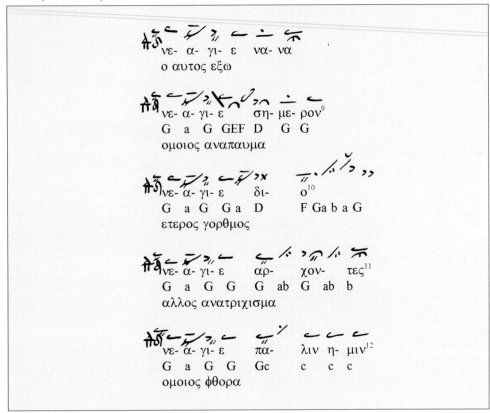

Ἴσον, ὀλίγον, ὀξεῖα, πετασθή, βαρεῖα, διπλῆ, κούφισμα, πετασθοκούφισμα, ἦχ. α' (ανανεανες), κύλισμα, πετασθοκατάβασμα ἤγουν πελασθόν, κατάβασμα καὶ ἀνάβασμα, ἦχ. β' (νεανες), ἀντικενοκύλισμα, ἕτερον τοῦ ψαλτικοῦ, γοργόν [= *tromikon*], στρεπτόν, τρομικόν, ὁμαλόν, κράτημα, θεματισμὸς ἔσω (text: διο), ἕτερος ἔξω (text: μεθ'ων), ἐπέγερμα, παρακάλεσμα καὶ ἕτερον σημάδιον, ἕτερον παρακάλεσμα, ὁμαλὸν μετὰ θέματος (text: ο θεος), ὄρθιον (text: σημερον χορειαν), λαρύγγισμα, ἀργοσύνθετον, δίπλωμα, ἦχ. γ' (ανεανες), σταυρός, ἄλλος, ὁ αὐτός, ἀπόθετον, ἀνάβασις καὶ κατάβασις, κροῦσμα, ἕτερον, ἦχ. δ' (αγια), ψηφιστοκατάβασμα μετὰ ἀντικενώμα[τος], πίασμα, ψηφιστοσύναγμα, θὲς καὶ ἀπόθες, ἄλλον τοῦ ψαλτικοῦ, στραγγίσματα, ἀπορροή, λυγίσματα, καὶ ἔτι λυγίσματα, ξηρὸν

κλάσμα οὕτως, καὶ ἄλλον, ἦχ. πλ. α' (ανεανες), οὐράνισμα, κρατημοϋπορροοκατάβασις, παρακλητική, τοῦτο δὲ ὅλον λέγεται κολαφισμός (text: ουτε ουτος ημαρτε), θέμα ἁπλοῦν, ἦχ. πλ. β' (νενανω), χόρευμα μετὰ ἑτέρων σημαδίων (text: χαιρετε), θὲς καὶ ἀπόθες καὶ, ἀντικούντισμα, χαιρετισμός (text: χαιρε), βυθογρόνθισμα (text: χαιρετε), χαιρετισμός (text: χαιροις), σύρμα (text: σημερον), δαρμός (text: σημερον), ἦχ. βαρ. (ανες), βαρύς, ἕτερος τετράφωνος, βαρύς, ἦχ. πλ. δ' (νεαγιε), ἀνατρίχισμα (text: αρχοντες), ἀνάσταμα, φθορά (text: παλιν ημιν), γορθμός (text: διο), ταῦτα δὲ εἰσὶν πάντα δαρτά :–

Type C appears to represent a further development of type B'⁸. The first signs are here fully integrated in the structure of the poem. The red text (ie. the echemata–syllables, the asmatic syllables and

Kostamonitu 86. Ἀρχὴ τῶν σημαδίων τῆς παπαδικῆς τέχνης, ψαλλομένων κατ' ἦχον. Ἀρχή, μέση καὶ τέλος, σύστημα πάντων τῶν σημαδίων τῶν ἀνιόντων καὶ κατιόντων, τὸ ἴσον ἐστί. χωρὶς γὰρ τοῦ ἴσου, ὅλα ἄφωνα. ποιηθέντα παρὰ τοῦ πρωτοψάλτου κυροῦ ἰωάννου τοῦ γλυκέως, ἦχος α'.

(fol. 13v)

Ισον   ολιγον   οξεια

πετασθη   βαρεια   διπλη

κουφισμα   πετασθοκουφισμα   κρατημοκουφισμα

κυλισμα   πετασθοκαταβασ(14r)μα ηγουν πελασθον

[κτλ.]

the short quotations) has disappeared and instead the various names of the *hypostaseis* are set skillfully to the melody of themselves. Thus, the character of the piece has changed from a diagram or a list of signs into a coherent didactic poem. Much more attention has been paid to the transitions between the modes, and here again, some extra *hypostaseis* have been added, and some have been set in a different mode. In type C almost all traces of the echemata-list have been eliminated, only βαρὺς τετρά–φωνος remains as a relic of its former state. Finally, a return into the first authentic mode has been attached. In short, the C-type of the ison-poem ascribed to Ioannes Glykys is rather similar to the more widespread Μέγα ἴσον by Ioannes Koukouzeles. Here follows a synopsis of the signs included in these two poems[9]. To facilitate the comparison, the principal shifts of mode are indicated in parentheses.

EBE 2269 (Glykys)	EBE 2458 (Koukouzeles)
Ἴσον	Ἴσον
ὀλίγον	ὀλίγον
ὀξεῖα	ὀξεῖα
καὶ πετασθή	καὶ πετασθή
βαρεῖα	
διπλῆ	καὶ διπλῆ
κούφισμα	
πετασθοκούφισμα	
τρομικὸν καὶ	
ἐκτρεπτόν	
κράτημα	κράτημα
κρατημοκούφισμα	κρατημοκατάβασμα
κύλισμα	τρομικόν
πελασθόν	στρεπτόν
κατάβασμα	θὲς καὶ ἀπόθες
(β')	(β')
ἀντικενοκύλισμα	
ἕτερον	
ὁμαλόν	
θεματισμὸς ἔσω	θεματισμός
ἕτερος ἔξω	
ἐπέγερμα μετὰ ὁμαλοῦ	
παρακάλεσμα καὶ ἑτέρων σημαδίων	
ἕτερον	
ὄρθιον	ὄρθιον σὺν τούτοις
λαρύγγισμα	οὐράνισμα
ἀργοσύνθετον	σεῖσμα
δίπλωμα	ἀνατρίχισμα
κροῦσμα	σύναγμα
ἄλλον	κύλισμα
σταυρός	στραγγίσματα
(γ')	(γ')
ἄλλος	κροῦσμα
ἀπόθετον	ἄλλον
(δ')	(δ')
ἀνάβασις καὶ	ἀνάβασμα καὶ
κατάβασις	κατάβασμα
	ὁμαλόν
ψηφιστοκατάβασμα μετὰ ἐλαφροῦ	ψηφιστοκατάβασμα
ἀντικένωμα	
παρακάλεσμα ἕτερον	παρακάλεσμα
τρομικοπαρακάλεσμα	
στραγγίσματα	
ἀπορροολυγίσματα	ἀπορροή
ἕτερα λυγίσματα	ἀντικένωμα
ξηρὸν κλάσμα	ἀντικενοκύλισμα
(πλ. α')	(πλ. α')
καὶ ἄλλον	ἀργοσύνθετον
πίασμα	κολαφισμός
οὐράνισμα	κούφισμα
κρατημοκατάβασμα καὶ	κρατημοκούφισμα
(πλ. β')	τρομικοπαρακάλεσμα
παρακλητική	καὶ παρακλητική
τοῦτο δὲ λέγεται κολαφισμός	(πλ. β')

θέμα ἁπλοῦν
θὲς καὶ ἀπόθες καὶ
χαιρετισμός
τοῦτο δὲ λέγεται ἀντικούντισμα
σύναγμα
χόρευμα
σεῖσμα

σύρμα καὶ ἕτερον
δαρμός

τοῦτο δὲ λέγεται ἀντικούντισμα
χορεύμα
ἕτερον ὅμοιον
σύνθεσις τοῦ μεγάλου ἄσματος

ἑτέρα σύνθεσις ἐξ αὐτῶν (in marg.)
ἕτερον βυθογρόνθισμα
κλάσματα ἀμφότερα
χαιρετισμός καὶ βαρεῖα ὁμοῦ
πίασμα
ἠχάδιν
ὃ λέγεται διπλοπέλασμα
θέμα ἁπλοῦν

βύθον γρόνθισμα
σύρμα
δαρτά

καὶ τέλος στιχηροῦ ἐν τούτῳ
(βαρυς)

τέλος στιχηροῦ ἐν τούτῳ
(βαρυς)
βαρύς

βαρὺς τετράφωνος
ἀνάσταμα
δαρτά
ταὐτὸ μετὰ ἐπεγέρματος
(πλ. δ')
ἀνάπαυμα
γορθμός
ἀνατρίχισμα
διπλοπελασθόν
φθορά
ἔναρξις
γοργόν
ἀργόν
θέμα ἁπλοῦν

ἕτερος τετράφωνος
ἀνάσταμα
δαρτά
ταῦτα πάντα μετὰ ἐπεγέρματος
(πλ. δ')
ἀνάπαυμα σήμερον
νε γορθμός

διπλοπετασθόν
φθορά
ἔναρξις
γοργόν
ἀργόν

καὶ προόσχες μαθητά
πνεύματα τέσσαρα
ἑπτὰ φωναὶ διπλασμός
καὶ τρία κρατήματα ἐντέχνως
συντεθέντα
(α')
παρὰ ἰωάννου τοῦ κουκουζέλη
καὶ μαΐστορος :-

(α')
ἡμίφωνον καὶ πρόσχες ὦ μαθητά :-

This accounts for a correlation of the overall design of these two didactic poems. Apart from the beginning, also a longer identical sequence of neumes is found in the *barys* and *plagios tetartos* sections. But the intricate relationship between the Koukouzelean poem and the B and C types of the one ascribed to Glykys must be studied also in details. The figuration *orthion* is exemplified through a quotation from the sticheron Δεῦτε πιστοὶ σήμερον (see example 4). Both text and melody of type B differ from the Ambrosian sticherarion regarding the last part, but in principle all versions follow the melody of the sticheron until the caesura after χορεῖαν. Type C has adapted the text ὄρθιον to the melody, but in the Koukouzelean poem a syllabic texting has been maintained through the addition of σὺν τούτοις, maybe inspired by the μετὰ καὶ ἄλλων σημαδίων of type B. Melodically, the Koukouzelean *orthion* cadences on G instead of a, and thus it deviates from the melody of the traditional sticherarion in favour of the contextual demands of the ison-poem.

Ex. 4

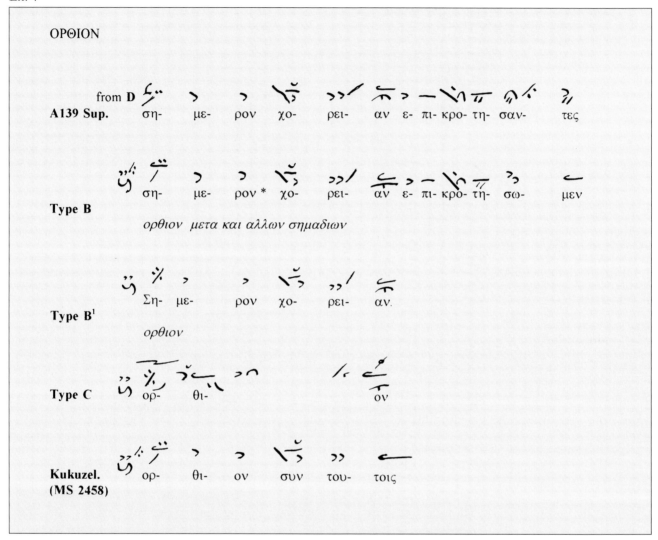

In the sticherarion the *choreuma*-figure occurs three times in combination with the word χαίρετε[10]. The B and C types cover a shorter portion of the melody than B'; it looks as if it is only the first part of the figure that is assigned to the name *choreuma* in these versions. The Koukouzelean poem is more elaborate as it exemplifies both the continuation with two *oliga* plus *diple* (texted ἕτερον ὅμοιον) and, together with B', another possible continuation with the figure *seisma* (texted χόρευμα, see example 5).

In most of the figurations it is difficult to determine the exact interrelation between the different *ison*-poems, but in the case of *anapauma* plus *gorthmos* it appears that the Koukouzelean poem and Glykys C are secondary to the B-type of the Glykys piece. The word Σήμερον has been preserved in the Koukouzelean poem, as a remnant of an earlier stage of development, and what was originally a sung intonation, νε–ά–γι–ε, has now been beautifully dressed by the four syllables of ἀ –νά –παυμα. Thus, *anapau-*

XOPEYMA

A(272r)

χαι- αι- αι- αι- ρε- ε- ε- τε- ε- ε- ε- ε- ε- ε

Type B

χαι- αι- αι- ρε- ε- ε- τε

χορευμα μετα και αλλων σημαδιων

Type B'

χαι- αι- αι- ρε- ε- ε- ε- τε- ε- ε- ε

χορευμα μετα ετερων σημαδιων

Type C

Χο- ρε- ε- ε- ευ- μα

Kukuzel. (MS 2458)

Χο- ο- ο- ρε- ε- ευ- μα- α- α- α- α- α

Ε- ε- ε- τε- ε-ε- ε- ρο- ο- ο- ο- ον ο- ο- μοι- ον

ma appears to be the term for the *apechema*, a differentiation that adapts the fourth plagal intonation to a continuation from low D. Exactly the same function is performed by the following figuration, *gorthmos*. The Koukouzelean poem uses the nonword νε (see the synopsis above) to fill out at the beginning, in the position of the last syllable of the former νεάγιε, and the text γορθμός replaces the equally accentuated διό of the sticherarion. In both cases it appears that Koukouzeles, if not systematically, then extremely pedagogically, has adapted the technical nomenclature of some melodic turns of the sticherarion to their own melody. Again in this example, the notation of the late C type is the most developed of them all. Besides, it is set in the *barys* mode, and also because of its fusing together the two figurations into one phrase it appears to be the version mostly removed from the point of departure (see example 6).

I have now presented the three main types of the *ison*-poem ascribed to Ioannes Glykys as it is found in the musical MSS. Each of these types seems to represent a stage of development, ranging from a schematic exercise of *cheironomia*, through the double-text types to a coherent didactic poem. I have already mentioned that the Koukouzelean ison-poem on the one hand incorporates features from the B types[11], but on the other

Ex. 6

ΑΝΑΠΑΥΜΑ + ΓΟΡΘΜΟΣ

A(100r)   Ση- με- ρον

A(64r)   from a   δι- ο- ο

Type B   ομοιος αναπαυμα
νε- α- γι- ε Ση- με- ρον   νε- α- γι- ε δι- ο
     ετερος γορθμος

Type C   α- να- α- παυ- μα-α γορ-   θμο- ος

Kuk.   α- να- παυ- μα Ση- με- ρον   νε γορ-θμο-ο-ος
(MS 2458)

---

hand, in its basic concept and in many details, matches type C. The development of the *ison*-poem seems to have been accomplished through integration of a number of different elements, at least some of which can be identified with probability, as shown in fig. 1.

Beside type A existed another, anonymous, exercise of cheironomic signs, maybe more. The evidence of this is a list found in MS Vat. gr. 791[12]. This exercise includes the sign *bareia*, exactly the feature that was significant of type B' (MS Kostamonitu 86). In addition, the wording of the rubric links these two MSS together[13]. Consequently, I consider it very likely that a list of the type we know from Vat. gr. 791 influenced the formation of type B'.

I have already mentioned that a list of intonations with differentiations, the so-called *apechemata*, seems to have played a part in the development of the B-types. Such lists are documented in round notation sources already from the 12th cent.[14]. Eventually, these lists were incorporated in the *propaideia*-block of the anthologia-MSS, I think, in the shape of a set of intonations linked with typical incipits of the sticherarion. This accounts for the eight mode design of the B types.

Fig. 1

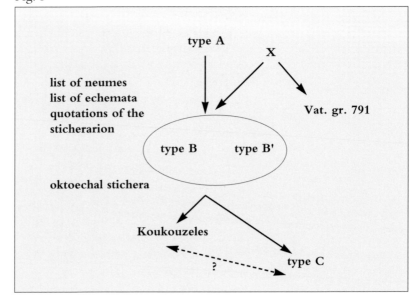

Another qualified contributor to the establishment of the B types is the lists of simple and great signs. Already Jørgen Raasted has placed the neume-lists of the old MS Laura Γ. 67 and the sticherarion Paris, BN ancien fonds gr. 261 (A.D. 1289) in connection with the *Ison* by Glykys[15]. Of these, especially the list of the Paris MS calls for attention. It is entitled Ἀρχή τῶν σημαδί[ων] τῆς παπαδ[ι]κῆς τέχνης, a wording exactly corresponding to the first phrase of the rubric in Kostamonitu 86 (see above Ex. 3). Although Paris gr. 261 includes roughly the same selection of signs as Glykys B, only three exactly identical sequences, ἴσον / ὀλίγον / ὀξεία, τρομικόν / ἄλλον (=*strepton*) / ἕτερον (=*ekstrepton*) and σύναγμα / ἄλλον (=*tromikosynagma*) appear in both sources. Further, the hypothesis of a coherence between the Paris list and the B types is supported by the existence of another 14th century list of neumes in MS Jerusalem, Saba 602 fols. 10rv. The rubric of this list is identical to the above mentioned, and regarding the selection and sequence of signs it relates to both type B and the Paris list. All neumes and figurations of these lists belong to the round notation of the sticherarion and the psaltikon. However, just like the *ison*-poems, it does not follow any particular classification of neumes. The Paris list is in the MS followed by another list of simple signs, a selection of group signs and rhythmical signs, tables of ascending and descending intervals, and finally, a diagram that relates the ἦχοι to the ancient modes. It is obvious to me that this very early *papadike*, or a corresponding block of educational-musical material from before the year 1300, played an important part in the development of the ison-poems[16].

A selection of short musical and textual quotations from stichera is a characteristic from the B-types onwards. These may have been applied to exemplify some characteristic turns of the sticherarion, in the manner known from the *echemata*-list with incipits of stichera appended. It cannot be determined whether such a list of memorable turns or typical melodic movements existed independently, or the quotations were selected *ad hoc*, specifically with the purpose of enhancing the B and C types of the *ison*-poem.

Finally, a thorough composed oktoechal form, returning to *protos* in the conclusion, is known from three traditional stichera[17]. We have information that the most famous of these, Θεαρχίῳ νεύματι, was used as for educational purposes[18]. The modal structure of these stichera might have inspired Koukouzeles to compile his Μέγα ἴσον, and similarly to the transformation of the Glykean poem into type C.

Most of these constituent elements pertain to the sticherarion. Nevertheless, also many features from the psaltikon are included, thus making the poem more suitable for a general "method" of Byzantine chant. In this respect, the ison-poems did not in themselves claim any measure of innovation, but they represent a step by step improved tool for teachers to train their pupils in the traditional Byzantine sticherarion and psaltikon. The codification of the *ison*-poems in the *anthologiai* may on the other hand have contributed to a more extended use of great *hypostaseis* in the musical MSS from the beginning of the 14th cent. From this point of view the more developed forms of the *ison*-poem, type C and Koukouzeles' Μέγα ἴσον, might be looked at as intermediates between the traditional genres and the kalophonic style, which seems to have matured approximately contemporaneously with the creation of the *ison*-poems[19]. While some melodic and structural features of the kalophonic sticherarion depend on the traditional sticherarion, the melismatic character of the kalophonic style is most certainly linked to the tradition of the psaltikon and the asmatikon[20].

The close relationship between the Koukouzelean *ison*-poem (of which the earliest dated witness is MS Athens, EBE 2458, 1336 A.D.) and the B types of the poem ascribed to Glykys suggests that the bringing together of these different elements was accomplished very early, i.e. at least before 1336. Thus, there exists a possibility that Ioannes Glykys, the Protopsaltes, was involved not only in the creation of type A, but also in type B. Our manuscript evidence of the B types, at best, goes back only to the late 14th cent.[21], and therefore, the precise dating and the authorship of the different types are topics open to discussion and reasoning within the given limits. Type C of the Glykys ἴσον is on the one hand a clear genetic continuation of the B types, on the other hand it appears very closely related to the Koukouzelean poem. A closer study of the manuscript tradition of type C will be necessary to arrive at a more precise date of composition. There is, however, no doubt that exactly in the late 13th and early 14th cent. an enormous activity in the field of musical education took place, an activity in which Ioannes Glykys, ὁ διδάσκαλος τῶν διδασκάλων[22], was a very significant character.

Bibliography

Chatzegiakoumis, M. 1972
Μουσικά Χειρόγραφα
Τουρκοκρατείας (1453-1832), Athens.

Dévai, G. 1958
The Musical Study of Koukouzeles in a
14th Century Manuscript", Acta Antiqua
Academiae Scientiarum Hungaricae VI
(1958), 213-235.

Gertsman, E.V. 1994
Petersburg Theoretikon, Odessa.

Hannick, C./Wolfram, G. 1985
Gabriel Hieromonachos, Abhandlung über
den Kirchenmusik, Monumenta Musicae
Byzantinae, Corpus Scriptorum de Re
Musica I, edd. Christian Hannick and Ger-
da Wolfram, Vienna.

Husmann, H. 1970
Die Oktomodalen Stichera und die
Entwicklung des Byzantinischen Oktoechos, Archiv für Musikwissenschaft 27
(1970) 304-325.

Husmann, H. 1981
Chromatik und Enharmonik in der byzantinischen Musik, Byzantion 51 (1981) 169-
200.

Jakovljević, A. 1988
Δίγλωσση Παλαιογραφία και
Μελωδοί–Υμνογράφοι του Κώδικα
των Αθηνών 928, Leukosia (Cyprus).

Petrescu, J.D. 1932
Les idiomèles et le canon de l'office de
Noël, Paris

Raasted, J. 1961
Diskussionsbeiträge zum XI. international-
en Byzantinistenkongress, München 1958,
edd. Franz Dölger and Hans-Georg Beck,
München 1961.

Raasted, J. 1966
Intonation Formulas and Modal Signatures
in Byzantine Musical Manuscripts, MMB
Subsidia VII, Copenhagen.

Raasted, J./Perria, L. 1992
Sticherarium Ambrosianum, MS A 139 sup.,
Facsimile edition in MMB XI, edd. Jørgen
Raasted and Lidia Perria, Copenhagen.

di Salvo, B. 1959-60
Gli asmata nella musica bizantina, Bolletino
della Badia greca di Grottaferrata, vols. 13
(1959) 45-50 and 135-178 and 14 (1960)
145-178.

Stathis, G.Th. 1975
Τὰ Χειρόγραφα Βυζαντινῆς Μουσικῆς, Ἅγιον Ὄρος. Κατάλογος
περιγραφικὸς τῶν χειρογράφων
κωδίκων Βυζαντινῆς Μουσικῆς τῶν
ἀποκειμένων ἐν
ταῖς Βιβλιοθήκαις τῶν ἱερῶν Μονῶ
ν καὶ Σκητῶν τοῦ Ἁγίου Ὄρους,
Vol. I, Athens

Stathis, G.Th. 1979
Οἱ ἀναγραμματισμοὶ καὶ τὰ μαθήματα τῆς βυζαντινῆς μελοποιί–
ας, (second ed. Athens 1992), Athens.

Tardo, L. 1938
L'antica melurgia bizantina, Grottaferrata.

Notes

NOTE 1

cf. Chazegiakoumis 1975 280, "εἰσὶ καὶ διὰ μόνην χειρονομίαν ταῦτα, οὐ μὴν δὲ ψάλλονται." In MS Laura I 165 (1656) (15th cent.), fol. 16v we find the following rubric in top of a slightly different list of neumes: "Τὰ αὐτὰ σημάδια μετὰ τῶν χειρονομιῶν αὐτῶν. χειρονομοῦνται οὖν χωρὶς μέλους."

NOTE 2

Cf. Gabriel Hieromonachos, Hannick/Wolfram 1985, lines 154 - 162.

NOTE 3

Until now, I have localized Type A in the following MSS.:
St. Petersburg gr. 497 (early 14th cent.) fol. 1r
St. Petersburg gr. 498 (16th cent.) fol. 4r (facsimiles of the two St. Petersburg MSS in Gertsman 1994)
Athens, EBE 899 (end of the 14th cent.) fol. 20rv.
Athens, EBE 2837 (15th-16th) fol. 2v-3r.
Athos, Laura E 148 (610) (15th-16th) fol. 12r.
Athos, Laura E 173 (635) (A.D. 1436) 1v.
Athos, Pantokratoros 214, (A.D. 1433) fol. 10v (without ascription).
Athos, Vatopediu 1530 (15th cent.) fol. 2v.

NOTE 4

Type B is recorded in:
Athens, EBE 885 (14th cent., second half) fols. 7r-8r. Parts of this version are shown in Gabriel Hieromonachos, Hannick/Wolfram 1985 129-132 (Commentary).
Athos, Laura E 165 (1656) (15th cent.) fols. 16v-17r (without ascription to Glykys).

Slightly different is type B' = Athos, Kostamonitu 86 (15th, first half) 13v-15r.

NOTE 5

Notes for Example 2:
1. This opening is found in the following stichera (references to the Ambrosian Sticherarion, A 139 sup. = MMB XI, edd. Jørgen Raasted and Lidia Perria, Copenhagen 1992):

Σήμερον ὁ Χριστὸς ἐν Βηθλεέμ (80v), Σήμερον ὁ Χριστὸς ἐν ἰορδάνη (97v), Σήμερον συμεών ἐν ταῖς αγκάλαις (114v), Σήμερον συμεών ὁ πρεσβύτης (115v), Σήμερον τῷναῷ(54r) and Σήμερον ἐκ ρίζης (64v).
2. From the sticheron Δεῦτε πιστοὶ σήμερον (fol. 271v), "ἐπικροτήσωμεν" instead of "ἐπικροτήσαντες".
3. I have not been able to localize this place in the sticherarion. The formula χαιρετισμός is often denoted with a θέμα ἀπλοῦν in the old sticheraria, see eg. in Vind. theol. gr. 136 (MMB vol. X) fol. 172, on the word χαῖρε in Ὡς στέφανον.
4. From Ἀπεστάλη ἄγγελος (122v).
5. From Δεῦτε πιστοὶ σήμερον (271v) or Ἑορτὴ χαρμόσυνος (142r).
6. The following stichera have this opening: Σήμερον τῆς παγκοσμίου (9r), Σήμερον συγκαλεῖται (37r), Σήμερον ἡ ψαλμική (94r), Σήμερον γεννᾶται (78r), Σήμερον τὸστίφη (55r), Σήμερον ὁ τοῖς νοεροῖς (8r) and Σήμερον ἡ χάρις (223r).
7. I have not been able to localize this opening, it may be a variant of the above.
8. From Ἀσκητικὸν γυμνάσιον (fol. 104v)
9. Examples of this opening are: Σήμερον ἡ κτίσις (100r), Σήμερον τῶν ὑδάτων (93r), Σήμερον ὁ ἀπρόσιτος (234v), Σήμερον τοῦ ναοῦ (238v).
10. From Εἰς αἶνον ἔδραμες (64r).
11. From Ἄρχοντες λαῶν (234v)
12. From Πάλιν ἡμῖν χρυσορρόας νείλος (106v), the original main signature is tritos.

NOTE 6

Description of this MS. in Stathis 1975 656.

NOTE 7

Note the shift of left margin and the interlinear correction of the kouphisma.

NOTE 8

Until now I have localized Type C in two late MSS:

Athens, EBE 2269 (17th cent.) pp. 48-50
Bruxelles, Bibl. Royale IV.515 (ca. 1700) fols. 6r-7v.

NOTE 9

Glykys after Athens, EBE 2269, pp. 48-50 (17th cent.), Rubric: Σημάδια ψαλλόμενα κατ᾽ἦχον ἐντέχνως ποιηθέντα παρὰ κὺρ ἰωάννου τοῦ γλυκέως. Koukouzeles after EBE 2458 (1336 A.D) fol. 3r, Rubric: Σημάδια ψαλλόμενα κατ᾽ἦχον. ποίημα τοῦ μαΐστορος κυροῦ ἰωάννου τοῦ κουκουζέλη. Edition in Dévai 1958. A new, critical edition by Maria Alexandru in preparation.

NOTE 10

In A 139 Sup. fol. 142v (Ἡ πάνσεπτος ἀποστόλων) and twice in fol. 272r (Δεῦτε πιστοὶ σήμερον).

NOTE 11

Judging from the sequence and selection of signs, the Μέγαῖσον by Koukouzeles seems to be somewhat closer to the B' type. A good illustration of this is the figuration of *darta*, that is absent in B but has approximately the same texting in B' and in Koukouzeles's composition. On the other hand, the sequence *anapauma/gorthmos* is found exclusively in B and Koukouzeles. Other contradictory examples could be mentioned.

NOTE 12

Facsimile in Tardo 1938 174.

NOTE 13

Vat. gr. 791 reads: Ἀρχὴ μέσης (sic) καὶ πλήρωσις. σύστημα πάντων τῶν ἀνιόντων. καὶ κατιόντων φωνῶν. τὸ ἴσον χωρὶς τούτων οὐ κατωρθοῦται φωνή. Cf. above, Ex. 3.

NOTE 14

Cf. Raasted 1966 48-49.

NOTE 15
Raated 1961 74: "Später seien aus diesen Listen (Laura Γ 67/Paris 261) einerseits die Papadiken entstanden, anderseits die Ison-gedichte, deren bekanntestes das von Kou-kouzeles sei. Älter als dieses sei ein sehr ähnliches von Joh. Glykys, der gewissermas-sen im Zentrum dieser Tradition zu stehen scheine".

NOTE 16
The importance of the Paris MS in relation to the Koukouzelean ison-poem was already suggested by Petrescu 1932 48 - 51, and was elaborated by Husmann 1981 169 - 200, especially 181 - 82.

NOTE 17
Cf. Husmann 1970.

NOTE 18
Cf. Raasted 1966 53.

NOTE 19
The inclusion of the kalophonic group σύνθεσις τοῦ μεγάλου ἄσματος in the Koukouzelean poem may be seen in con-nection with the early kalophonic reper-toire, named "asma" in Italian MSS, described and indexed by di Salvo 1959-60.

NOTE 20
cf. Stathis 1979 60-61.

NOTE 21
On the date of Athens 885 (Type B), see Jakovljević 1988 A'.

NOTE 22
Glykys is given this epithet in MS Chilan-dar 146 (ca. 1330-40) fol. 287r.

Μία περίπτωση επιβίωσης βυζαντινών μελωδικών στοιχείων σ' ένα πασχαλινό τροπάριο από τη Ζάκυνθο

**Μ.Φ.
Δραγούμης**

Η επτανησιακή εκκλησιαστική μουσική διαφέρει σημαντικά από το λεγόμενο νεο-βυζαντινό μέλος, που βρίσκεται σήμερα σε χρήση στις περισσότερες ελληνικές εκκλησίες. Κατάγεται από την Κρήτη και μεταφυτεύτηκε στα Επτάνησα στα 1669, όταν πολυάριθμες κρητικές οικογένειες μετανάστευσαν στα Επτάνησα μετά την άλωση του βενετοκρατούμενου Χάνδακα από τους Τούρκους. Η εκκλησιαστική μουσική που μετέφεραν οι κρητικοί πρόσφυγες στην καινούρια τους πατρίδα δεν άργησε να πέσει σε αχρηστία στην ίδια την Κρήτη, ενώ στα Επτάνησα γνώρισε μια δεύτερη περίοδο ακμής και διατήρησε τη δημοτικότητά της σχεδόν ως τις μέρες μας.

Όπως όλες οι μορφές του βυζαντινού μέλους, έτσι και το κρητοεπτανησιακό ιδίωμα διαιρείται σε οκτώ ήχους, χωρίς όμως να υπάρχουν μεταξύ τους διακρίσεις γένους, γιατί είναι όλοι διατονικοί. Αλλά από την άλλη το χτίσιμο των μελωδιών γίνεται χωρίς εξαίρεση σύμφωνα με την βυζαντινή φουρμουλαϊκή τεχνοτροπία, που περιγράφεται από τον Wellesz και άλλους μελετητές. Αυτό φυσικά δεν σημαίνει ότι το ιδίωμα αυτό δεν έχει ενσωματώσει και ορισμένα δυτικά στοιχεία σε κάποια μελωδικά του γυρίσματα. Εξάλλου έχει υιοθετήσει ένα είδος τετραφωνίας, που οπωσδήποτε έχει δυτική προέλευση. Στο είδος αυτό της τετραφωνίας ο πρωτοψάλτης εκτελεί τη γραμμή του μέλους, όπως διαμορφώθηκε από την παράδοση, ενώ η υπόλοιπη χορωδία (συνήθως ένας δεύτερος τενόρος και δύο μπάσοι) αυτοσχεδιάζουν μια απλή αρμονική συνοδεία που περιλαμβάνει αρκετές ταυτοφωνίες, παράλληλες πέμπτες και όγδοες.

Μέχρι σήμερα οι περισσότεροι Έλληνες μη Επτανήσιοι μουσικολόγοι και μουσικογράφοι υποτιμούσαν το κρητοεπτανησιακό μέλος, χαρακτηρίζοντας το συνοθύλευμα αναφομοίωτων επιδράσεων από τη Δύση και την Ανατολή. Σήμερα όμως η άποψη αυτή έχει αναθεωρηθεί και γίνονται προσπάθειες από τη μια να μελετηθεί σοβαρά σύμφωνα με τις μεθόδους της σύγχρονης μουσικολογίας κι από την άλλη να παρουσιαστεί στο ευρύτερο κοινό ζωντανά και από δίσκους.

Σε μια πρόσφατη μελέτη μου του 1986 για το κρητοεπτανησιακό μέλος, όπως καλλιεργείται στη Ζάκυνθο – και που για ευκολία το αποκαλώ "ζακυνθινό μέλος" – έχω παραθέσει ένα μουσικό παράδειγμα, όπου δείχνω ότι η ζακυνθινή μουσική παραλλαγή του ειρμού της πρώτης ωδής τα κανόνα του Πάσχα *Αναστάσεως Ημε ρα* (στο εξής Α. Η.) παρουσιάζει πολύ λιγότερες αναλογίες με το αντίστοιχο νεοβυζαντινό μέλος, που συνηθίζεται σήμερα ανατολικά από τα Επτάνησα, απ' ό, τι με την παλιότερη, ξεχασμένη σήμερα βυζαντινή εκδοχή του, που

Ex. 1

δημοσιεύτηκε επανειλημμένα από τον Wellesz (βλ. Παρ. 1). Την διαπίστωση αυτή την έκανα το Πάσχα του 1985, όταν ηχογραφούσα στο χωριό Καστάρι τον Νίκο Λειβαδά, άριστο γνώστη του τοπικού ψαλτικού ιδιώματος.

Εντωμεταξύ ηχογράφησα τον ίδιο ειρμό και σε τρεις ακόμα παραλλαγές από ισάριθμους λαμπρούς φορείς του ιδιώματος: τους Στάθη Χριστοδουλόπουλο (1926–1992), Γιώργο Μουζάκη και Τάκη Τσουκαλά (βλ. Παρ. 2).

Ακολουθεί τώρα η αναλυτική έκθεση των συμπερασμάτων που βγαίνουν από τη σύγκριση των τριών εκδοχών του Παρ. 1. Μετά την έκθεση αυτή, που δεν είχε γίνει στην προηγούμενή μου μελέτη, θα προχωρίσω σε μια γενικότερη σύγκριση, όπου θα παραβάλλω το ξεχασμένο βυζαντινό *Αναστάσεως Ημέρα* με τις υπόλοιπες τρεις ζακυνθινές εκδοχές του που συγκέντρωσα μετά το 1985.

Παραλληλίζοντας λοιπόν τα τρία μέλη του Παρ. 1 παρατηρούμε ότι παρά τις αρκετές διαφορές τους έχουν και τα εξής δώδεκα κοινά χαρακτηριστικά.

1) Η τονική τους είναι το *Λα* και το *Ρε* και κινούνται μέσα στα πλαίσια της διατονικής οκτάβας του *Ρε*. Η νεοβυζαντινή εκδοχή αν και κινείται στην ίδια οκτάβα δεν αγγίζει το ψηλό *Ρε* κι έχει για βάση μόνο το *Ρε*.

2) Αρχίζουν απ'το *Λα* που είναι και η σημαντικότερή τους νότα. Στη νεοβυζαντινή εκδοχή η θέση αυτή ανήκει στο *Σολ*.

3) Αν και το *Ντο* χρησιμοποιείται ως δεσπόζων φθόγγος μόνο στη βυζαντινή εκδοχή (φράσεις αρ.1 και 4) και το *Φα* μόνο στη ζακυνθινή (φράση αρ.2), οι υπόλοιποι τρεις δεσπόζοντες φθόγγοι είναι κοινοί (*Λα, Σολ* και *Ρε*). Το νεοβυζαντινό μέλος χρησιμοποιεί για το σκοπό αυτό μόνο το *Σολ* και το *Ρε*.

4) Οι περισσότερο σε χρήση φθόγγοι είναι κατά σειράν συχνότητας τόσο στη βυζαντινή, όσο και στη ζακυνθινή εκδοχή το *Λα* (31–25) και το *Σολ* (12–12). Στη νεοβυζαντινή εκδοχή επικρατούν το *Σολ* (22) και το *Φα* (14).

5) Οι μεσαίοι σε χρήση φθόγγοι είναι κατά σειράν συχνότητας στη βυζαντινή εκδοχή το *Ντο* (11), *Σι* (7), *Φα* (6) και στη ζακυνθινή οι ίδιοι με λίγο διαφορετική σειρά, δηλαδή το *Φα* (8), *Σι* (7), και *Ντο* (5). Οι αντίστοιχοι φθόγγοι στην νεοβυζαντινή εκδοχή είναι το *Λα* (9), το *Μι* (8) και το *Ρε* (6).

6) Οι λιγότερο σε χρήση φθόγγοι συμπίπτουν στις δυο εκδοχές Β. και Λ. και είναι: τα δυο *Ρε* και το *Μι* (*Ρε* χαμηλό 2–5, *Μι* 2–2 και *Ρε* ψηλό 2–1). Στην νεοβυζαντινή εκδοχή τη λιγότερη χρήση έχουν οι φθόγγοι *Σι* (4) και το *Ντο* (1).

7) Τρεις από τις οκτώ φράσεις, η τρίτη (*Πάσχα Κυρίου Πάσχα*), η πέμπτη (*και εκ γης προς ουρανόν*) και η έκτη (*Χριστός ο Θεός*) τόσο στη βυζαντινή, όσο και στη ζακυνθινή εκδοχή, καταλήγουν στις ίδιες νότες, δηλαδή στο *Σολ*, το *Λα* και το *Λα* αντίστοιχα. Η νεοβυζαντινή εκδοχή μοριάζεται την ίδια κατάληξη με τη βυζαντινή μόνο μια φορά (3η φράση).

8) Το κατιόν διάστημα *Λα – Ρε* που παρουσιάζεται συχνά στον αρχαίο βυζαντινό πρώτο και πλάγιο πρώτο ήχο (Παρ. 1, Β. 1) και που το συντάμε στο νεοβυζαντινό μέλος μόνο στην ανιούσα του μορφή (Παρ. 1, ΝΒ 7) βρίσκεται σε χρήση στη Ζάκυνθο εμφανιζόμενο κυρίως στις καταλήξεις των μελωδιών του πρώτου ήχου, όπως βλέπουμε ότι συμβαίνει στην περίπτωση της εκδοχής Λ. του Α. Η. (Παρ. 3).

9) Το *Πάσχα Κυρίου Πάσχα* (3η φρ.) λέγεται στις εκδοχές Β. και Λ. πάνω στις ίδιες περίπου νότες (Παρ.4).

Ex. 3

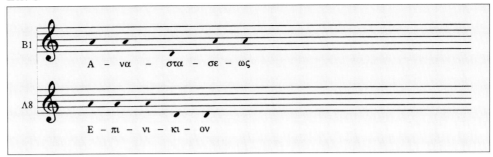

Ex. 4

Ex. 5

Ex. 6

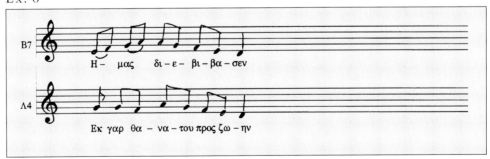

10) Η πέμπτη φράση στη βυζαντινή εκδοχή (και εκ γης προς ουρανόν) και η έκτη στη ζακυνθινή (Χριστός ο Θεός) είναι σχεδόν ίδιες (Παρ.5).

11) Το ίδιο ισχύει για την έβδομη φράση στη βυζαντινή εκδο-

χή (ημάς διεβίβασεν) και την τέταρτη (εκ γαρ θανάτου προς ζωήν) στη ζακυνθινή (Παρ.6).

12) Στη βυζαντινή εκδοχή εμφανίζονται οι φράσεις 2 και 8 (λαμπρυνθώμεν λαοί – επινίκιον άδοντας) μελοποιημήνες με ακρι-

Ex. 7

Ex. 8

βώς τον ίδιο τρόπο. Η φόρμουλα αυτή εμφανίζεται κάπως διαφοροποιημένη και στη φράση 5 (*και εκ γης προς ουρανόν*) της ζακυνθινής εκδοχής (Παρ.7).

Από τη σύγκριση του βυζαντινού Α.Η. με τις υπόλοιπες ζακυνθινές παραλλαγές (Χ–Μ και Τ) του ίδιου μέλους προκύπτουν μερικές ακόμα, εξίσου αποκαλυπτικές ομοιότητες (Παρ. 8–10).

1) Όπως φαίνεται στο Παρ.8

στην εκδοχή Χ (Χριστοδουλόπουλος) η διάταξη των φθόγγων που αντιστοιχούν με το *λαμπρυνθώμεν λαοί* (2η φρ.) και το *ημάς διεβίβασεν* (7η φρ.) είναι σχεδόν απαράλλαχτη μ' εκείνην που χρησιμοποιεί στα σημεία αυτά ο βυζαντινός μελοποιός. Επίσης υπάρχουν κάποιες μικρές ομοιότητες ανάμεσα στα δυο μέλη στο *εκ γαρ θανάτου προς ζωήν* (4η φρ.).

2) Στην εκδοχή Μ (Μουζάκης) η

92

Ex. 9

Ex. 10

διάταξη των φθόγγων που αντιστοιχούν με το *εκ γαρ θανάτου προς ζωήν* (4η φρ.) συμπίπτει μ' εκείνην που χρησιμοποιεί ο βυζαντινός μελοποιός για να κάνει την τελική του κατάληξη (8η φρ.) στις λέξεις *επινίκιον άδοντας* (Παρ.9).

Όπως φαίνεται στο Παρ.10 στην εκδοχή Τ (Τσουκαλάς) στο *Χριστός ο Θεός* (6η φρ.) γίνεται ένα ρετσιτατίβο πάνω στο *Ντο*, ακριβώς όπως συμβαίνει στη βυζαντινή εκδοχή στο *εκ γαρ θανάτου προς ζωήν* (4η φρ.). Επίσης το *ημάς διεβίβασεν* (7η φρ.) στην ίδια ζακυνθινή μελοποίηση χρησιμοποιεί παρόμοια κατάληξη μ' εκείνην που συναντούμε στην αντίστοιχη βυζαντινή μελοποίηση στο *Πάσχα Κυρίου Πάσχα* (3η φρ.).

Μια βασική διαφορά ανάμεσα στο Βυζαντινό και Ζακυνθινό μέλος αναφορικά με τη χρήση το Α' ήχου στο Α.Η, είναι ότι ενώ και στις δυο περιπτώσεις η τονική βρίσκεται τόσο στο *Λα* όσο και στο *Ρε*, το βυζαντινό παράδειγμα κάνει την τελική του πτώση στο *Λα*, ενώ το ζακυνθινό στο *Ρε*. Στη Ζάκυνθο ο ειρμολογικός πρώτος ήχος καταλήγει πάντα στο *Ρε* κι αυτό είναι ένας κανόνας που δεν υπόκειται σε εξαιρέσεις. Στην αρχαία βυζαντινή μουσική ωστόσο τα πράγματα ήταν πιο ελαστικά και το *Ρε* χρησιμοποιούνταν σαν καταληκτικός φθόγγος, όχι μόνο στον ειρμολογικό πλάγιο του πρώτου ήχο, αλλά και στον αντίστοιχο πρώτο, αν κι εδώ εμφανιζόταν στο ρόλο αυτό σπανιότερα απ' το Λα. Στους Ειρμούς των Ωδών του κανόνα του Πάσχα, όπως μας τους παραδίδει ο Κωδ. Ε.γ ΙΙ της βιβλιοθήκης της ιεράς μονής της Γκροτταφερράτα (έτος γραφής 1281), το Ρε παρουσιάζεται ως τελικός φθόγγος σε δυο περιπτώσεις, στην έκτη και στην όγδοην Ωδή. Οι υπόλοιποι έξη Ειρμοί καταλήγουν στο Λα, ακριβώς όπως το Α.Η.

Θα κάνω ακόμα μια παρατήρηση για τις διαφορές που χωρίζουν τις συγκρινόμενες παραδόσεις αναφορικά με το Α.Η. Σε συνδυασμούς όπως Σολ–Φα–Σολ ή Σολ–Φα–Λα, όπως επίσης Λα–Σι–Λα ή Ντο–Σι–Λα οι ζακυνθινές παραλλαγές του Α.Η. ανεβάζουν το Φα στη θέση δίεση ή κατεβάζουν το Σι στη θέση ύφεση. Η συνήθεια αυτή που υπαγορεύεται από τον λεγόμενο "νόμο της έλξης" δεν παρατηρείται μόνο στα Επτάνησα, αλλά και σε κάθε ελληνική ορθόδοξη εκκλησία. Αλλά η παλαιότητα της καταγωγής της δεν είναι εύκολο να καθοριστεί, αφού οι βυζαντινοί σπάνια σημείωναν στα χειρόγραφά τους σημάδια που να δηλώνουν διέσεις ή υφέσεις. Μπορούμε όμως να υποθέσουμε (πάντα με επιφύλαξη) πως οι έλξεις υπήρχαν ήδη από την εποχή που κυκλοφόρησαν τα πρώτα βυζαντινά μουσικά χειρόγραφα στα μέσα του 10ου αιώνα.

Απομένει τώρα να εξετάσουμε ποιο από τα εκκλησιαστικά μέλη που προέκυψαν από τη βυζαντινή μουσική έχουν στενότερη σχέση μαζί της, το ζακυνθινό μέλος ή το νεοβυζαντινό. Το ερώτημα αυτό είναι δύσκολο να απαντηθεί γιατί η συγκριτική μελέτη του απέραντου σε όγκο υλικού, τόσο του βυζαντινού και νεοβυζαντινού μέλους, όσο και του ζακυνθινού βρίσκεται ακόμα στα εντελώς πρώτα της βήματα. Ήδη από τώρα ωστόσο, μπορούμε να ισχυριστούμε ότι το νεοβυζαντινό μέλος απορρέει από το βυζαντινό, τόσο όσο και το ζακυνθινό, με τη μόνη διαφορά ότι το νεοβυζαντινό μέλος κληρονόμησε σε μερικές περιπτώσεις στοιχεία που το ζακυνθινό τα απέρριψε, όπως και το αντίθετο. Το Α.Η. είναι ένα ενδιαφέρον παράδειγμα υιοθέτησης από μια μειοψηφία μιας παλαιάς μελωδίας που η πλειοψηφία – άγνωστο γιατί – την απέρριψε.

Bibliography

Δραγούμης, Μ.Φ. 1978
Η δυτικίζουσα εκκλησιαστική μουσική μας στην Κρήτη και τα Επτάνησα, Λαογραφία, τομ. Λα΄ (31ος) (Δελτίο της Ελληνικής Λαογραφικής Εταιρείας), Αθήνα, 272–293.

Δραγούμης, Μ.Φ. 1986
Πρόσφατες έρευνες στη Ζάκυνθο για την εκκλησιαστική μας μουσική, Δελτίον της Ιονίου Ακαδημίας, τομ. Β΄. Κέρκυρα, 270–280.

Δραγούμης, Μ.Φ. 1989
Παρατηρήσεις για την τροπική δομή των οκτώ Αναστάσιμων Απολυτικίων της Ζακύνθου σε αντιπαραβολή με τα αντι΄στοιζα νεοβυζαντινά μέλη, Απόψεις, τομ.

5ος, (Περιοδική έκδοση του Συλλόγου Εκπαιδευτικών Λειτουργών του Κολλεγίου Αθηνών), Αθήνα, 177–190.

Μαργαζιώτης, Ι. 1968
Θεωρητικόν της Βυζαντινής Εκκλησιαστικής Μουσικής, πρώτη έκδοση, Αθήνα.

Wellesz, E. 1961
A history of Byzantine Music and Hymnography, second edition, Oxford 1961.

Wellesz, E. 1963
Melody construction in Byzantine Chant, Actes du XIIe Congres International d'Études Byzantine à Ochride, 1961, Belgrad, Vol. I, 135-151.

Summary:
A case of survival of 13th – 14th century melodic traits in an Easter chant from the island of Zakynthos

Markos
Ph. Dragoumis

The church music of the Eptanesa or Ionian islands differs considerably from the so-called Neo-Byzantine Chant which is presently in use in most Greek churches. It is of Cretan origin and was brought over to the Eptanesa in 1669. That was the year when a large number of Cretans fled to the Eptanesa to escape from the Turks who had just taken over the island from the hands of the Venetians. In Crete this music soon fell into disuse, whereas in the Eptanesa it was adopted and developed in most of the " Seven Islands " and maintained its popularity up to today. On account of its origin the Eptanesians refer to this music as " Cretan " or " Cretoeptanesian ".

Just like all forms of Byzantine Chant the Cretoeptanesian idiom is divided into eight groups or modes (echoi) and the melodies belonging to each mode are composed according to the formulaic techniques described by Wellesz and other specialists. On the other hand the idiom has incorporated some Western elements in certain melodic features and in the fact that it is performed in four parts. The first tenor sings the line of the melody, as handed down by tradition, while the three other singers (a second tenor and two bass voices) improvise a simple harmonic accompaniment including several parallel fifths and octaves.

The Cretoeptanesian chant was enjoyed and cultivated especially in the island of Zakynthos, where it acquired an independence of its own. Up to today most Greek writers on music considered the various forms of Cretoeptanesian chant and especially that of Zakynthos as being a hotchpotch of unassimilated influences from the East and the West. But recent studies have shown that they were totally mistaken.

One of the most expressive melodies of the Zakynthian repertory is the Hirmos of the First Ode of the Easter Canon which starts with the words $A\nu\alpha-\sigma\tau\acute{\alpha}\sigma\epsilon\omega\varsigma$ $H\mu\acute{\epsilon}\rho\alpha$. When I first recorded this melody in Zakynthos in 1985 I was struck by its similarity to its much older medieval – and for many centuries obsolete – Byzantine counterpart. On the other hand I was quite impressed by the fact that it had almost no relationship to its more or less contemporary Neo-Byzantine counterpart (see Exx. 1 and 3-7).

Between 1985 and 1992 I recorded in Zakynthos three more variants of the same melody (see Ex. 2). The comparison of these additional versions to their Byzantine counterpart reveals a series of even more striking similarities (see Exx. 8-10).

It would be a mistake to jump to the conclusion that because of these similarities the Zakynthian Chant has a stronger Byzantine flavour than the Neobyzantine Chant. Both stem directly from the Middle Ages, but each of them has retained in some cases more or less the same Byzantine elements and in others somewhat different ones for reasons which have yet to be explored.

Some Byzantine Chironomic survivals in the tradition of Balkan Church Music: The case of Roumanian Orthodox Chant

Marios D. Mavroïdis

It is a commonplace to say that common history and common religion lead to common culture. In the case of the Balkan nations, the state of the Byzantine empire, followed historically by the Ottoman regime, together with the Christian Orthodox religion, formed, apart from the many differences between the various national groups that inhabit the Balkan area, certain common social and cultural axes which, to varying degrees, kept on functioning up to our times.

Such is the case of the church music of the Orthodox national groups, the origin of which is to be found in the so-called Byzantine music, during the late Byzantine period as well as the post Byzantine period. This music, as it usually happens, followed different trends of evolution in the different ethnic environments, yet it kept certain common characteristics all over the Balkan states. These characteristics pertain to the modal structure of the church music, the rules and aesthetics of the musical composition, and the musical notation.

I believe that these survivals have been possible because of the close and functional relation between the local churches and the mother Church, the Patriarchate of Constantinople. This relation has been reinforcing them spiritually and practically on the field of religion. And through this, the Orthodox musical culture has survived up to our times. I also believe that this survival was greatly aided by the Orthodox monasterial situation, especially that of Mount Athos, where Slavic Orthodox monks could come in close contact with the greek-speaking ones.

Practically speaking, the most significant of these survivals is that of the musical notation. For, as it is well-known, a great part of the systematic features of this music is embodied in the nature and the operation of the musical signs and characters. And it is worth noticing that one finds Slavic publications of ecclesiastical music in 'παρασημαντική' musical notation even in recent times, when the use of the so-called western musical notation is generally applied all over the world. Because by means of the παρασημαντική, these features are, more or less, maintained in contemporary music interpretation.

Several such publications were produced for the needs of the various Slavic churches. I happened to see a Slavonic Anthology, published probably at the beginning of the century, similar to those published by Θεόδωρος Φωκαεύς in Constantinople in the second half of the 19th century. It belongs to my friend and dear colleague, Lykourgos Angelopoulos, and it contains chants in all Byzantine modes; some of the pieces also indicate the name of the composer: e.g., the Αναστάσιμα Ευλογητάρια του Πέτρου Λαμπαδαρίου in the 5th mode (= plagal of 1st mode).

I also happened to see a Bulgarian publication of Σύντομον Ειρμολόγιον Πέτρου του Πελοποννησίου, which is in the possession of Simon Karas. All the above publications keep the main melodic formulas of the original compositions, and arrange the melodic phrases so that they fit to the new language.

In the case of Roumania, the phenomenon is rather more intense. It is the particular history of the area, of course, that makes the Greek influence much more strong and evident: the Greek princes of Constantinople, who governed the territories around the Danube for a long period up to the eruption of the Greek revolution of independence, were not only authorized as governors of *Moldovlahia* by the Ottoman power; they were also ambassadours of Greek culture from the capital of the oriental world. And in that culture church music has a great share. Therefore, the activity in publishing is remarkably higher, and the same stands for the activity of composition.

I shall here mention two characteristic examples of this fruitful publishing activity: the publication, in 1891 at Bucharest, of the *Encomia of Holy Friday* in arrangement from the Greek original by *Dimitrie Suceveanu*. And the publication in 1925 of the Holy Liturgy by *Popescu-Pasărea*, a brilliant Roumanian cantor and ecclesiastical composer.

Yet, in all the above cases, we have only the musical texts, but no further indications of how these texts must be sung. We find no rules concerning the musical interpretation and performance. Until now, I have not been able to find any theoretical works on the exact explanation of signs in the actual music of our days. On the other hand, disk recordings give only a very slight idea of that reality; they are usually taped down where the music is easy to get hold of, mainly the big cities. And, generally, this material suffers from a major western influence. In some cases too, there has been a cultural antagonism towards the Greeks, leading to a differentiation in the field of music. One characteristic example is the Bulgarian interpretations of compositions by Ioannis Koukouzelis, which form part of the efforts to demonstrate the hypothetical Bulgarian origin of the great melodist.

Shortly after the fall of the Ceauçescu regime in Roumania, the Institute of Biblical Mission of the Roumanian Orthodox Church, published the *Cântările Sfintei Liturghii*, "The chants of the Roumanian ecclesiastical liturgy" (1992). In this publication are included the most representative compositions of Roumanian melodists starting from 18th century up to our times. This material covers the three big Orthodox liturgies, and all the periods of the ecclesiastical year.

Furthermore, in the publication are included some *Calofonikee Heermee* composed by Roumanian musicians, some Roumanian carols and other spiritual folk songs, and some Matheemata in the 8 modes. The material of this book comes from the living oral Roumanian tradition, and it was selected and codified by Nicu Moldoveanu, professor of the Department of Orthodox Theology at the University of Bucharest. The work of Prof. Moldoveanu was supervised by a committee, consisting mainly of theologians and clergymen, whose task, according to the preface of the edition, was to choose the chants with the purest possible Roumanian essence and character.

Whether the pieces included in this anthology are of a discrete compositional character or not, it is not the place to discuss here; this is the subject of a future structural and comparative study of the melodies. What makes the edition extremely interesting though, is the fact that, although Prof. Moldoveanu uses sources that are much older and written in the παρασημαντική[1], he gives the musical texts in both Byzantine and Western musical notation. And furthermore, in his transcriptions he tries to present in a most accurate and consequent way the melismatic particularities of the actual musical performance. And in doing so, he reveals the survival of a living and functional chironomic code in the Roumanian church music of today.

The existence of chironomy in the Roumanian interpretation of Byzantine music is of great importance, not only for the Roumanians, who managed to carry and save a very old tradition up to our days, but also for the Greeks, who, as we all know, even today, cannot come to an agreement on how their own sacred music is to be sung.

In the long history of Greek presence and influence in the areas around the Danube, one could search for indications of strong similarities between the savant musical cultures of the Roumanians and the Greeks. I believe that it is not at all incidental that the first musical editions according to the new method were realized in Bucharest in 1820. It is enough, just to have a look at the long catalogue of donators of the Δοξαστάριον, published by Petros Efessios: this catalogue is full of names of citizens from Bucharest, among which some are obviously Roumanian[2].

On the other hand, as Lykourgos Angelopoulos pointed out convincingly in his exposition during the International Musicological Symposium at Delphi on 1986[3], it is very likely that at the time of the musical reform (1st half of 19th cent.), the chironomy was generally a living reality. So, in order to make it the simplest possible, the three establishers of the new method neglected quite a few of the signs of the old method, having confidence in the oral tradition. Whether they were right or wrong, one can easily judge. But, if at that time, chironomy existed in Greek interpretations, it certainly existed in Roumanian interpretations too.

Considering now the particularities of the Roumanian society, and the events of Roumanian History, old and recent, one could discover the terms that made the maintenance of this old tradition possible. So, if we co-examine these two factors, (that is, chironomy on one hand, and a non-communicational and slow-developing society on the other), we may arrive at the conclusion that contemporary Roumanian church music can offer an answer to the question: *"How should the Greeks sing their church music?"*.

But, let us come back to the chiro-nomic code. The preliminary study I carried out revealed practically all the chironomic positions (θέσεις) described by the Greek theoreticians: I shall here mention positions with melismatic functions of various types that can be identified as operations of different qualities of character, some of which are not used by the new method. Although, as it is obvious, the musical texts are written in the new method of παρασημαντική, their transcriptions give a plethora of citations or figures for the following signs: οξεία, πεταστή, βαρεία, ομαλό, αντικέ-νωμα, έτερον, τζάκισμα, λύγισμα, στρεπτό, τρομικό as well as terminating positions using μικρόν ίσον[4]; all these positions have many different possibilities of performance.

It is certain, of course, that the subject needs a complete study, theoretical and practical. Nevertheless, we are going to take a quick look at this code, examining the function of only a few signs and combinations, as they appear in the transcriptions by Prof. Moldoveanu. But before that, some remarks have to be made:

a. Examining the material offered by the book, we should always have the Greek interpretation of Byzantine music in our minds, and its theory, which forms the point of departure for this study.

b. Under such a point of view, we discover a modal system which, of course, needs to be examined separately, but at first glimpse it is almost identical to that of the Greeks, although some of its functions are different: e.g. there is no sharpening or flattening of the notes towards the dominant ones, unless it is indicated in the Byzantine text. In spite of these differences, the modal system cites directly to its greco-oriental origin. A very characteristic example is that of the long " ″Αξιον" of the Sunday, a composition of *Macarie Ieromonahul*

(1770 - 1836), with the indication *glasul III* ("3d voice" ~ Ἦχος Τρίτος). In fact, the composition is written in Ἦχος πλάγιος του τρίτου επτάφωνος, which is a major mode based on B flat (= Ζω ὑφεση). Similar to what many Greeks did, mainly in Constantinople, the composer adds also the indication *Agem Syrian*, which is the mistaken Arabic term *Ajem Ashiran*, the name of the makam of Turkish and Arabic music that corresponds exactly to this Byzantine Ἦχος.

c. In the texts there are few violations of the rules of musical orthography. The most frequent is that of the replacement of υπορροή by other signs:

Ex. 1

It is probable, though, that such "faults" have their origin in the differences between the Greek and the Roumanian language, and the difficulties of transcribing the original poetry into Roumanian, mainly because of the different number of syllables, while keeping the same melodic formulas.

d. Given that all musical scales are described by the well tempered western scale, there is no accurate representation of the intervals actually intoned by the Roumanian cantors. There is no information at all about this matter in the edition. And finally,

e. The chironomic system is only valid for the church music, exactly as it does not pertain to Greek folk songs.

Now, we will deal successively with two different paradigms of chironomic positions, that of οξεία and that of πεταστή.

1. Positions of Οξεία
In these positions, we are dealing with signs of the new method, ολίγον, κεντήματα and ψηφιστόν.

(a) Ολίγον as a simple accent
The ολίγον is functioning as στήριγμα (= basis). Example (2) and Example (3)

(b) Ολίγον as Οξεία
Example (4)
The operation of οξεία is indicated by the small note before the main φωνή (= note), in the form of an *appoggiatura*.

Ex. 2

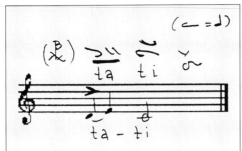

Ex. 3

Ex. 4

Ex. 5

Ex. 6

Ex. 7

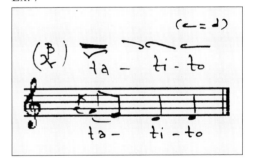

(c) Ψηφιστόν **as** Οξεία
Example (5) and Example (6) and Example(7)

As it is obvious, it can be combined with ίσον, or any ascending character.

This also happens in a series of successive descents: Example (8)

Sometimes, always according to the transcriptions of Moldoveanu, the function of ψηφιστόν is extended to the following descending character as well: Example (9)

(d) Κεντήματα **as** Οξεία
Example (10)
In this case, κεντήματα give an ascending *appoggiatura* which works as a bridge,

eliminating the difference between the first and the last and higher note.

(e) Κεντήματα **together with** Ολίγον **as** Οξεία
Example (11)

(f) Κεντήματα **together with** Ολίγον **and** Ψηφιστόν **as** Οξεία
Example (12) and Example (13)

In both examples, the embellishing note comes before the second sign which is the κεντήματα. When the κεντήματα come first, then the embellishing note follows: Example (14)

Ex. 8

Ex. 9

Ex. 10

Ex. 11

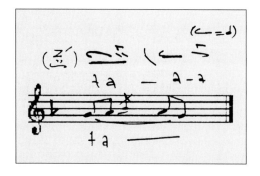

Ex. 12

(g) Κεντήματα, Ολίγον **and** Ψηφιστόν **in position of** Στρεπτόν
The following is found to be a very common analysis in the texts, especially in those with a slow tempo: Example (15)

(h) Ολίγον **and** Ψηφιστόν **in position of** Στρεπτόν
This position combines always a character with κλάσμα, that is of double duration, under which is placed the ψηφιστόν, and it is always followed by a descending character carrying a γοργόν.

This grouping is equivalent to an analysis of the character carrying the κλάσμα: Example (16)

In some texts, the analysis is even more detailed:
    Example (17) shows this with a grace-note, and in
    Example (18) we observe the same phenomenon with real notes.

2. Operation of Πεταστή
Πεταστή is the more ambiguous character in the Roumanian texts, exactly

102

Ex. 13

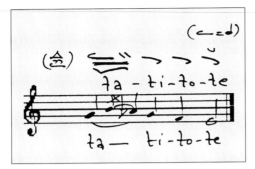

Ex. 14

Ex. 15

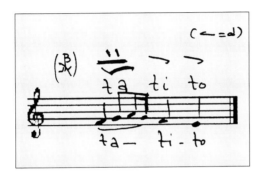

Ex. 16

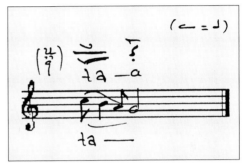

Ex. 17

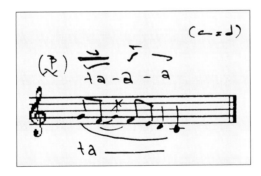

Ex. 18

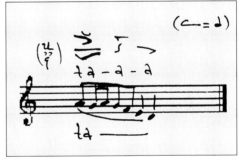

like it is in the Greek ones. Therefore, one discovers many different possibilities of this character in the transcriptions of Moldoveanu.

(a) Πεταστή as a simply ascending character

In this case, πεταστή has no action other than the ascending second. Sometimes, this behaviour is explicable: that is when the πεταστή reaches a stable and immovable note like, for instance, the Ζω flat of Ἦχος Βαρύς. Example (19) In the Greek texts also, the πεταστή does not move in cases like this.

(b) Πεταστή as an accent

Example (20) and Example (21) Πεταστή is normally followed by descending characters in the Roumanian texts, as it happens in Greek texts also.

(c) Πεταστή before long descending characters

Example (22) with grace-note and Example (23) with real notes.

(d) Πεταστή before short descending characters

Example (24) We notice here that in ex. 24, as well as

Ex. 19

Ex. 20

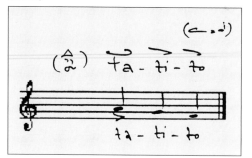

Ex. 21

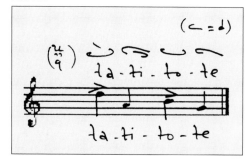

Ex. 22

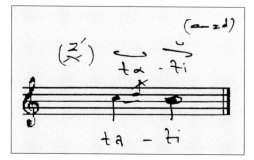

Ex. 23

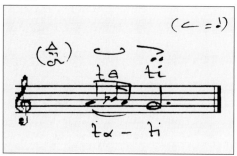

Ex. 24

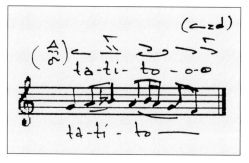

in ex. 23, the embellishing action of πεταστή is applied to the second half of the duration of the note.

(e) Πεταστή with κλάσμα before descending characters
Example (25)

In this case, the embellishing action of πεταστή is now applied to the first half of the duration of the note. Πεταστή has the same action if followed by a descending note with κλάσμα:
Example (26)

(f) Πεταστή with κλάσμα before short descending characters
Example (27) and Example (28)

As it is obvious from ex. 27, this combination can support two syllables.

Speaking about πεταστή in the transcriptions of Moldoveanu, it should be pointed out that its chironomic nature is sometimes suppressed, and there seems to be no evident explanation for this phenomenon. Generally speaking, it is not at all obvious why πεταστή sometimes looses its embellishing function. It is likely that its performance can be embellished or left without ornamentation, depending on the mood of the performer, something that often happens with Greek ψάλτες too.

On the other hand, in several cases, the πεταστή is used in a way violating

Ex. 25

Ex. 26

Ex. 27

Ex. 28

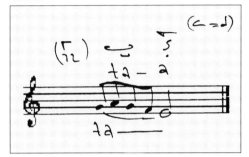

Ex. 29

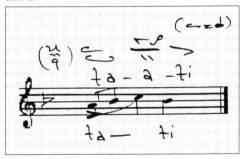

Ex. 30

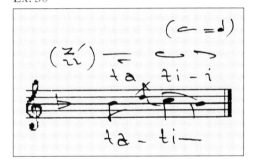

the rules of musical orthography: for instance, as an accent followed by ascending characters: Example (29)

In other cases, πεταστή is transcribed in a way which fits rather to the οξεία: Example (30)

And vice versa, ψηφιστόν is sometimes transcribed as πεταστή: Example (31)

It is probable, however, that errors like these originated in the editing procedure. Or during the collection of the material, what is especially likely to happen when one deals with an oral tradition.

Unfortunately, the space available does not permit the presentation of other paradigms. Yet, it is necessary to make some

Ex. 31

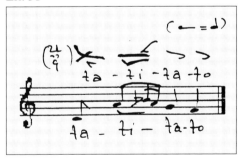

remarks on the consequences of the phenomenon that I, though partially and insufficiently, have tried to describe here. For the above mentioned reasons, indicating a close relation between Greek and Roumanian church music, I believe that this phenomenon offers a strong argument in favour of those Greek theoreticians of modern times who support a rather 'melismatic' interpretation of the Byzantine music. In many of the Roumanian interpretations, I clearly discover the doctrine of scholars like Παναγιώτης Κηλτζανίδης[5], like Αγαθάγγελος Κυριαζίδης[6], like Βασίλειος Παπαρούννης[7], like Θεοδόσιος Γεωργιάδης[8], like Χαράλαμπος Οικονόμου[9], and like Αβραάμ Ευθυμιάδης[10]. And above all, the doctrine of Simon Karas who, in his Θεωρητικόν[11], deals in detail with the chironomic function of the signs and the characters of Byzantine music, not hesitating to use some of the signs belonging to the old παρασημααντική, in order to describe the melismatic nature of the art of melurgy in a most accurate and precise way. It is very well known that these ideas find a strong opposition. Yet, the oral tradition has in many cases verified such a point of view, as Lykourgos Angelopoulos has very clearly stated in his above mentioned exposition at Delphi (1986). And, I think that the case of Roumanian church music offers yet another verification.

Bibliography

Karas, S.I. 1982
Μέθοδος της Ελληνικής Μουσικής,
Θεωρητικόν, Vol. I, Athens.

Efessios, P. 1820
Σύντομον Δοξαστάριον του αοιδίμου
Πέτρου Λαμπαδαρίου του Πελοπον-
νησίου, Bucharest.

Moldoveanu, N. 1992 (ed.)
Cântările Sfintei Liturghii, Bucharest.

Notes

NOTE 1
Makarie Ieromonahul, Vienna, 1823/ Anton
Pann, Bucharest, 1835/ Anthology of
Neamt, Ierodiakonul Nectarie Frimu,
1840/ Ștefanache Popescu, Bucharest,
1860-1875, and many others. There are also
publications of the Holy Synod of the
Roumanian Orthodox Church from 1951
and 1961 etc.

NOTE 2
e.g. Γιάνκος Ρακκοβίζας, Μιχαήλ
Φιλλιπέσκος and Τίτος Μαϊνέσκος etc.

NOTE 3
Unfortunately, the Acta of this symposium
have not yet been published.

NOTE 4
The term should be understood not as an
element of the old Παρασημαντική, but
as it is used by Simon Karas, in order to
describe certain types of chironomies, Karas
1982 181- 83.

NOTE 5
Constantinople, 1881.

NOTE 6
Constantinople, 1906.

NOTE 7
Athens, 1939.

NOTE 8
Athens, 1963.

NOTE 9
Paphos, Cyprus, 1940.

NOTE 10
Thessaloniki, 1972.

NOTE 11
Karas 1982.

The "Exegesis" of Chourmouzios Hartofylax on certain compositions by Ioannis Koukouzelis

Lycourgos Ant. Angelopoulos

Chourmouzios Hartofylax, one of the three founders of the new musical method which is still in use today, transcribed (by means of "exegesis") a great part of the works by the famous Byzantine composer Ioannis Koukouzelis, who is referred to as the second source of the Greek ecclesiastical music[1] (the first being John of Damascus).

On the basis of the preserved manuscripts by Chourmouzios Hartofylax[2] we can here present a preliminary list[3] of all the transcribed works by the great Byzantine maïstor (referring only to the number of chants contained in the manuscripts – a more detailed and analytic study will follow, including the texts of the chants as well)[4]:

MS 703 ΜΠΤ
1) The great ison {1}
2) Verses of Anoixantaria (including the verses with the indication "απο χορού" that repeat the same melody) {14}
3) Verses of the first Kathisma of the Psalter (with the verses "απο χορού", repeating the same melody) {16}
4) Kalophonic verses from the first Kathisma of the Psalter {8}
5) Exclamations {2}
6) Theotokion, anagrammatismos of Theotoke Parthene for the Artoklasia service Κεχαριτωμένη χαίρε {1}
7) Verses of the Polyeleos "Koukoumas" {2}

MS 704 ΜΠΤ
8) Verses of the Polyeleos "Latrinos"[5] {4}
9) Anagrammmatismos of Polyeleos (Ευλογητός Κύριος) {1}
10) Pasapnoarion of Matins, 1st mode {1}
11) Δόξα Πατρί of Polyeleos' Perissi {1}

MS 705 ΜΠΤ
12) Alleluiarion, 1st plagal mode {1}
13) Cheroubikon "Palatinon", 2nd plagal mode {1}
14) Cheroubikon for the Liturgy of the Presanctified Gifts, 1st plagal mode. {1}
15) Koinonikon of ordinary Sundays, 1st plagal mode {1}
16) Koinonikon for the Liturgy of the Presanctified Gifts {1}

MS 706 ΜΠΤ
17) Theotokia Την όντως Θεοτόκον, Άνωθεν (2) {3}
18) Kratemata MS 710 ΜΠΤ (2nd plagal mode (4), nenano (1), barys (2), 4th plagal mode (17)) {24}

Kratemata MS 711 ΜΠΤ (1st mode (4), 2nd mode (6), 3rd mode (3),
4th mode (3), 1st plagal mode (10))   {26}
19) Kratemata in other composer's compositions MSS 730, 731, 732   {7}
20) Akathistos, Oikoi MS 714 ΜΠΤ   {2}
21) With the indication "Ἀναποδισμός" MS 732 ΜΠΤ   {1}
22) With the indication "Ἀναγραμματισμός" MS 722 ΜΠΤ (3),
727 (4), 728 (8), 729 (10), 730 (7), 731 (6), 732 (9), 733 (10), 734 (1)   {58}
23) With the indication "Στιχηρόν"⁶ MS ΜΠΤ 727 (4), 728 (4),
729 (1), 730 (10), 731 (4), 732 (4), 733 (3), 734 (1)   {31}
24) With the indication "Καλλωπισμός" MS ΜΠΤ 727 (3), 728(4),
729 (4), 730 (2), 731 (4), 732 (7), 733 (4)   {28}
25) With the indication "πους" (πόδες with name of composer,
anonymous and shortened by other composers) MS ΜΠΤ 727 (2),
728 (7), 729 (1), 730 (11), 731 (10), 732 (10)   {41}
26) With the indication "Πρόλογος" MS 730 ΜΠΤ, MS 731 ΜΠΤ   {2}
27) With the indication "Ἐπιβολή" (named or anonymous)
MS ΜΠΤ 729 (1), 730 (4), 731 (2), 732 (1), 734 (1)   {9}
28) With the indication "Παρεκβολή"
MS ΜΠΤ 729 (6), 730 (1), 732 (2), 733 (2), 734 (1)   {13}
29) With the indication "Σταυροθεοτοκίον" MS ΜΠΤ 733   {17}
30) With the indication "Μεγαλυνάριον"
MS 729 ΜΠΤ (1), 730 (2), 731 (2)   {5}
31) With the indication "Πεντηκοστάριον" MS ΜΠΤ 731 (1), 732 (2) {3}
32) With the indication "Στίχος" MS ΜΠΤ 704 (2), 728 (1), 734 (1)   {4}
33) Ἐκ τῶν Περισσῶ MS ΜΠΤ 733   {1}

According to my opinion, one of the most important compositions by Ioannis Koukouzelis is the Theotokion Ἄνωθεν οἱ Προφῆται, composed in the 2nd plagal mode (Example 1). This composition should be distinguished from another piece with more or less the same text, but set in the 3rd plagal mode (ba-rys). Of these, only the latter has been published previously[7].

Example 1:
    The composition divides into three parts: the text, a kratema and the termination. The "text" constitutes the first two thirds of the composition, while the

Ἄνωθεν οἱ προφῆται σὲ προκατῆγγειλαν Κόρη (twice)
Κόρη σέ προκατήγγειλαν ἄνωθεν οἱ προφῆται
Στάμνον, ῥάβδον, πλάκα, τράπεζαν λυχνίαν κιβωτόν
γέφυραν καὶ κλίμακα.
Στάμνον, ῥάβδον, πλάκα, τράπεζαν λυχνίαν κιβωτόν
ὄρος ἀλατόμητον καὶ χρυσοῦν θυμιατήριον
παλάτιον καὶ θρόνον τοῦ βασιλέως.
Κόρη σὲ προκατῆγγειλαν οἱ προφῆται
στάμνον χρυσοῦ τὸ μάννα φέρουσαν
Σὲ προκατῆγγειλαν οἱ θαυμαστοὶ προφῆται
ΚΡΑΤΕΜΑ
Σὲ προκατῆγγειλαν Κόρη

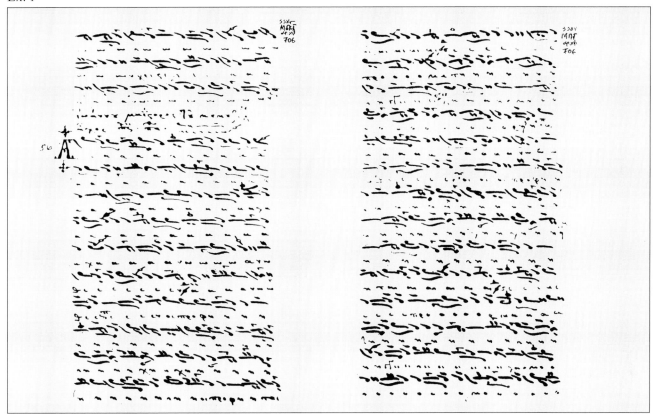

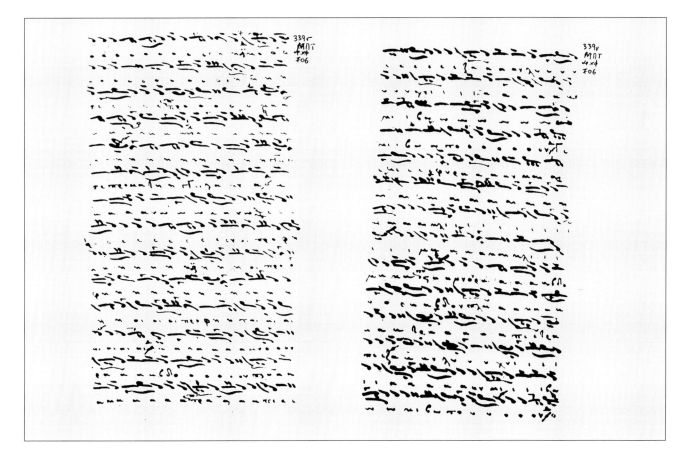

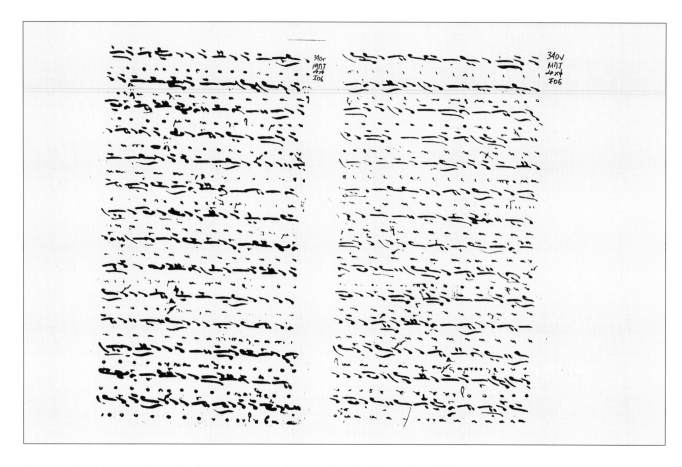

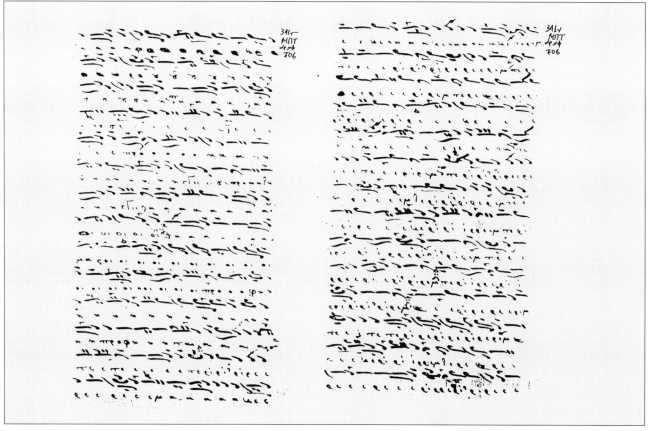

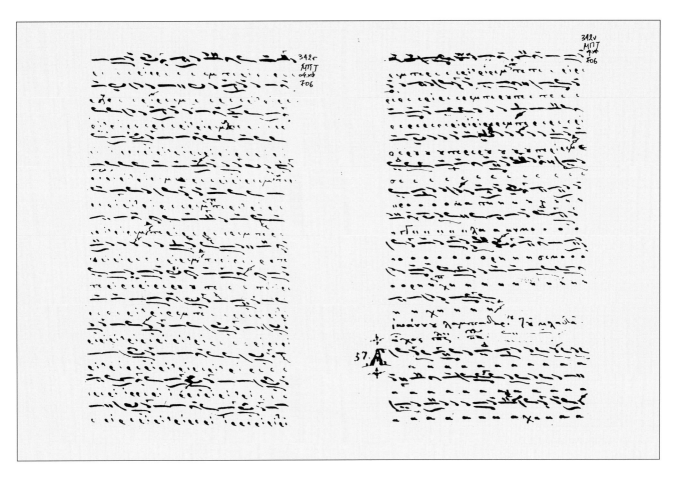

remainder consists of the kratema followed by a brief musical termination, beginning and ending in 2nd plagal mode trifonos (nenano):

Fig. A

Fig. B

Fig. C

The Kratema after the text begins with the syllables *te-te-ee-te-rim-rem* and *a-ne-ne-na-ne-na-a-na-ne*. In the rest of the Kratema, variations of the syllables *te-ri-rem* are used. Regarding the vocal range of the compositions, we notice the following:

The upper limit is the note Bου with oxeia (that reaches the note Γα as well) in the thesis (fig. A) and shortly after this thesis a similar phrase is repeated with kratemata (instead of oxeia) (fig. B). Also, with the action of the *petasthe*, which is "latent" under the ison in the thesis and in all the similar phrases, the composition reaches again the note Γα (fig. C).

The lowest note is Δι, to which the kratema descends twice in the soft diatonic mode.

Regarding the rhythm, we notice the prevailing use of a four-unit pattern, with frequent insertions of meters in 5 units, 6 units iambic and 7 units.

The composition opens on Ἄνωθεν with a characteristic introduction in *nenano* where "ἔνατος ἦχος πέλει"[8]. Then, a very skillfully made succession of modes follows (- nenano- 1st tetraphonos - nenano - 1st tetraphonos - nena- no- agia) and a termination in nenano after the phrase in 2nd plagal mode on the repetition of the word Ἄνωθεν:

Words	Modes
οἱ προφῆται	: νενανῶ– ἅγια (alternating)
σὲ προκατήγγειλαν κόρη	: ανανές – νεχεανές
Ἄνωθεν	: νενανῶ– νεχεανές
οἱ προφῆται	: νενανῶ– ἅγια – ανανές 4/φωνος – ἅγια – νενανῶ
σὲ προκατήγγειλαν κόρη	: ἅγια– ανεανές – ανανές 4/φωνος – ἅγια – ανεανές – ἅγια - κόρη σὲ
νεχεανές 4/φωνος – νεχεανές	: προκατήγγειλαν αρχίζει νεχεανές – ανανές 4/φωνος, ανεανές 5/φωνος – ἅγια – νενανῶ
Ἄνωθεν οἱ προφη	: νεχεανές 4/φωνος
η–οι–προφῆται	: ἅγια[9] ending in νενανῶ
στάμνον, ράβδον, πλάκα, τράπεζαν, λυχνίαν, κιβω	: νεχεανές
κιβωτόν	: ἅγια – νενανῶ
γέφυραν καὶ κλίμακα	: νεχεανές
στάμνον	: ανανές 4/φωνος
ράβδον, πλάκα, τρα-	: ἅγια
πε-τράπεζαν,	: ανανές
λυχνίαν, κιβωτόν	: ἅγια – ανεανές – ἅγια – νενανῶ
ὅρος	: ἅγια – ανανές 4/φωνος – ἅγια
ἀλατόμητον	: ἅγια – ανανές 4/φωνος – ἅγια – ανανές 4/φωνος
καὶ χρυσούν θυμια-	: ἅγια – νενανῶ– ἅγια– ανανές 4/φωνος
τήριον	: ἅγια[10] – νενανῶ
παλάτιον καὶ θρόνον	: ανανές 4/φωνος – ἅγια – νενανῶ
τοῦ βασιλέως	: ανανές 4/φωνος – νεχεανές
κο (νο) ρη	: νεχεανές – νενανῶ
σὲ προκατήγγειλαν	: ανανές 4/φωνος – ἅγια – ανανές 4/φωνος
οἱ προφῆται	: νενανῶ – ἅγια – νενανῶ
στάμνον χρυσού τὸ μάννα	: νενανῶ – νεχεανές – ἅγια
φέρουσαν	: νεχεανές ending in ἅγια
σὲ προκατήγγειλαν	: ἅγια – ανανές 4/φωνος νεχεανές
οἱ θαυμαστοί	: νεχεανές – ἅγια – νεχεανές – ἅγια– ανανές 4/φωνος
προφῆται	: ανανές 4/φωνος – ἅγια – νενανῶ

The kratema is as follows:

κε]α]ω — αγια — κε]α]ω — αγια — κε]α]ω
τε ε   α κε

κε]α]ω   κεχεαμες — αγια — κεχεαμες —
τε ρεμ   τε ρε

π   κεχεαμες   π   αγια — κεχεαμες —
ε]α   τε ε   ει ρεμ   τε ει ει

αγια — α]αμες τετράφωνος — αγια —   αγια — α]αμες τε-
ει ρεμ   τε

τράφωνος — αγια —   α]αμες τετράφωνος — αγια —
ει ρεμ   ε ε

αμεαμες   π   α]αμες αντίφωνος   τετράφωνς — αγια
εεε   ει]ει ρε ε

αντίφωνος — κεαγιε   αγια αντίφωνος   κεαγιε — α]αμες
εε   ει]ει   τε ει

— βαεὺς — κεαγιε   κεχεαμες   π   κεχεαμες
εε   εεεμ   τε ει

π   κεαγιε — κε]α]ω   κεχεαμες — αγια — κε]α]ω
εεμ   τε   εεμ   τε ει

Δ   αγια   κεχεαμες   αγια —   κεχεαμες
ρεμ   τε   ε τε   εεμ τε ε ε   ει ρεε

αγια — α]αμες τετράφωνον — κεχεαμες   π   κεχεαμες
ρε ε ε ε   εεμ   τε τε

αγια μὲ κατάχηξη κε]α]ω   α]αμες τετράφωνος — αγια —
ρου   ρεμ   ε δε ε (προκατηγesιαν)

α]αμες τετράφωνος — κεχεαμες — κε]α]ω —   α]αμες τετράφωνος
κο ο(ρη)

αγια — κεχεαμες   π   κε]α]ω   Δ
εη η   χη η   η η η

Further, it is worth mentioning the survival of numerous musical phrases from compositions by Koukouzelis in later compositions, dating both from the period before and after the Fall of Constantinople. For example, in the Theotokion Ἄνωθεν οἱ προφῆται by Ioannis Kladas, the introduction is identical with that of the Koukouzelean piece with the same name (see Example 2), while the composition as a whole is very similar to another composition by Koukouzelis, the Ρι̣φεί̣ς.

Ex. 2

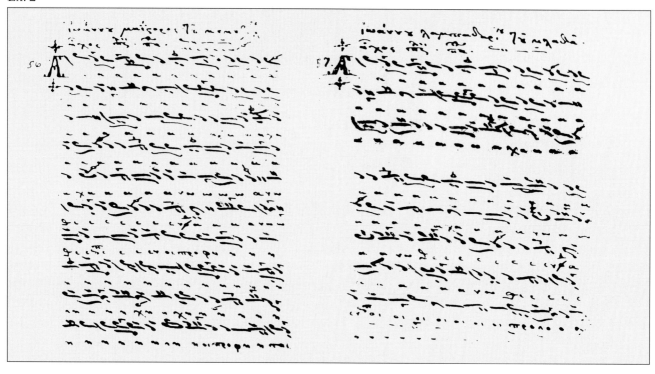

Another example is the phrase Ἀλληλού–ια which is repeated in the Koinonikon Αἰνεῖτε τόν Κύριον by Koukouzelis, and reoccurs in the Cheroubikon in 1st plagal mode by Theofanis Karykis, protopsalt in the Great Church and later Ecumenical Patriarch (see Example 3).

a) Koinonikon of Sunday Αἰνεῖτε τόν Κύριον by Ioannis Koukouzelis, 1st plagal mode, MS ΜΠΤ 705, f. 118v
b) Cheroubikon by Theophanis Karykis, 1st plagal mode [18r-19v] MS ΜΠΤ 705, f. 19v

We find another characteristic phrase in the *agia* mode (fourth mode) of the papadike, when the composition moves into the first plagal and returns to *agia* mode (see Example 4), sticheron Φρού–ρησον by Ioannis Koukouzelis, 2nd pla-

gal mode [175v - 178r], MS ΜΠΤ 728 f.177r.

The same phrase is, according to my opinion, found in the Ambrosian chant "Ecce apertum" (offertorium) (see Example 5)[11].

This particular musical phrase guided my interpretation of the offertorium according to the theoretical teaching of the *agia* mode of the *papadike*, when I studied it together with Marcel Pérès, conductor of "Ensemble Organum".

Finally, this *agia*-phrase is also found twice in the Cheroubikon for week-days (in *agia* mode) by Petros Lampadarios. As it is well known, the Cheroubikon by Petros Lampadarios was composed according to old musical phrases (see Example 6, on the word ...τῆ ...).

I think that the systematical study, analysis, and presentation of the works by

Ex. 3

the renowned Byzantine maïstor – through the "exegesis" of Chourmouzios Hartofylax – will not only offer inestimable and new knowledge, but also contribute to the acquaintance of one of the most important Greek composers through the ages, one of the creators of the Greek musical civilization, as it has frequently and correctly been emphasized by Michael Adamis[12]. However, this musical treasure, that reveals such a variety, melodical richness and high technical standard, remains for the most part unknown and is still waiting for its emergence.

Ex. 4

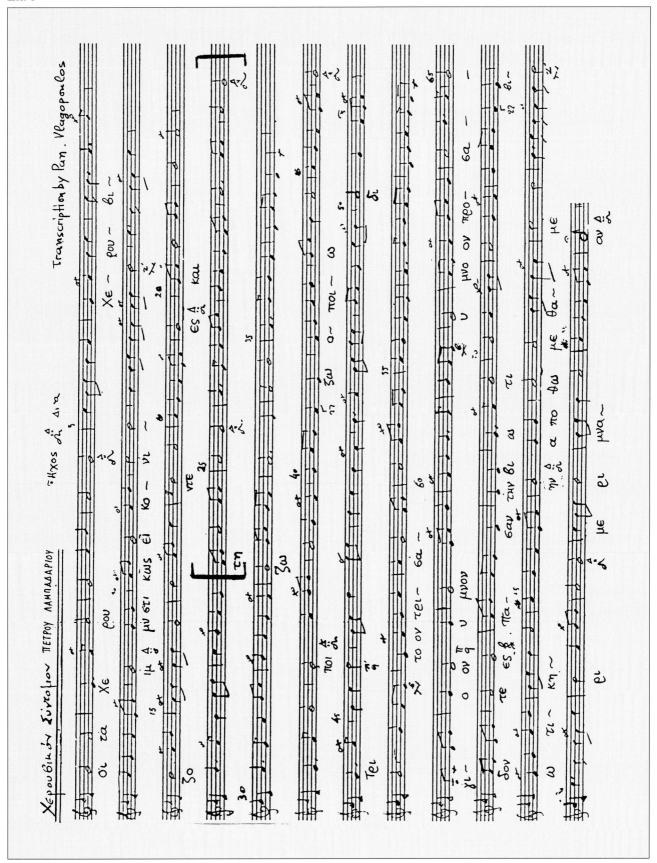

Bibliography

Adamis, M. 1992
From Byzantine to contemporary music, address held at the Palermo congress of Music, May 1992.

Alygizakis, A.E. 1985
Ἡ Ὀκταηχία στὴν ελληνικὴ λειτουργικὴ ὑμνογραφία. Thessaloniki.

Chatzegiakoumis, M. 1972
Μουσικά Χειρόγραφα Τουρκοκρατείας (1453-1832), Athens.

Chatzigiakoumis, M.K. 1980
Χειρόγραφα Εκκλησιαστικῆς Μουσικῆς, Athens.

Chourmouzios 1824
Anthologia, Constantinople.

Jakovljević, A. 1982
Ο μέγας Μαΐστωρ Ιωάννης Κουκουζέλης Παπαδόπουλος, Κληρονομία 14,2.

Karas, S.I. 1992
Ιωάννης Μαΐστωρ ο Κουκουζέλης και η εποχή του, Athens.

Stathis, G. Th. 1977
Η δεκαπεντασύλλαβος υμνογραφία εν τη βυζαντινή μελοποιία, Athens.

Stathis, G. Th. 1979
Οἱ ἀναγραμματισμοὶ καὶ τὰ μαθήματα τῆς βυζαντινῆς μελοποιίᾳ ας, (second ed. Athens 1992), Athens.

Stathis, G. Th. 1989
Ἡ ασματικὴ διαφοροποίηση ὅπως καταγράφεται στὸν κώδικα ΕΒΕ 2458 τοῦ ἔτους 1336, in Χριστιανικὴ Θεσσαλονίκη Παλαιολόγειος ἐποχή, Κέντρο ιστορίας θεσσαλονίκης τοῦ Δήμου θεσσαλονίκης, 3, Thessaloniki, 165-212.

Williams, E.W. 1968
John Koukouzeles' reform of Byzantine chanting for Great Vespers in the 14th century, Yale Univ. Ph.D.-thesis.

Notes

NOTE 1

cf. Williams 1968 304 and
Jakovljevic 1982 357.

NOTE 2

Manuscripts of the National Library, Athens, ΜΠΤ 703, 704, 705, 706, 710, 711, 714, 722, 728, 730, 731, 732, 733, and 734.

NOTE 3

Many transcribed chants by Koukouzelis can be found in Chatzegiakoumis 1975 and 1980, Stathis 1977 and 1979 (including the following list of MSS: ΜΠΤ 706, 712, 722, 727, 728, 729, 730, 731, 732, 733, 734), and Stathis' recordings *Ο Μαΐστωρ Ιωάννης Παπαδόπολος Κουκουζέλης* (1270 περίπου - α' ημ. ιδ' αι.) η ζωή και το έργο του, records I - III (IBM album no. 6), Athens 1988.

NOTE 4

Together with Costas Angelides and George Konstantinou, graduate students of the Alexandros A. Onassis Foundation, I am working on a project for the study and analysis of Koukouzelis' work as transcribed by the three Teachers.

NOTE 5

There are probably 3 - 4 more verses of Polyeleos "Latrinos" that should be attributed to Koukouzelis, those beginning with the word "Ευλογήσατε"; they are not referred to by Chourmouzios under the name of Koukouzelis, and must be identified with the corresponding verses in the older MSS (the verses of the Polyeleos which in a later MS of the 15th century are characterized as "voulgara" should not be taken into account, because it is almost certain that this composition belongs to Ioannis Glykys). In the MS EBE 2458 the verses *τὸ μνημόσυνόν σου* are accredited to Panaretos. Cf. Karas 1992 66, Jakovlević 1982 367-368, and Stathis 1989 176.

NOTE 6

These are considered to be compositions by Koukouzelis. Also the anonymous "podes" that follow the above mentioned stichera and *kalopismata* must be ascribed to Koukouzelis.

NOTE 7

In the *Ανθολογία* by Χουρμούζιος Χαρτοφύλαξ, See Chourmouzios 1824, Vol. I 566-574.

NOTE 8

According to verses of Ioannis Lampadarios (Kladas) for the method of Koronis. This method is found in MSS Dionysiou 570 f. 103v, Koutloumousiou 447 p. 47 and Koutloumousiou 461 f. 27 v. The verses are a.o. edited in Alygizakis 1985 163.

NOTE 9

The well-known characteristic phrase of agia is suitable for chanting by one voice. We have found this very often (See the corresponding thesis in the slow Τῆ Ὑπερμάχῳ).

NOTE 10

The characteristic thesis of "agia".

NOTE 11

Antiphonarium Ambrosianum, Paleographie Musicale V (Brit. Mus. add. 34 209), 61-62. Recorded on compact disc, HARMONIA MUNDI / HMC 901295, Chants de l'eglise Milanaise, Ensemble Organum (dir. Marcel Pérès).

NOTE 12

e.g. Adamis 1992.

A Way to the Transcription of Old Byzantine Chant by means of Written and Oral Tradition

Ioannis Arvanitis

A.

In the Greek Orthodox Church there has been an uninterrupted tradition of chant, each composer following, usually, in the footsteps of his predecessors. Correspondingly, there is a continuity between the various appearances of a hymn, or classes of hymns, through a very long period up to the time of Petros Lampadarios, who gave the music a form which through the transcriptions by the Three Teachers is still in use today.

Starting from these transcriptions (that constitute a written tradition but at the same time are based on an oral tradition that indicates the specific function of the various musical signs), one can trace a way to the transcription of Old Byzantine Chant, especially that of the Heirmologion and the Sticherarion, having in mind the continuity of the chant tradition.

In this paper will be dealt only with the subject of transcription in relation to the melodic movements, without examining the subject of scales and intervals. It is presupposed that there is a close relation or identity of the modern *echoi* with the old ones, despite the differences caused by the evolution of the *melopoiía*.

The starting point for my way of transcribing the Old Sticherarion and Heirmologion is the close relation between the Heirmologion of Petros Lampadarios (18th cent.) and that of Balasios (17th cent.), especially in the Heirmoi of Holy Week. This period of the ecclesiastical year seems to be very conservative in the earlier as well as in later times. Thus, many melodies are preserved in the same, or almost the same form, despite the fact that the style of the *melopoiía* may have changed for the hymns of the rest of the year. We can conclude from the *heirmoi* of the Holy Week that Petros and Balasios followed a common tradition, based on the same or closely related formulas.

Table A shows some *heirmoi* of the Holy Week from the Heirmologia of Balasios and Petros that verify this close relation (or identity).
Se table A

In Table B there is given an example of a formula in the Second Mode from the Heirmologion of Petros. This formula is contained in the Heirmoi of Table A too. There are two forms of this formula: one 'stenographic', given by Balasios, but also found in the version by Petros, and one analytic' given only by Petros. But in Table B we can see that for the heirmos and the troparia of the same *ode* Petros uses both the 'stenographic' and the '-analytic' form. From the similarity of the music of the *heirmos* and the corresponding *troparia* of an *ode*, we can conclude that the 'analytic' form in fact is an analysis of the 'stenographic' one and that they produce the same music, a music through exegesis given by the Three Teachers.
Se table B

But this and other related formulas have counterparts in the Old Sticherarion and Heirmologion, as one can see in Table C. The earlier and later forms (note especially that of Balasios) have at least the same interval ('phonetical') signs. Therefore, they are likely to produce the same music.
Se table C

Table D presents some further examples of the close relations between the

Hirmoi of the Holy Week from Hirmologion of Balasios.
MS of the National Library of Athens [EBE] 946.

ω την α βα τον κυ μαι νο μενην θαλασσαν θει

ω αν του προ σταγματι α ναξη ρα ναν τι ι ι

ι και πε ζευ σαι δι αν της τον ι σρα η λι την

λα ον κα το δη γη σαν τι κυ ρι ω α σα

μεν εν δο ξως γαρ δε δο ξα σται ⁘

Τω δο γμα τι ι τω τυ ραν νι κω οι ο

οι οι τρεις παιδες μη η η πει σθεντες εν τη κα μι

νω ελη θεν τες θε ο ο ο ο ον ω μο ο ο λο

Γουν ψαλλοντες ε ε ευλο γη τε ε τα εργα κυ

ρι ου τον κυ υ ρι ον ⁘

Τον α χω ρη τον θε ον εν γα στρι

χω ρη σα σα και χα ρα αν α αν τω

κο ο ο σμω κυ η σα σα σε ε ε ν υμνουμεν

Ρ

πα να γι ι α παρ θε ε νε :+

η μα τυ ρα αν νου ε πει υ πε

ρι ι σχυ σεν ε πτα πλα σι ως κα μι νος ε ξε

και θη πο τε εν η η η η παι δε ε ες

ουκ ε φλε χθη σαν βα α α σι λε ως πα τη

σα α αν τες δο γμα αλλ ε βο ο ο ο ον παν

τα τα ερ γα κυ ρι ου τον κυ ρι ο ο ον υ μνει τε

και υ πε ρυ ψου τε εις παν τας τους αι ω ω ναςτ.

The same Hirmoi from Hirmologion of Petros Lampadarios.

ἦχος

Τ

ω την α βα τον κυ μαι νο με νην θα λασ σαν θει

ω αυ τον προ στα γμα τι α να ξη ρα ναν τι ι ι

ι ι ι ι και πε ζευ σαι δι αυ της τον ι ερα

η λι ι ι την λα ον κα θο δη γη σαν τι κυ ρι

ω α σω μεν εν δο ξως γαρ δε δο ξα σται :+

125

ω δο γμα τι τω τυ ραν νι κω οι ο ει

οι τρεις παιδες μη η η πει σθεν τες εν τη κα

μι νω βλη θεντε ες θε ο ο ο ο ο ον

ω μο ο ο λο γου ουν τα α λλο ον τες ε

ε ευ λο γει τε τα ε ε ερ γα κυ ρι ι ου

τον κυ υ υ ρι ον :†

η η τον α χω ρη τον θε ον εν γα

στρι χω ρη σα σα και χα ρα α α αν τω

κο ο ο ορω κυ υ η η σα α σα σε ε ε

υ μνουμεν πα να γι ι ι α πα αρ θε ε νε :†

η μα τυ ρα αν νου ε πει υπε ρι ι εσχυσεν

ε πτα πλα σι ως κα μι νος ε ξε και θη πο τε ε

εν η η η η παι δε ε ες κη ε φλε ε χθη

η σαν βα α α ει λε ως πα τη σα α αν τες δογμα

Table A (continued)

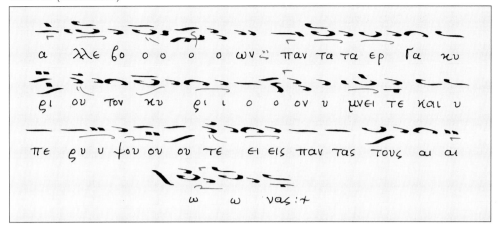

α λλε βο ο ο ο ο ωνͅ παν τα τα ερ Γα κυ

ρι ου τον κυ ρι ι ο ο ον υ μνει τε και υ

πε ρυ υ ϯου ου ου τε ει εις παν τας τους αι αι

ω ω νας ⁘

Table B

"Ἡ τὸν ἀχώρητον θεόν", Εἱρμὸς τῆς θ´ Ὠδῆς

κο ο ο ο σμω κυ υ η η σα α α σα

"Τοῖς μαθηταῖς", τροπάριον τῆς θ´ Ὠδῆς

η η η ξει ο κυ ρι ος

"Ἐν τῇ δευτέρᾳ", τροπάριον τῆς θ´ Ὠδῆς

προ βα α α τοις με ε συ υγ τα α ξον

"Ῥῆμα τυράννου", Εἱρμὸς τῆς Η´ Ὠδῆς

παι δε ε ες ουι ε φλε ε χθη η σαν

"Ἀποκενοῦσα γυνή", τροπάριον τῆς Η´ ᾠδῆς

των ι χνων σου ου ου ε πε λα βε το

"Δάκρυσι πλύνει", τροπάριον τῆς Η´ ᾠδῆς

των εν βι ω ω ω ου δι η μαρ τε

"Ἱερουργεῖται", τροπάριον τῆς Η´ ᾠδῆς

δι α της ε ε ε ξα γο ρευ σε ως

Table C

A. Examples from the Sticherarium (Codex Ambrosianus)

(f. 278 v)

ε σκυ λευ σας τον θα να τον

(f. 80 v)

τω δδ Γμα τι του και σα ρος

(f. 79 v)

αν αυ τω βο η σω μεν

(EBE 883)

α ρε των δα τι λως

B. Examples from the Hirmologium (Cod. Cryptensis E.γ. II)

(f. 58 r)

ε δρο σι σεν ο α ΓΊε λος

(f. 36 v)

παι δας δι ε φυ λα ξας

θε ο λο γουν τες χει λε σιν ε μελ πον

α μαρ τι αν ε ξη λει τε

(f. 39 v)

θε ο ο ο ον ω μο λο Γουν τα ξλον Τες

Heirmologia of Petros and Balasios on the one hand and the and the old ones on the other.
Se table D

But also the Sticherarion of Petros contains formulas which can be found in the Heirmologion of Balasios and in the Old Sticherarion and Heirmologion, as can be seen in Table E.
Se table E

From the preceding material we can confirm, I think, the importance of the Heirmologion of Balasios as a guide to the transcription of Byzantine Chant. Another example will be useful. Balasios' Heirmologion has not been transcribed by the Three Teachers, but there is an

exegesis of it in a manuscript of the Monastery of Koutloumousi on Mount Athos (No. 440), written in a stage of notation previous to that of the Three Teachers. Gr. Stathis gives two photographs from this MS in his catalogue of the manuscripts of Mount Athos[1]. We see here the sticheron ῞Οσιε Πάτερ in a form of exegesis. From the MS of the National Library of Athens No. 946 I transcribe the same sticheron in two forms, 'heirmologikon' and 'sticherarikon'[2] (see Table F).
Se table F

Table G shows some examples of formulas from these stichera, including the exegesis of Koutloumousiou 440 and an exegesis by me in modern Byzantine nota-

Table D

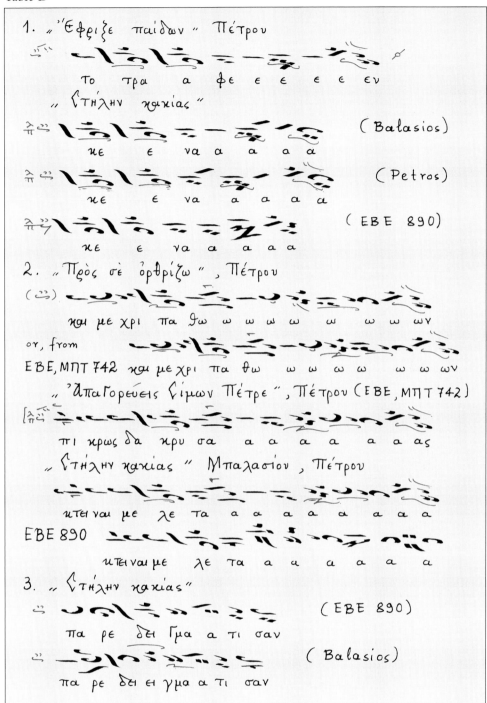

tion (i.e. an 'exegesis of the exegesis' in Koutloumousiou 440 and other corresponding exegeseis), as well as a few additional comments.
Se table G

It is necessary to take into account not only the theseis cited above, but also the whole tradition written in the short melismatic style, i.e. the short Doxologies, the short Polyeleoi etc. Only on this basis can we, with the help of the theoretical treatises, accomplish a transcription of the Old Sticherarion and Heirmologion in short melismatic style. According to my opinion, this style permits the neumatic

πα ρε δει ει γμα α τι σαν

or

πα ρε δει ει Γμα α τι σαν

"Ῥῆμα τυράννου", [⌣]

Πέτρου   ε πει υ πε ρι ι εχυ σεν

"Δάκρυσι πλύνει",

Πέτρου   τας πο δας υ πε ευ θυ νος

"Τὸ τάλαντον", 𝄐

Πέτρου   κυ ρι ι ι ου τον κυ υ ρι ον

4. "Στήλην κακίας"

    (EBE 890)

μου λε ευ ε ε ται

    (Balasios)

βου λε ε ε ευ ε ται

    (Petros)

βου λε ε ε ευ ε ται

5. "Πνευματικῶς ἡμᾶς πιστοί", EBE 2490, f. 64υ-65r

α Γα Γων η μα α α ας

"Τῆς πίστεως",

Πέτρου   α α Γι ο ο ο ος

"Τῷ τὴν ἄβατον", Πέτρου (analytic form)

α να ξη ρα α ναντι ι ι ι ι ι ι

(Note: The MSS EBE 890 and EBE 2490 belong to the 14th cent.)

Table E

a) Balasios, EBE. 946 , „ Θεός Κύριος "

και κλαδων υ μνοις κραυ Γα ζον τες

Εχέγ.

και κλαα δων υ μνοι οι οις κραυ Γα α α ζο ο ον

τες   The same by Petros

και κλαδων υ μνοι οι οις κραυ Γα α α ζο ον τες

Εχέγέσις by the Three Teachers :

και αι κλαα δων υ μνοι οι οις κραυ Γα α α α ζο ο ο ον τες

Petros , Doxastarion , December 24 th :

ο ρα α α Ται πλα α α 6μα α Τος

Εχέγέσις (25)

(3 Teachers)   ο ο ο ρα α α Ται πλα α α α 6μα α α Τος

Old forms of this formula , found in Stichera
and Hirmoi of the 4̈, π̈ 3̈ and ο2̈ Modes , are :

b) E.γ. II

η υ πε ρο πλος δυ ρα μις

Χρυσάφης
ὁ νέος :   Του πνευ μα τος σαλ πι γγας

Πέτρος :

Του πνευ μα α Τος σαλ πι ι σΓας

131

«Εἱρμολογικόν», EBE 946 φ.243r, ἦχος πλ β΄ ...

ο ο ο σι ε πα α α τερ θε ο φο ο ρε

θε ο δο ο ο σι ι ε με γα λως η γω νι ι

ι σω εν τη προ ε και αι αι ρω ζω η εν υ

μνοις και νη ζει ει ει αι αις και α γρυ πνι ι ι αις

τυ πος γε νο με ε ε νος τω ω ω ων σων φοι τη η η

των νυν δε συγ χο ρε ευ εις με ε τα των α

σω μα α των χρι ζον α πα α αυ ζως δο ο ο

ξο ο ο λο γω ω με ων το ο ον ευ θε ρ θε ον

λο ο ο γον και λυ τρω την τον υ πο κλι να

αν τα τη ην κα ραν τω προ δρο ο μω και α

γι α σα αν τα τη ην φυ σιν των υ δα α των αυ

τον ι κε τευ ε αυ τον δυ σω πει ο σι ε

δω ρη θη η η ναι αι τη ευ κλη σι ι ια ο μο νοι αν

ει ρη η η νην και με ε γα ε λε ε ος :+

Table F (continued)

«στιχηραρικόν», EBE 946 f 281 r-v, ἦχος πα

σι ε πα τερ θε ο φο ρε θε ο δο σι ι

ε με γα λως η γω νι ι ι σω ερ τη προ εκαι

ρω ζω η εν υ μνοις και νη στει ει ει αι αις

και α γευ πνι ι ι ι αις τυ πος γε νο με νος

των σων φοι οι τη των ρυμ δε συγχορε ε ευ εις με τα α

των α σω μα α α των Χρι στον α παυγως δο ξο λο

γω ω ω ω ω ω ων τον εκ θε ου θε ον λο ο ο ο ο γον

δ λυ τρω την τον υ πο κλι να α αν τα τη ην κα

ραν τω προ δρο ο μω και α γι α σα αν τα

τη ην φυ σιν των υ δα α των αυ τον ι με

τευ ε αυ τον δυ σω πει ο σι ε δω ρη θη ναι

τη εκ λη σι α ο μο νοι αν ει ρη η η νην

και με ε γα ε λε ε ος: +

Table G

a) Analysis of eso thematismos on αγια

(EBE 946)

δδ ο ο ο ξο ο ο λο Γω ω (με) ων

δδ ο ο ο ξο ο ο λο Γω ω ω ω ω ω ω

(Koutloumousi 440)

ω ω ω ω

Exégésis of Koutl. 440

δδ ο ο ο ο ο ξο ο ο ο λο

Γω ω ω ω ω ω ω ω ω ω ω ω ων

Another synonymous exégésis

... Γω ω ω ω ω ω ω ω ω ω ω ω ω ω ω ω ων

b) EBE 946, „Εἱρμολογικόν":

Το ο ον εκ θε χ θε ον

Koutl. 440:

Το ο ον εκ θε ου ου ου θε ον

Exégésis of Koutl. 440 (ε/χ)

θε ε ου ου ου θε ε ον

Another shorter (ε/χ)
exégésis:

θε ε ου ου ου θε ε ον

c)

και α Γρυ πνι ι ι αις

και α α Γρυ πνι ι ι ι ι αις

Exég. (Koutl 440)

και α α α Γρυ πνι ι ι ι ι αις

134

The egegésis of the syllable „-πνί-" has the shape of the strepton ꝛ . It could have the shape of the tromikon ς as well , that is :

πνι ι ι αις   πνι ι ι αις   (EBE 946)

σων φοι ΤΗ Η Η Των

σω ων φοι ΤΗ Η Η Των   (Κουτλ. 440)

Exégésis : σω ω ων φοι ΤΗ Η Η Η Των

„Cτιχηραριϰόν" :

θε ον λο ο ο ο Γον ϰαι λυ Τρω ΤΗν   (EBE 946)

θε ον λο ο ο ο ο Γο ον ϰαι λυ υ υ Τρω ΤΗν   (Κουτλ. 440)

Ex. θε ον λο ο ο ο ο Γο ο ον ϰαι λυ υ υ υ Τρω ΤΗν

It could also be transcribed as follows , with an antikenoma on the word „λυτρωτήν" , that is :

θε ον λο ο ο ο Γον ϰαι λυ Τρω ΤΗν

θε ον λο ο ο ο Γο ον ϰαι λυ υ Τρω ω ΤΗν

The same in „Ειρμολογιϰόν" (Shape of strepton) (EBE 946)

Γον ϰαι λυ υ Τρω ΤΗν

λο ο ο ο Γο ον ϰαι λυ υ υ Τρω ΤΗν   (Κουτλ. 440)

135

Ex.

λο ο ο ο ο Γο ο ον χαι λυ υ υ Τρω την

d) „Στιχηραρικόν"

Ο σι ε πα τερ Ο σι ε πα α α τερ

Petros Lampadarios, Doxastarion, September 1st:

Ο σι ε πα α α τερ

Exegesis of this „Thesis" by the Three Teachers:

Ο σι ι ε ε πα α τερ

„Στιχηραρικόν"

δω ρη θη ναι τη ευ κλη σι α

Petros Lampadarios, December 24th.

των Γε νε θλι ι ι ων Τα α ας ει σο ο ο δους

Exegeseis of the above formulas:

δω ρη θη η ναι τη ε ε ευ κλη η σι ι ι α

των Γε νε θλι ι ι ων Τα α ας ει ει σο ο

(The latter by the Three Teachers)

δους

These formulas can be found in the old Sticherarium and Hirmologium, too.

characters to be performed in their full melismatic interpretation.

As an example, and as a result of the *theseis* and their exegeseis from the Heirmologion or the Sticherarion of Petros Lampadarios and from the Heirmologion of Balasios contained in Tables B-E, we can say that the (later) presence of *antikenoma* in *theseis* like (a) of Table H gives us the well-known endings of the new Sticheraric and the 'new' long Heirmologic style and, according to the examples above, of the Old Sticheraric and Heirmologic style as well.

In addition, we can from the study of the *sticheron* Ὅσιε Πάτερ (Tables F-G) verify the close relation (or identity) of *theseis* like those of Table H (b) and (c), and, finally, we can show the possible identity of the *syndesmoi* (double *apostrophos*) in the *analysis* of the *tromikon*. This could be taken as an indication for us to transcribe similar *theseis* in the same way (see Table H, *theseis* (d)-(f)).

Table H

B.

In many cases this way of exegesis can be justified sign by sign according to the rhythmical value and the cheironomic function of each sign in the theoretical treatises. However, the concept of *synagma* ('grouping') is of crucial importance as it sometimes diminishes the time value of the signs (see Table I).

C.

The 'long *exegesis*' do in many cases result from the short one by duplicating, quadrupling etc. the time values of the short melodic movements and, eventually, by elaborating and enriching the parts of the composition. Through that procedure,

the long *exegesis* sometimes appears very different from the short one.

The structural relation between the short and the long *exegesis* may by the inverse procedure give us some indication which, with the help of the theoretical treatises, can lead from the 'long exegesis' backwards to the 'short' one, a procedure especially useful regarding the 'short *exegesis*' of the Old Papadike (see Table J).

D.

Finally, there is a possibility of a syllabic or 'mixed' *exegesis* for a group of old chants, for example the short *prokeimena*, the *'Triadika'* of Lent a.o. (see Table K).

137

Table I

2 + 1 t.u.   1 t.u.   4 t.u.

(total : 4)

b)

Notes:
i) The numbers indicate the units of duration according to the present musical theory. Each interval neume of the old notation without a subsidiary rhythmical sign has the duration of two time units.
ii) The formulas in brackets are the later forms with red subsidiary signs.
iii) After the = follows a transcription into modern Byzantine notation.

Table J

a) [notation] = [notation] or [notation] . By dublicating the time values, it gives [notation]
or [notation] . Dublicating again, we have:
[notation] or [notation] or
[notation]

Examples from the transcriptions of the Three Teachers.

[notation] = [notation]
E ξα πο στε λεις το   E ξα πο στε χει ει ει εις το

[notation] = [notation]
Και εις το ον   Και ει ει ει εις το ον

b) [notation] = [notation] ×2 → [notation]
Example: From „Κατευθυνθήτω", ῆχος ğ

[notation]
Των χει ...   τω ω ω ω ων χει ....

c) [notation] = [[notation] |= [notation]] ×2 →
[notation] or [notation]
Example: Apéchema of the Barys echos.

[notation]
α α κες α α α α α α α κε ε κε ε ες

d) [notation] ×2 →
[notation] or [notation] or
[notation]
[notation] ×2 → [notation]
or [notation]
or [notation]
Example: From „Τὸ προσταχθέν."
[notation] α νυ νμφευτε α α νυν ν νμφε ε ε ε κε ε ευτε

Table K

Προκείμενον, ἦχος αʹ   (ΕΒΕ 2406)

ε   νοι το κυ ρι ε   το ε λε ος θου εφ η μας κα θα

περ ηλπι σα μεν ε ε   πι ι σοι :+

Τῇ Ἁγίᾳ καὶ Μεγάλῃ Τεσσαρακοστῇ, Τριαδικόν, ἦχος γʹ

ω   μα τι καις μορ φω σε σι των α σω μα των Δυ να με

ω ων προς νο ε ραν και α ϋ λον α να γο με   νοι οι

εν νοι α αν και Τρι σα γι ω μελω δη μα τι Τρι συ πο ζα

του   θε ο τη τος ος δε χο με   νοι ε κλαμ ψιν χα ρυ

ε κω, βο η   η σω με εν   α   Γι ο ο

ο ο ος α   Γι ο ο ο ο ο ς α

α Γι ος ει ε σ θε ος δι α της θε ο το κυ ε λε   η

σο ον η η μα ας :+

Bibliography

Stathis, G. 1993
Τὰ Χειρόγραφα Βυζαντινῆ ς
Μουσικῆ ς, Ἅγιον Ὄρος. Κατάλογος
περιγραφικὸ ς τῶν χειρογράφων
κωδίκων Βυζαντινῆ ς Μουσικῆ ς τῶν
ἀποκειμένων ἐν ταῖ ς Βιβλιοθήκαις
τῶν ἱερῶν Μονῶν καὶ Σκητῶν τοῦ
Ἁγίου Ὄρους, Vol. III, Athens.

Notes

NOTE 1
Stathis 1993 300-301. This volume was
published just a week before the Symposium.

NOTE 2
These names are attributed by me. The
rubric of Koutloumousiou 440 signifying '-
sticherarikon' reads: "Τὸ παρὸν ὑπάρχει
ἀργότερον μεμιγμένον μὲ στιχηρόν".

Interpretation of Tones and Modes in Theoretical Handbooks of the 15th century

Antonios E. Alygizakis

Introduction

Undoubtedly, the ecclesiastical modes, as is also the case for the musical modal system in general, constitute one of the most interesting, yet at the same time one of the most difficult chapters in the history of music[1]. This has to do with the fact that the aforementioned subjects are shaped by various factors, such as, mathematics, the physical sciences, philosophy, by theology, etc.[2] Christianity adopted some of the theoretical and technical principles of the ancient Greek modal system, but it related the eight *echoi* (modes) and the *octaechia* as a liturgical phenomenon to its own practice within the bounds of the theological symbolisms and the doctrine of the Church[3]. On the other hand, the musical system of the Christian East remains basically polymodal and the whole structure of Byzantine and post-Byzantine liturgical melody is founded on that perspective[4].

Concerning the Byzantine polymodal system, certain theoretical handbooks of the late Middle Ages are particularly enlightening. Among these is an anonymous text having the following characteristic inscription:

Ἑτέρα παραλλαγὴ καὶ μέθοδος καὶ μητροφωνία τῆς ψαλτικῆς τέχνης, περιέχουσα ἅπασαν τῶν η′ ἤχων τὴν ἑρμηνείαν, ποῦ καταντᾷ εἶς ἕκαστος καὶ ποῦ κεῖται καὶ πῶς εἶς ἕκαστος ἦχος ἔχει. ἤγουν οἱ κύριοι, μέσους καὶ παραμέσους, καὶ οἱ πλάγιοι, διφώνους, καὶ τριφώνους, καὶ τετραφώνους. καὶ διερμηνεύει ταῦτα ὁ μακαρίτης ἐκεῖνος κὺρ Ἰωάννης μαΐστωρ ὁ Κουκουζέλης, ἐν τῇ σοφωτάτη αὐτοῦ μεθόδῳ: Αὕτη ἐστὶν ἡ ἑρμηνεία τῶν φωνῶν καὶ ἤχων[5].

The text above is the first, amongst two other related interpretations which were formulated by the well-known music theoreticians: Ioannes Plousiadenos[6] and Ioannes Laskares[7]. All three texts refer to the great Maestor Ioannes Koukouzeles, who appears to introduce and systematically form the Byzantine polymodal system. A fact that, from the beginning, takes for granted the significance of the musical theory of that kind[8].

This paper is an attempt at an analytical presentation of the content of the aforementioned anonymous text, which bears the specific title: "Interpretation of tones and modes". This presentation will be in two parts: First we shall examine the manuscript tradition of the text and its content and secondly we shall analyze its relation to the other two similar interpretations of the polymodal system and its significance in the development and formulation of Byzantine and post-Byzantine musical theory as a whole.

1. Manuscript tradition and content

Our text is partially of a theoretical nature which was common in theoretical treatises and methods concerning Byzantine music. We find it in two important manuscripts: MS Athonite Dionysiou 570 (15th century) and MS Athens 968 (17th century). We are mainly interested in the Athonite MS[9]. It is the most complete selection of theoretical dissertations and methods, which coexists along with the *Mathematarion*. The most important point regarding this MS though appears to be that it was written by the priest Ioannes Plousiadenos, a great representative of Psaltic Art in the late 15th century[10]. Here then, our text occupies a significant place. It constitutes the apogee of a major unity, which includes the first elements of theory, as seen by the titles of the chapters: 'Concerning the tones', 'Division of music' and 'Interpretation of *echemata*', along with various methods: the '*octaecho*', the '*diplophonia*' and finally 'the classification of the great *hypostases*'[11]. It seems, however, that the 'Interpretation of tones and modes' was not only a learning method of primary importance for the student. At the same time its theoretical material is of particular importance and is related to older levels of theory. It may belong to the group known as the anonymous handbooks A, B, C, D, etc., given that the Athonite MS 570 presents our text after these[12].

It is also characteristic that our text is presented first in MS Dionysiou 570, which goes on to compile Ioannes Laskares' similar interpretation; the well known dissertation of Hieromonachos Gabriel; several pre-theories and methods and also another method similar to the method of *parallage* (παραλλαγή) of Ioannes Plousiadenos[13]. Therefore it would seem that the very important Athonite MS Dionysiou 570 forms a complete coverage of almost the entire theoretical material of Byzantine music, where the methods of interpretation and *parallage* of the modal system hold a significant place. Furthermore, the depth, the arrangement and the philological formation of the content, as we shall see below, show our text to be superior to the other two similar texts within the same MS, that of Ioannes Laskares and that of Ioannes Plousiadenos. Thus, despite Plousiadenos' flattering title to

Laskares' interpretation: Ἑτέρα παραλλαγὴ τῆς μουσικῆς τέχνης, σοφωτέρα καὶ ἀκριβεστέρα εἰς ἄκρον[14], our text seems to supply information on both interpretations (Laskares - Plousiadenos).

The content of our text is specified in its long title, which refers to the proper technical terminology[15]. The terms *parallage* and *metrophonia* are of course two of the most difficult aspects of music theory. It is characteristic, nevertheless, that in every reference to the modes - according to the interpretation of their *parallage* - their signatures are included. Thus, the term *metrophonia* in the title possibly refers to this fact and it prepares us for the relationship of primary importance between *parallage* and *metrophonia*. In the title, as well, are defined the groups of modes: κύριοι, πλάγιοι, μέσοι, παραμέσοι, δίφωνοι, τρίφωνοι and τετράφωνοι[16]. Finally there exists also the significant evidence which presents Maestor Ioannes Koukouzeles as the instigator (architect) of the polymodal system. The master in question, analyses all the types of modes "ἐν τῇ σοφωτάτῃ αὐτοῦ μεθόδῳ"[17].

Our text is divided basically into two parts, in which the *parallage* and *metrophonia* of the two principal categories of modes: the authentic and the plagal modes are described[18]. In this way, every part refers separately to the four cases of every category. A smaller part constitutes a kind of short preface, while an even smaller part with general instructions, brings the text to an end[19].

The preface gives the basic theory for the creation of the first categories of the modes which are the plagal and the *mesoi*, then a corresponding descent of voice every four tones and every two tones is described. Furthermore, it is here that, for the first time, the term *parakyrioi* modes is mentioned, which refers to the second *tetrades* of modes, to the plagal modes upon which the *mesoi* conclude. At this point also, it is made clear that because there is an organic relationship among the first four categories of modes (authentic, plagal, *mesoi*, *mesoi* of the *mesoi*), their distinction is made by the length of time during which the melody stays at every category of mode and their conclusions which coincide.

In all cases of the four authentic and the four plagal modes, the *parallage* of our text applies the same technique. That is, it ascends successively four tones and then descends in the same way. With this technique, the rest of the modal groups and their cases are created from the different rungs and bases of the authentic modes.

This entire technique above is simplified by Hieromonachos Gabriel's *'Kanonion'*, where only the signatures of the eight modes are mentioned[20]. Thus, while we know exactly the *metrophonia*, we do not know the specific characteristics of the modes' various categories. Because of this, we are obliged to consider in detail the whole text of our interpretation.

In the case of the First mode, ascending to the fourth tone our text refers to the proper *tetraphonos* First mode[21]. Descending three tones we have diphonos of Plagal Fourth[22].

In the Second mode by ascending four tones we find *tetraphonos* Second[23]. One tone downwards is Plagal First *Nenanos*[24]. At this point it is verified that *Nenanos* is Third and Fourth modes because, Third mode was created from Second mode and Second from First mode and because: "τὰ γὰρ μέλη πολλάκις εἴωθε νικᾶν τὴν μετροφωνίαν"[25]. Moreover, the mesos of Second *tetraphonos* is Third, because Third mode is *triphonos* of Plagal fourth, thus, "πᾶσα τριφωνία τὸν αὐτὸν ἦχον ποιεῖ"[26]. In addition, three tones below Second mode is Barys, which changes into Plagal Second and *Legetos*[27]. Finally, four tones below is Plagal Second or eso Second mode, because Second mode is the *diphonia* of Plagal Fourth and *triphonia* of Barys mode[28].

Three tones above Third mode is Second mode, also named 'tied' (δεμένος) Third and four tones above is *tetraphonos*

Third or 'double' Third[29]. Finally, three tones below Third mode is Plagal Fourth, which is again Third mode, because it is *triphonos* of Plagal Fourth[30].

Three tones above Plagal First mode is *tetraphonos* First mode, which is also its authentic mode[31].

Three tones above Plagal Second mode is *Nenano*, which is Third and Fourth modes[32]. Because three tones above is also First, which (decays) and changes into *Nenano*[33]. Further, ascending four tones it turns into *tetraphonos* Second, which is first and second and because of *phthora* it becomes Third[34]. Three tones below is *Barys* mode, which is Plagal Second and *Legetos*, because *Legetos* changes into *Barys* mode and Plagal Second[35].

With regards to *Barys* mode, when we refer to its *tetraphonos* it is again the authentic mode. In the same way that one tone above Third mode is Fourth mode, one tone above *Barys* mode is Fourth mode, which is a Third mode from the *parallage* and not Fourth mode, Finally, four tones above *Barys* mode is Third mode, its authentic mode, which is called Nanas (νανάς), while a tone below is *tetraphonos Barys* mode[36].

The Plagal Fourth mode, which is also *tetraphonos Barys* mode which in turn is Third mode as its authentic, is similar to Third mode, as its *triphonos* mode according to the canon "πᾶσα τριφωνία τὸν αὐτὸν ἦχον ποιεῖ"[37]. Four tones above Plagal Fourth mode is *tetraphonos* Fourth mode, which is its authentic, the beginning of the plagal tones[38].

Our text comes to its conclusion with two precepts that refer to the following categories of modes: to *Legetos*, to *tetraphonos Barys*, and to eso First, Second, Third and Fourth modes[39].

2. Relation to other interpretations and importance

Our text, as is evident from its place in the selection of the theoretical material of the MS Athos Dionysiou 570, is an anonymous dissertation, which, obviously, was taken into consideration and completed by our two well known representatives of Psaltic Art, Ioannes Plousiadenos[40] and Ioannes Laskares Kalomisides[41]. The material concerning the interpretation of the tones and modes must have been known by Hieromonachos Gabriel too. However, having a more practical and orderly mind, he worked out the '-Kanonion', which not only simplifies the *parallage*, but also presents the latter in a more systematic and pedagogical way, easier to memorize[42]. Specifically the rule "πᾶσα τριφωνία τὸν αὐτὸν ἦχον ποιεῖ", is used by both the music theoreticians Ioannes Plousiadenos[43] and Ioannes Laskares[44]. We also encounter the same matter in the references concerning the great Maestor Ioannes Koukouzeles, who is the undisputed instructor of the rules and methods of the polymodal system[45]. We can not ignore, of course, the intimate relation of all interpretations and methods of *parallage* to the *Agiopolites'* basic theory[46]. But this treatise, in spite of its significance in the technical arrangement of the Byzantine modal system, has only archaic elements of theory, which lack the detailed analyses and applications of Koukouzeles' practice.

Finally, with regard to the philological structure, our text apparently belongs to the theoretical material and to the group of the known anonymous dissertations A, B, C, D, etc., which are included in the collection bearing the title "Ἐρωταπο-κρίσεις τῆς παπαδικῆς τέχνης", ascribed to Saint John of Damascus[47].

Concluding our reference to the text *Interpretation of tones and modes*, we find that its content includes important elements and thorough analyses on the Byzantine polymodal systems' complicated mechanism. Moreover, the relation of the modes' system to Maestor Ioannes Koukouzeles on the one hand, and, its deeper relation to the modal system of Hellenic antiquity on the other hand, makes the text in question, as well as texts related with it, a witness to the vitality of the Byzantine musical civilization. The latter is also confirmed by the fact that the majority of the elements of Byzantine polymodal system were preserved during the post-Byzantine period, providing material even for the three masters' analytical method of writing[48]. Chrysanthos in his *Theoritikon* refers with clarity to modal systems, such as *triphonia, pentachordo, trocho,* etc.. Considering those, he admits that "ταῦτα πάντα ἐξη–κριβώθησαν ἀπὸ Ἰωάννην τὸν Πλουσιαδηνόν"[49]. Furthermore, contemporary music books include a great number of melodies whose terminology belongs to the old Byzantine polymodal system[50].

So beyond any formulation of a conclusion, the Interpretation of tones and modes, among the theoretical handbooks of the 15th century, constitutes a very useful method for the study and research even of the contemporary traditional Byzantine melody.

Plate 1

Plate 2

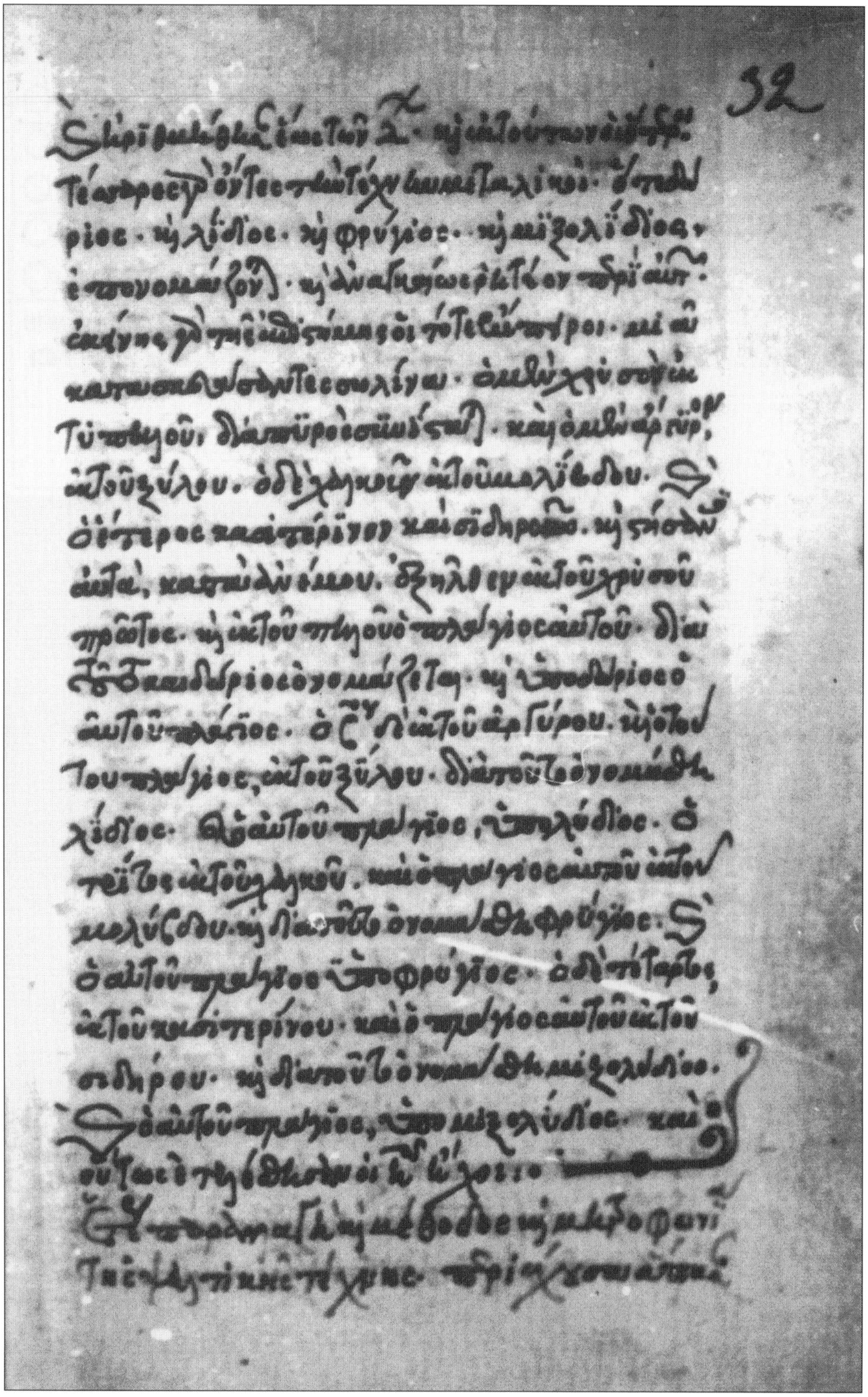

Παραλλαγή

Τοῦ — **Γα**

(left margin, vertical) Ἐνταῦθα τὰς κατιούσας εὑρήσεις πᾶν πλαγίας

⸭					ͱ
α					ζ
β					ϛ
γ					ε
δ					δ
ε					γ
ϛ					β
ζ					α
η					⸭

(right margin)
ἐνταῦθα
λάμβανε
τοὺς αὐτοὺ-
σας φωνὰς
καὶ εὑρήσης
πάντας
κινεῖὸς

μέθοδος
σοφωτάτη
τῷ δεῖ ὀιεχε
σθαι τὰῳαπ
φωνιζην
Δομέστια

βρι — **ηλ**

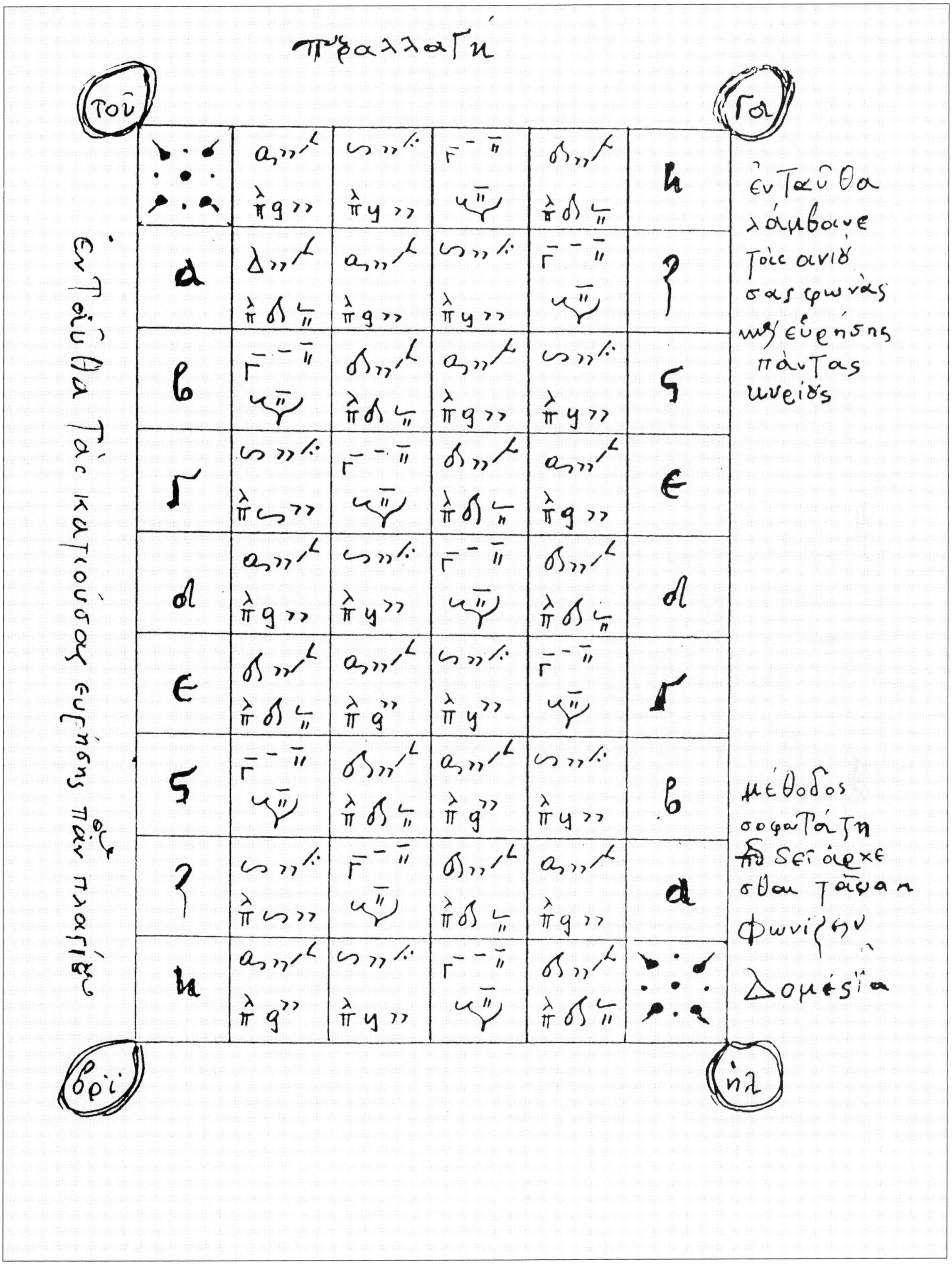

Appendix
English translation of the 'Interpretation of the Tones and Modes' from MS Athos Dionysiou 570
(Edition of the Greek text in Alygizakis 1985, pp. 230-34)

*Antonios
E. Alygizakis*

Another *parallage* and method and *metrophonia* of the Psaltic Art, which contains the whole interpretation of the eight modes, the extent of each one of them and where they are to be found and the nature of each mode. That is, the authentic modes, the mesos and the paramesos and the plagals with its *diphonoi* and *triphonoi* and *tetraphonoi*. These are what he the blessed Mr. Ioannes Maestor and Koukouzeles interprets in his most wise method.

This is the interpretation of the tones and modes:
One must know that the authentic modes are on the whole four. From these then authentic modes are produced the plagal modes. That is, from the First its Plagal and similarly from the Second its Plagal and from the Third similarly its Plagal, that is the *Barys* and from the Fourth similarly its Plagal. And with both authentic and plagal they became eight modes. Furthermore, the plagal of each mode is found by descending four tones, for this reason also there are no more than four authentic modes. We refer to the para-authentic modes because such are needed so that each *mesos* mode can find its final cadence upon such para-authentics, upon these they naturally rest, as it were, and are rendered with their characteristic melodic sound. How this occurs we shall explain immediately. And let us begin with the Plagal First mode and its *mesos*, the *Barys*; by comparing this to the others you may understand the other *mesos* modes, ie., that of the Second the Third and the Fourth modes. If you move down from the First mode two tones it becomes *Barys* mode, which is

the plagal of the Third; and this is the *mesos* of First. If from this *mesos*, that is the *Barys* we move down another two tones it becomes Plagal First. Similarly, with the Second mode, when you follow this process exactly you shall find its *mesos* (Plag. Fourth) and for the Third the Plagal First and for the Fourth the Plagal Second. The authentic modes sometimes act as if taking precedence over their *mesos* and their plagal and at other times they act as a *mesos* of the *mesos* and as the authentic mode of the particular *mesos*. For example, we chant First Mode and its *mesos* is *Barys*. The authentic for *Barys* is Third and the melody sometimes is placed as *Barys* and other times as Third or even as the First Mode itself. And when the melody persists either on Third mode as on *Barys* it must change itself from that mode in which it has lingered.

Know, oh musician!, that if you move up one tone from the First mode you shall find the Second, if you move up two tones you shall find the Third, if you move up three you shall find the Fourth, if you move up four you again shall find the First and this is the authentic *tetraphonos*. If you thus move down from this *tetraphonos* one tone you will find the Plagal Fourth and this is Fourth mode. And if you move down from the afore-mentioned First mode two tones you shall find the *Barys* mode and this is the Third. If you move down from this First, three tones you shall find the Plagal Second and this is the Second, that is, the *diphonos* of Plagal Fourth. And if you move down from this afore-mentioned First tone four tones you find its plagal that is the Plagal First, which is both First and

Fourth and Plagal First: Plagal First (?), Fourth, First, Plagal First.

If you move up one tone from the Second mode you find the Third mode, if you move up two tones you find the Fourth, if you move up three tones you shall find the First mode and this is the Second Mode, because the First mode is one and the same with the Second. If you thus move up four tones we again shall find the Second authentic mode, which is Third with the *phthora*, for it is known that the *phthora* creates another mode; (Second mode *tetraphonos*). If you thus move down from this Second mode one tone you shall finds the Plagal First mode and this is *Nenanos*; for *Nenanos* is Third mode and Fourth; because the Third mode was born from the Second and the Second was born from the First; for the melody often wins out over *metrophonia*. And if you move down from the above mentioned Second mode two tones you shall find the Plagal Fourth and it is the *mesos* of this Second and this is the Third; for the *mesos* of the Second of the *tetraphonos* is the Third, because the Third is the *triphonos* of the Plagal of the Fourth mode, thus every triphony creates its own mode. And if you move down from this mode three tones you shall find the *Barys* mode and he becomes Plagal Second and into *Legetos*. And if you move down from this mode four tones you shall find its plagal, that is Plagal Second and he is called esos Second, because the Second is a *diphonos* of Plagal Fourth mode and *triphonos* of *Barys*, thus: *Barys*, Second.

Similarly again, if you move up from the Third mode one tone you shall find the Fourth mode. If you move up two tones you shall find the First mode, if you move up three tones you shall find the Second mode and he is tied Third, for from the Second was born the Third. If you move up four voices you shall find again the authentic Third mode, which is named also as double-Third and this is the *tetraphonos* Third mode. Similarly if you move down from this *tetraphonos*

Third one tone you shall find the Plagal Second mode and this is Second, for the plagals are created from the authentic modes. Therefore know this, oh! listener, that the modes have a tendency towards transformation and that is why the authentic transform into plagal and the plagal towards the authentic, as the blessed Maestor Ioannes Koukouzeles has shown in his most wise method and *parallage*, on the one hand by moving up with the *oligon* he showed the plagal modes as authentic and on the other hand moving down with the *apostrophos* he proved the opposite; the authentic modes as plagal. Let us return to our topic. If you move down from the Third mode two tones you shall find the Plagal First and this is the authentic First: First, Second and Fourth and Plagal First, be careful then, in the case that you move down one tone from the Second you shall find the Fourth tone, for the First and the Second are of one essence. And in the case of moving down from the First one tone you shall find the Plagal Fourth mode and this is Fourth, the very same thing as in Second (Pl. Second). If you move down from the Third three tones you shall find Plagal Fourth mode and this is again Third, because this is the *triphonos* of Plagal Fourth. If you move down from this *tetraphonos* Third the four tones you shall find its plagal, that is, *Barys*.

Similarly again, if you ascend from the Fourth mode one tone up you shall find the First Mode and he is Second because the Fourth and the Plagal First are transformed into one and because in moving up from the Plagal First one tone you shall find the Second tone, similarly with the Fourth. And if you move up two tones you shall find the Second mode and this is Third. Because when upon the Fourth you make a *diphonia* you shall find the Third, as occurs from the First. And if you move up from the Fourth mode three tones you shall find the Third mode and he is Fourth, as is from the First and Plagal First. If you move up from the Fourth mode four tones you shall find again the authentic Fourth and this is the authentic First, as from the Plagal First.

Beginning of the Plagal modes

Plagal First mode
If you move up from the Plagal First one tone you shall find the Second mode. And if you move up two tones you shall find the Third mode. If you move up three tones you shall find the Fourth mode. If you move up four tones you shall find the First mode the *tetraphonos*, whom is its authentic.

Plagal Second mode
If you move up from the Plagal Second one tone you shall find the Third tone and he is the Second, because the Plagal First is one and the same with the Plagal Second, as is the case with the First and the Second. If you move up from the Plagal Second two tones you shall find the Third as Fourth and this is Third as from the Plagal First. If you move up three tones you shall find the Nenano, which is both Third and Fourth. Because if you move up three tones from the Plagal Second you shall find the First mode and the *phthora* of the Nenano makes this a perfect Nenano. If you move up from the Plagal Second four tones you shall find his authentic the Second *tetraphonos* and he is First and Second and from the *phthora* of the Third.

Barys mode
If you move up from the *Barys* one tone you shall find the Fourth mode and he is Third. When you say *Barys tetraphonos* consider that it is its authentic, that is to say the Third, for when you move one tone from the Third and find the Fourth mode, in the same manner when you move up from the *Barys* you shall find the Fourth mode, except that by *parallage* it is Third and not Fourth. If you move up from this *Barys* two tones you shall

find the First mode and this is Fourth and Plagal Second. If you move up three tones you shall find the Second tone and this is First and Second. If you move up four tones you shall find the Third mode and he is its authentic, which is named *Nanas*.

Plagal Fourth mode
If you move up from the Plagal Fourth one tone you shall find the First mode and this one is Plagal First and Fourth, because the Plagal Fourth is the *mesos* of the Second. Because the First and Second are one and he therefore is *mesos* of the Second and of the First, thus he concludes both on the Fourth and on the Plagal First. If you move up from the Plagal Fourth two tones you shall find the Second mode. If you move up three tones you shall find the Third mode, who is also *mesos* of the Second, as from the First for which the *mesos* is *Barys*. Because the *tetraphonos Barys* is its own authentic, that is, the Third. And the Third and the Plagal Fourth are one, because it is its *triphonos*, according to the rule that states that every *triphonia* creates the same mode. If you move from this Plagal Fourth four tones you shall find the fourth mode the *tetraphonos* and this is its authentic. The beginning of the plagals.

If you move from the Plagal First one tone you shall find the Plagal Fourth mode. If you move down two tones you shall find the *Barys* mode. If you move down three tones you shall find the Plagal Second mode. If you move down four tones you shall find the Plagal First mode and this is the Plagal Fourth, because the Plagal First is transformed to the Fourth. Fourth (???) First and Plagal First.

If you move down from the Plagal Second one tone you shall find the Plagal First mode and this is the Plagal Fourth, because the Plagal First and the Plagal Second have the same power and are one, only their *phthora*s are what distinguishes them. If you move down two tones you shall find the Plagal Fourth and this is *Barys*, as with the Plagal First. If you move down three tones you shall find the *Barys* mode and this is the Plagal Second and *Legetos*. Because the *Legetos* turns into the *Barys* and to Plagal Second.

Know therefore, oh musician, how things are with the modes, either authentic or plagals, that is, if you move up three tones the same mode you find again, similarly with the plagals the same thing occurs. If you move down three tones from any of the plagals you again will find the same plagal mode. If you move down from this Plagal Second four tones you shall the Plagal Second and this is the Plagal First the Plagal Second and the Plagal Fourth.

If you move down from the *Barys* one tone you shall find the Plagal Second mode and he is both Plagal Second and Plagal First. Understand that there is also *Barys tetraphonos* and he is Third. If you move down two tones you shall find the Plagal Second mode and he is the Plagal Fourth mode. If you move down three tones you shall find the Plagal Fourth mode and he is again *Barys*. If you move

down four tones you shall find again the *Barys* mode and he is Plagal Second and Plagal First.

If you move down one tone from the Plagal Fourth you shall find the *Barys* mode. If you move down two tones you shall find the Plagal Second mode and this is also Plagal First and Plagal Second. If you move down three tones you shall find the Plagal First mode and he is again Plagal Fourth mode. If you move four tones you shall find again the Plagal Fourth and he is *Barys* mode.

Know, oh musician, that the *mesos* of the First mode is the *Barys* and the *mesos* of the Second mode is the Plagal Fourth, that is, the *Neanes* and the *mesos* of the Third mode is Plagal First and the *mesos* of the Fourth mode is the Plagal Second, that is to say the *Legetos*. *Legetos* is also *Barys*, that is to say, the Plagal Third, because this is *Barys tetraphonos*, which is named also *Nanas*.

Know that the *eso* First is the Plagal First and the *eso* Second the Plagal Second and the *eso* Third the Plagal Third, which is named *Barys* and the *eso* Fourth is the Plagal Fourth.

Bibliography

Alygizakis, A.E. 1985
Ἡ Ὀκταηχία στην ἑλληνικὴ λειτουργικὴ ὑμνογραφία. Thessalonike.

Alygizakis, A.E. 1990
Χαρακτηριστικὲς περιπτώσεις
ἐκκλησιαστικῶν ἤχων ἐκτὸς τῶν ὀ
κτώ, in Προσφορὰ Παντελεήμονι Β᾽
τῷ Παναγιωτάτω Μητροπολίτη
Θεσσαλονίκης, ἐπὶ τῇ εἰκοσιπεντα–
ετηρίδι τῆς ἀρχιερατείας αὐτοῦ,
reprinted Thessalonike 1991, Thessalonike.

Bentas, Ch. 1971
"The Treatise on Music by John Laskaris",
Studies in Eastern Chant II, 21-27.

Chrysanthos of Madytos 1832
Θεωρητικὸν μέγα τῆς μουσικῆς
(reprinted Athens 1977), Tergeste.

Chrysaphes 1985
The Treatise of Manuel Chrysaphes, the
Lampadarios, Monumenta Musicae Byzantinae, Corpus Scriptorum de Re Musica II,
ed. Conomos, D.E., Vienna.

Gabriel Hieromonachos 1985
Abhandlung über den Kirchengesang,
Monumenta Musicae Byzantinae, Corpus
Scriptorum de Re Musica I, edd. Wolfram,
G. and Hannick, Ch., Wien 1985.

Raasted, J. 1983
The Hagiopolites, A Byzantine Treatise on
Musical Theory, Preliminary edition,
Cahiers de l'Institut du Moyen-Âge Grec et
Latin (Université de Copenhaque) 45,
Copenhagen.

Stathis, G. Th. 1976
Τὰ Χειρόγραφα Βυζατινῆς Μουσικῆς,
Ἅγιον Ὄρος. Κατάλογος περιγραφι-
κὸς τῶν χειρογράφων κωδίκων
Βυζαντιῆς Μουσικῆς τῶν ἀποκει-
μένων ἐν ταῖς Βιβλιοθήκαις τῶν ἱ-
ερῶν Μονῶν καὶ Σκητῶν τοῦ
Ἁγίου Ὄρους, 2, Athens.

Thomas, I. 1967-79
"Octoechos", New Catholic Encyclopedia
X.

Wellesz, E. 1947
Eastern Elements in Western Chant, Monu-
menta Musicae Byzantinae, Subsidia II,
Second edition Copenhagen 1962, Oxford-
Boston.

Werner, E. 1959
The Sacred Bridge, The Interdependence of
Liturgy and Music in Synagogue and
Church during the First Millennium, Lon-
don-New York

Plates
1. The text of Anonymous: 'Interpretation
of the tones and modes', MS Athos, Dionysiou 570, f 32r.

2. The text of Anonymous: 'Interpretation
of the tones and modes', MS Athos, Dionysiou 570, f 32v.

3. A copy of Gabriel's 'Kanonion'. MS
Athos, Dionysiou 570, f 56v.

Notes

NOTE 1
cf. Alygizakis 1985 13. See also Wellesz 1947 30 ff. and Thomas 1967-79 640.

NOTE 2
cf. Alygizakis 1985; also Werner 1959 373 and Alygizakis 1990 38.

NOTE 3
cf. A. Alygizakis 1985 55 ff.

NOTE 4
cf. A. Alygizakis 1990 37.

NOTE 5
See MS Athos, Dionysiou 570, f. 32 and from the National Library of Athens MS 968, f. 155v, published in A. Alygizakis 1985 230 ff.; cf. also Stathis 1976 701. An English translation of the text is published at the end of this work.

NOTE 6
cf., Ἑρμηνεία τῆς παραλλαγῆς, MS Athos, Dionysiou 570, fol. 119 and from the National Library of Athens 968, fol. 116v ff., in A. Alygizakis 1985 235 ff.; see also Gr. Stathis 1976 705.

NOTE 7
cf. Παραλλαγὴ τῆς μουσικῆς τέχνης, MS Athos, Dionysiou 570, fol. 40, in A. Aly-gizakis 1985 239 and in the National Library of Athens MS 2401, fol. 223r, ed. Bentas 1971 21-27; cf. Stathis 1976 701.

NOTE 8
cf., Anonymous, Ἑρμηνεία τῶν φωνῶν καὶ τῶν ἤχων, published in Alygizakis 1985 232,73: « καθὼς καὶ ἀ μακάριος Ἰωάννης ὁ Κουκουζέλης, ἐν τῇ σο-φωτάτῃ αὐτοῦ μεθόδῳ καὶ παραλλαγῇ τοῦτο ὑπέδειξεν»; Ἰωάννης Πλουσιαδενός, Ἑρμηνεία τῆς παραλλαγῆς, Alygizakis 1985 235,21: « Ὁ γοῦν θεμέλιος καὶ πά ντων ἡμῶν τῶν καλῶν ἡγεμὼν καὶ οἱ ον φωστὴρ τῆς καθ᾽ ἡμᾶς ἐπιστήμης, ὁ μακα-ρίτης μαίστωρ κύρις Ἰωάννης ὁ Κουκουζέλης ὀνομαζόμενος, παντ᾽

ἀρίστως ἐκθεὶς καὶ κανονίσας, ...»; Ἰωάννης Λάσκαρες, Παραλλαγὴ τῆς μου-σικῆς τέχνης, Alygizakis 1985 240,41: « καθὼς καὶ ὁ θαυμάσιος μαίστωρ Ἰωάννης ὁ Κουκουζέλης, ἐν τῇ σο-φωτάτῃ αὐτοῦ μεθόδῳ τῇ παραλλαγῇ τοῦτο ὑπέδειξεν».

NOTE 9
See above, note 5.

NOTE 10
cf. Stathis 1976 712.

NOTE 11
Stathis 1976 701.

NOTE 12
Stathis 1976 701.

NOTE 13
Stathis 1976 701.

NOTE 14
Cf. Alygizakis 1985 239.

NOTE 15
Alygizakis 1985 230.

NOTE 16
Alygizakis 1985 230.

NOTE 17
Alygizakis 1985 230.

NOTE 18
Alygizakis 1985 232.

NOTE 19
Alygizakis 1985 234.

NOTE 20
See MS Athos, Dionysiou 570, fol. 56v. The diagram is published by Stathis 1976 702 and Alygizakis 1985 271. The diagram of the *Kanonion* by Gabriel is also drawn by Ch. Hannick in Gabriel Hieromonachos 1985 92. The *Kanonion* from MS Athos, Chilandariou 53, fol. 3r is published by D.

Conomos in Chrysaphes 1985 76 with detailed comments on the subject of the *parallage*. See also plate 3 of this work.

NOTE 21
cf. Anonymous, Ἑρμηνεία τῶν φωνῶν καὶ τῶν ἤχων, in Alygizakis 1985 231,36.

NOTE 22
Alygizakis 1985 231, 41.

NOTE 23
Alygizakis 1985 231, 50.

NOTE 24
Alygizakis 1985 231, 51.

NOTE 25
Alygizakis 1985 231, 54.

NOTE 26
Alygizakis 1985 231, 58.

NOTE 27
Alygizakis 1985 231, 60.

NOTE 28
Alygizakis 1985 231-32, 60-63.

NOTE 29
Alygizakis 1985 232, 68.

NOTE 30
Alygizakis 1985 232, 86.

NOTE 31
Alygizakis 1985 233, 103.

NOTE 32
Alygizakis 1985 233, 111.

NOTE 33
Alygizakis 1985 233, 113.

NOTE 34
Alygizakis 1985 233, 115.

NOTE 35
Alygizakis 1985 234, 152.

36
Alygizakis 1985 233, 118-126.

37
Alygizakis 1985 233, 130-137.

38
Alygizakis 1985 233, 139.

39
Alygizakis 1985 234, 175.

40
See above, note 6.

41
See above, note 7.

42
See Gabriel Hieromonachos 20, Τί ἐστι ψαλτική.

43
cf. Ἑρμηνεία τῆς παραλλαγῆς, in Alygizakis 1985 235,14.

44
cf. Παραλλαγὴ τῆς μουσικῆς τέχνης, in Alygizakis 1985 240,61.

45
See above, note 8.

46
The Hagiopolites, ed. Raasted 1983; see also Alygizakis 1985 221 ff.

47
Alygizakis 1985 12.

48
Cf. Alygizakis 1990 46.

49
cf. Chrysanthos 1832 41.

50
Cf. Alygizakis 1990 46.

The Musical use of the Psalter in the 14th and 15th centuries[1]

Panagiotes Ch. Panagiotides

Introduction

At this Symposium we will be looking at the period of reform or, more correctly, blossoming, of a specific type of musical tradition, that of the *Papadike*. We prefer to label this as a period of blossoming rather than of reform because of the very fact that it is marked by a new form of written melody which preexisted, but was not recorded as such[2]. As is well known, the period immediately preceding the era in question is one of crucial political events. It was only a few decades before the Easterners were able to throw off the remnants of Latin rule in the city of Constantinople-New Rome and it was inevitable that this would create a climate of new hope, but also, as the events of the major part of the 13th century had shown, the danger of losing many treasures received from the forefathers. One of these treasures, amongst many others, was the tradition of ecclesiastical Chant or Psaltic Art (Ψαλτικὴ Τέχνη) as was its traditional name. Therefore, the blossoming of this new type of written melody, the *Papadike*, was to a certain degree a result of historical events.

Two types of musical books, namely the 'choir book', the *Asmatikon* and the book of the soloist, the *Psaltikon*, existed as forerunners of the *Papadike*[3]. Following we shall look briefly at the historical appearance of this new type of musical manuscripts, and then proceed to describe the use of psalms in some of these. The codices which we shall use are MS Athens, National Library 2458[4] and MSS Koutloumousiou 457[5], Iberon 973[6]

and Filotheou 122[7] from the monasterial libraries of Mount Athos.

Background and the Athenian codex 2458

Here a word must be said about the tradition before and after the appearance of the first codex of this type, i.e. the *Papadike* of Ioannes Papadopoulos the Koukouzeles in the year 1336, in the codex Athens 2458[8], the most important codex of its type.

Many scholars like, for instance, Egon Wellesz[9] take the date of Koukouzeles authorship as marking a period of reform in Psaltic Art. Thus, he divides the periods of the middle and late Byzantine notation around the time of Koukouzeles. While others, such as H. J. W. Tillyard[10] and Oliver Strunk[11], although they vary on the beginning of the middle Byzantine notation as being between the years c.1100 and c.1177, they agree on the beginning of the late Byzantine notation chronologically as the 15th century, citing the fall of Constantinople-New Rome as the cause of this point of demarcation. This apparent confusion on the ending and the beginning of middle and late Byzantine notation is also, we believe, a factor which contributed to the idea that around the time of the writing of Koukouzeles' *Papadike*, there was a '-reform' rather then an organic growth or embellishment in the field of Psaltic Art. We believe that the classification presented by G. Th. Stathis lies closer to the actual facts. He estimates that the period of the middle stage begins at c. 1177 and ends c. 1670, with a period of transition between this date and the introduction of the New Method with its analytical writing in the years 1814-15[12].

A final word here must also be said about the MS Athens 2458 to which we have already alluded to. This codex as Stathis himself states "forms the first and oldest dated edition of this new type of musical manuscript, which at the time became necessary so as to contain the numerous and varying, but also marvelous, melodic compositions of known and unknown, 'older and recent composers'"[13]. Hence, the other codices that we are going to look at in this study in tandem have this work as their precursor.

As we have tried to show thus far, and as we will proceed to explain, we are looking at a new type of book as opposed to a new or reformed repertoire as such. Although Koukouzeles writes a new type of book and no doubt codifies the contemporary florid and more embellished style of his own and immediate predecessors, he does not reform the melody as such, so as to justify labelling his work reformative or 'new'. We cited the example of Wellesz, as supporting his classification of the middle and later notational traditions around the time of Koukouzeles. Further, H.J.W. Tillyard propounded the hypothesis that the date of the later notation should be sought with the fall of Constantinople-New Rome, i.e. around the year 1453. Thus, his classification of the middle (Round) notation is between c.1100-1450 and of the later notation c.1400-1821[14].

A further point of interest is the apparent contradiction of the idea that this period of conquest by the advancing Turkish armies is one of decline and great external influence on the tradition of the Psaltic Art[15]. As G.Th. Stathis points out, there is an apparent point of weakness in this their own argument, since, in the opinion of all these scholars - Wellesz, Strunk and Tillyard - the trans-

mission of the Psaltic Art did not undergo radical changes between the middle and late stages[16].

Here though one must keep in mind their intractable, dogmatic hypothesis that Byzantine music originally was only diatonic. This hypothesis is, we believe, the basis for such views and opinions. For instance, Egon Wellesz characteristically - after referring to former comparative studies on surviving bilingual chants - draws the conclusion that when Charlemagne ordered the translation into Latin of some Greek hymns, the music used must have been diatonic, since these remaining western sources reveal no other form of music[17]. Hence we read: "The essential fact for us lies not so much in the investigation as to which of the Western manuscripts contain the best version for comparison, but in the confirmation of *the correctness of the assumption* (italic ours) which I held from the beginning, i.e. that Byzantine music was diatonic before the Empire came under the overwhelming influence of Arabic, and, even more, of Turkish music"[18]. This assumption is founded upon the fact that: "...Byzantine music cannot have sounded strange to Western ears. Would Charlemagne have told his clergy to translate the Greek texts into Latin, would he have ordered them to include a set of Greek antiphons in the Latin Service if the melodies had, on account of their intervals, sounded different from the liturgical Chant he was used to? Certainly not. Byzantine Chant must have been as diatonic as that of the Latin Church"[19]. Wellesz immediately in the next paragraph contradicts this hypothesis when he states that Greek music played a major part in the creation and development of Latin Chant from its introduction from the Syro-Palestinian Church and even later directly from the Eastern Church[20]. This is a contradiction in terms for if we are to accept this hypothesis that ecclesiastical chant was only diatonic, we must at the same time renounce its roots and links with the synagogue and nascent

Christian Church, which, as one must keep in mind, both originated in regions of Syria and Palestine, and which is known by scholars as not solely diatonic. Further, if we take into consideration the possible influences from ancient Hellenic musical theory, then it is evident again that Wellesz' hypothesis, does not take into account or explain such references as for instance those in the works of Boetius or Cassiodorus who adopt the systems of Ptolemy and Aristeides Quintilianus respectively; who themselves are inheritors in a long line of musical theorists before them; but this is another question deserving its own discussion[21].

The Psalter in some of the MSS of the 14th and 15th centuries

In the *Papadike* we find usually a collection of the lessons of Great Vespers, Orthros, the Divine Liturgy and the service of the Dead - the *Amomos*. The *Papadike* manuscripts that we will be looking at contain to a certain degree remnants of the *Asmatike akolouthia* of the city of Constantinople-New Rome, but they also represent the traditions of other regions such as Thessalonike. Taken as a whole, however, they represent mainly the monastic tradition of Mount Athos[22].

Since the codices are concerned with these services it is natural that the following Psalms are used: 1, 2, 3, 44, 88, 102, 103, 111, 117:27, 118, 134, 135, 136, 140, 145, 148, 149 and 150. The quotations from the Book of Psalms will be from the numbering of the Septuagint, for, as it is known in the Eastern Orthodox Church, this is the text used in prayer as opposed to the Masoretic text contained in the standard Common Bible.

We shall now turn our attention to the codices and proceed to look at these Psalms used at Vespers, at *Orthros* (Matins), at the Divine Liturgy and, finally, in the service of the Dead (the *Amomos*).

a) Vespers

In the MS. Athens 2458 we have right at the beginning of Vespers (11r) the chanting of the prayer «Δεῦτε προσκυνήσωμεν» which continues with Psalm 103 (11v) until the verse «Ἀνοίξαντός σου τὴν χεῖρα» (11v), ie. the Anoixantaria. The compositions are by Koukouzeles, Georgios Panaretos, Xenos Korones and for some verses we have a choice for more than one setting. Following on (13v-22v) we have the «Μακάριος ἀνήρ», Psalms 1, 2, and 3. Here, apart from the fact that pieces of various compositions are attributed to others than those already mentioned, such as, Georgios Kontopetres, Tzaknopoulos, Ioannes Xyros, and even *'Agiosophitika'* pieces, we have the occurrence of ἀλλάγματα which denotes sections where the Psalms are chanted either by a soloist or by the choir, or, in some cases, even by both choirs (131r)[23]. An example of this combined chanting of the choirs is the last phrase «πάντα ἐν σοφία ἐποίησας» of the «Μακάριος ἀνήρ». All these are chanted in the Plagal Fourth mode. Then there are selected verses from these Psalms written in the *kalophonic* style again in the same mode. It is within these melodies that this new embellished form of melodic expression is found. The first two verses from Psalm 140, ie. «Κύριε ἐκέκραξα» and «Κατευθυνθήτω», then follow (36r-39v), in all of the eight modes.

At this point, a word should be said about this embellished form of melody, the *kalophony*. This *kalophony*, as we have stated above, is a new form of melody which blossomed with the advent of the Palaeologian period at the end of the 13th and beginning of the 14th centuries24. This form of melody is found both in Psalmic hymns and hymns written by Christian hymnographers. Here, nonetheless, we are concerned with the Psalmic hymns. As we have just seen, the *Anoixantaria*, the *Makarios Aner* and, as we shall see following below, this form is to be also found in the *Polyeleos*. These embellishments are the zenith of the *ka*-

lophonic style. The three aspects which make up this style are the following as we read in G. Stathis: a) broad and eloquent; b) repetition of syllables, words, or phrases and rearrangements of the text that are *anagrammatismoi* (word inversions) and retrogrades, and c) the imposition of a *kratema* at the beginning, in the middle or at the end, once, twice, three times or even more, although the phenomenon was also evident, in seed form, in the simpler, quicker and older «πα-λαιά» compositions[25].

In the MS Koutloumousiou 457, which is written around the second half of the same century as MS Athens 2458, we have mentioned amongst the names of composers of the Anoixantaria (1v-6r) other names as well, i.e. Dokeianos, Gabalas and Nikon the monk. But of more importance is the fact that the first part of each verse is said quickly in a simple ekphonetic style and the rest of the verse is then chanted[26]. Again, the ending of the Anoixantaria is chanted by both choirs as above. Then we have the Psalms 1, 2, and 3 (6v-10v). Also here, the first and the second part of the verse is performed in two different ways, as in the *Anoixantaria*[27]. Some of the verses have individual names, for example the one called *'frankikon'* (8r) by Koukouzeles, and others are just designated '-older'. Other new names of composers that we meet are Constantine Ferentares, Athanasios the Monk, Theodore Glabas, Christophoros and Chaliboures. Again follow verses of *kalophony* by Koukouzeles, Korones, a piece by Tzaknopoulos and *kratemata* (23r-55v); these all are chanted in the Plagal Fourth mode. Then follow the first two verses of Psalm 140 in all eight modes (55r-57v).

Now, we turn to MS Iberon 973, written around the start of the 15th century. Here, the Psalms are used in the same form and practice as that mentioned regarding MS Athens 2458, with - as is to be expected - new compositions by Arkadios the Monk, Hieromonk Ananias, Agathon Korones, Georgios

Sgouropoulos and others. The important composer of this codex is, however, Ioannes Kladas the Lampadarios. In his 'new' Great Vespers he has just about all the *Anoixantaria* in his own composition apart from the last verse. Again we have here the Psalms of *Makarios Aner* in full with again more new names, e.g. Kladas, Markopoulos, Andreas Sigeros, Agallianos, Sgouropoulos, Theodoros Argyropoulos, and others. We also have Psalm 140 (84r) as above.

MS Filotheou 122, which dates from the first half of the 15th century, is another significant MS. This codex, unlike the others which we have studied, has Psalm 140 in all the modes at the start of the codex (26r) along with other lessons from *Orthros*. When the chanting of Psalm 103 follows (47r) we have at the position of the *Anoixantaria* the τριαδι-κά *Anoixantaria*. Some of them are labelled as "Korones against the Latins" (49v), and "by the same - i.e. Korones - against Barlaam and Akindynos" (49v). Given its date, this use of a short doxology referring to the Holy Trinity at the end of the embellished *Anoixantaria* is referring to a theological dispute in the early and middle 14th century[28]. The mode used here is still Plagal Fourth. Let us look briefly at one example with such a doxology. The verse «Ἀντανελεῖς τὸ πνεῦμα αὐτῶν καὶ ἐκλείψουσι» is chanted to this point and then we have following a small doxology to the Holy Trinity as follows: «Δόξα σοι, Πάτερ, δόξα σοι, Υἱέ, δόξα σοι, τὸ πνεῦ-μα τὸ ἅ...χαχα...γιον, δόξα σοι» (from the *Anoixantaria* of Koukouzeles in Plagal Fourth). The traditional and simpler ending for these hymns was the phrase «δόξα σοι ὁ θεός»[29]. The *Makarios Aner* which follows is again in the Plagal Fourth mode (54r) and the series concludes with *kalophonies* (57r).

b) *Orthros*

In the *Orthros* service we have the chanting of the Polyeleos. Before we discuss these codices, however, we must mention, the «Θεὸς Κύριος» (Psalm 117:26-27) and the «Πᾶσα πνοή» (Psalm 150:6). The former verse is sung right at the start of *Orthros* and the latter before the *Orthros* Gospel and it also forms a part of the *Pasapnoaria*. The *Prokeimenon* also makes use at times of psalmic verses from various Psalms, but at this particular point in time we will not reiterate further upon this point. A brief description will be made of the antiphon also since we have represented in this category such important Psalms as 136 and 44 in the *Orthros* service, but a more complete discussion on the question of the antiphon will follow in the future[30].

Thus, turning to the codex Athens 2458 and, more specifically, to the *Polyeleos* we read that this is the practice followed at "Constantinople and all the world" (75r), and that the melodies are ascribed to both past and present composers. We have, in the First mode, Psalm 134 «Δοῦλοι Κύριον»; we notice that the Psalm starts with an *anagrammatismos*. Instead of beginning with "Praise the name of the Lord", it takes a phrase from the middle of the verse and begins with "Servants of the Lord". We find here again the names of Koukouzeles, Dokeianos, Georgios Panaretos, Christophoros and Korones as composers. Psalm 135 «Ἐξομολογεῖσθε τῷ Κυρίῳ», called *'Latrinos'*, follows (81v). Here, apart from the frequent interchanges, «ἀλλάγματα», we have a variety of modes used. It starts off with Second mode, then moves to Plagal Second, then *Nenano*, then to Plagal Fourth, then Third, then finally again Plagal Fourth with which it ends. Amongst the traditional compositions we have alternatives by Koukouzeles, Georgios Panaretos, and Andreas. Psalm 136 (83v), «Ἐπὶ τῶν ποταμῶν Βαβυλῶνος», which is next, uses the Third mode until the end when a direction is given (86r) for all to sing together the Alleluia in the Plagal Fourth mode. Here most pieces bear the name of Korones but we also have I. Glykys, Gregory the Domestikos and Christo-

phoros mentioned. On folio 86r there is a variation of Psalm 134 which is chanted in Thessalonike, in the First mode. Some of these pieces bear the names of Kornelios the monk, Manouel Plagites and Glykys. On folio 96r we have another version of Psalm 135 which is called «τετράστιχος», it is chanted in all eight modes and the only part which bears a composer's name is the one in Barys mode(97v) which is attributed to Korones. Although this Psalm is called *tetrastichos*, it has only 26 verses and not 32, as it has to compromise on the Barys and the Plagal Fourth in order to use all the modes. The Barys has the last two verses and the *Doxa* is for two choirs with both choirs chanting the final Alleluia together in the Plagal Fourth mode. Then follows the *Polyeleos* sung by the monks which is shorter in duration, ie. Psalm 134 (98r) and Psalm 135 (99r) in Plagal Second and Psalm 136 (99v) in *Nenano*. The kalophonies which follow (100r) are by Koukouzeles and Korones and are mainly in the First mode. An exception is the Δόξα in Plagal First (107v), one piece in Second mode (110r) and one in Plagal Second (111r). It is notable here that there are no compositions of Psalm 136 in *kalophony*.

In the codex Koutloumousiou 457 we find again the *Polyeleos 'Latrinos'* (114v) in the First mode. The only variation is that this time we have other composers mentioned as well: Korones, Christophoros Mystakon, the Protopsaltes Gregorios Glykys, Dokeianos, the *Domestikos* Ferentares Konstantinos, Longinos the Monk, Agallianos, Amarianos, Kornelios and Georgios Kontopetres. Psalm 135 (124v) is exclusively in the Second mode with changes to *Nenano*; only three verses are ascribed to specific composers: two to Koukouzeles and one to Panaretos. Psalm 136 (130r) is chanted in the Third mode. This time, though, this psalm is named amongst the antiphons. In the direction of the rubrics we are told that this Psalm is chanted at the *Orthros* of Cheesefare and Meatfare Sundays. The composers mentioned here are Gregory the *Domestikos*, Korones, Ioannes Glykys, Dokeianos, Gratzianes Glabas and Xenophon. The *kalophonies* which follow (148r-161r) are by Koukouzeles and Korones. The *kalophonic* verses from Psalm 134 are all in the First mode and those of Psalm 135 are in Second and Plagal Second. The so-called *Polyeleos* Κουκουμᾶς in a version 'from Thessalonike' in the First mode is next (168r). The composition is anonymous apart from the *kalophonic* verses which are attributed to Koukouzeles, Ioannes Glykys, Kornelios the Monk, Manouel Plagites the Priest, Christophoros (Mystakon), Korones and Athanasios the Monk. On folio 181r a tetrastichon composition of Koukouzeles, of Psalm 135 is given. It is an octaechos composition starting with the First mode and changing mode on every verse. A condensed version of the *Polyeleos* which is chanted by the monks in Plagal Second *Nenano* mode follows, but only the music for the first verse of each of the psalms 134, 135 and 136 is given. In folio 186r we have the antiphon «Λόγον ἀγαθόν» (Psalm 44) in the First mode. It begins with the fifth word of the first verse, i.e. with an *anagrammatismos*. The composers mentioned are: Ioannes Glykys, Koukouzeles, Ananias, Panaretos, Korones and Athanasios the Monk.

The *Polyeleos* in the Codex Iberon 973, is set in a similar manner, first comes the *'Latrinos'* (107r) in the First mode, and then Psalm 135 (116r) in the same mode; and there are no new names of composers. The only change from the Codex Koutloumousiou 457 is the tone used for Psalm 135. The Thessalonian *Polyeleos* 'Koukoumas' in First mode follows. Here the *Koukoumas* is eponymous and, apart from those mentioned above as composers, we have: Koukoumas, Stamenitzes, Gregory, Agathon Korones the monk, Andreas Sigeres, Koukouzeles, Manouel Thebaios, Georgios Sgouropoulos, Kontopetres and Ioannes Lampadarios. Another quicker - but incomplete - *Polyeleos* in *Nenano*, chanted by the monks, follows. On folio 150r we find the antiphon for the feasts of the Theotokos and our Lord to be Psalm 44[31]. Other new names of composers found here are Gregorios Glykys, Andreas Sigetes, Ioannes the king Batatzes, Ioannes Protopsaltes, Georgios Sgouropoulos, Ethikos and Michael Koukoulas. Then Psalm 136 follows in the Third mode, again as an antiphon with the direction that it can be chanted «ὅπου βούλει».

Codex Filotheou 122, as the previous ones, has the *Polyeleos* *'Latrinos'* (69r) in the First mode. The composers are the same as in Koutloumousiou 457. The Thessalonian *'Koukoumas'* (80v) and *kalophonic* verses from this Psalm follow. Then the *Polyeleos* *'Latrinos'* continues (90r) with Psalm 135, but this time in the First mode; yet it is surprising to find that even at this late period - keeping in mind that these composers flourished at the beginning of the previous century – we find the compositions in the First mode attributed to Korones, Koukouzeles and others of their time. A condensed version of Psalm 135 in the Third mode is next, followed by a condensed version of Psalms 134 and 135 in Plagal Second *Nenano* mode (97r). For the feasts of our Lord and the Theotokos we have again Psalm 44 prescribed as an antiphon (108r). Psalm 136 in the Third Mode is here prescribed as an antiphon to be chanted only on Cheesefare Sunday. As new composers we find Agallianos, the priest Gauras and Georgios Sgouropoulos.

It is obvious that the practice of the *Polyeleos* was that Psalm 134 was chanted in the First mode, Psalm 135 in the Second, Plagal Second, *Nenano*, Third and Plagal Fourth modes and Psalm 136 chanted in the Third and *Nenano* modes. This practice had already ceased by the time Koutloumousiou 457 where the Second and Plagal Second are still there and by the time of Iberon 973 and Filotheou 122 the melody of both Psalm 134 and 135 is in the First mode. This is probably a tradition which arose in some monasteries while the older practice was still followed in other monasteries and in the city churches. However, remnants of the other tones are still evident in the quicker versions of the *Polyeleos* by the monks, i.e. the use of the Second, the Plagal Second and the *Nenano*.

We saw that Psalm 44, although not contained in Koukouzeles' codex as an antiphon, is consistently found as such in the later manuscripts and here Koukouzeles is named among the composers. Further, it is evident that there are no *kalophonic* compositions for Psalm 136. The rubrics may give us a clue for a possible reason. The infrequent use of this psalm, i.e. once a year (MS Filotheou 122) twice a year (MS Koutloumousiou 457) or even as MS Iberon 973 states «ὅπου βούλει», may have contributed to this phenomenon. Its apparent interchange as part of the *Polyeleos* and as an antiphon may also explain this fact, since we do not find *kalophonic* compositions amongst the antiphons.

c) Divine Liturgy

In the Divine Liturgy[32] we have first the Typika, which in the codex Athens 2458 consist of Psalms 102 and 145. The first Psalm is chanted in Plagal Fourth 'nana', and the second in Plagal Second (142v). The only difference from Athens 2458 in codex Koutloumousiou 457 (192r) is the mode used for the first Psalm which in this case is the Third, whereas the modes in Iberon 973 and Filotheou 122 (187v) are in agreement with those of Athens 2458.

Another main source of Psalmic verse in the Divine Liturgy are the communion hymns. All in all there are twenty six hymns, but in reality only twenty two are based on Psalms[33].

In MS Athens 2458 the communion hymns begin on folio 168r. The older compositions are mainly in the Second and Plagal Second mode. However, all the modes except the Third are used. It is of note that from the eighteen commun-ion hymns of this MS only three are not in a plagal mode. Also the two communion hymns for the Presanctified, one old and one by Koukouzeles are in Plagal Second[34]. The composers of this codex are: Ioannes Koukouzeles, Xenos Korones Ioannes Glykys and Geogrios Panaretos.

MS Koutloumousiou 457, like Athens 2458, starts with a composition by Koukouzeles on folio 213v. Here other composers are represented, ie. Agallianos, Kontopetres, Dokeianos, etc.. This time the communion hymns of the Presanctified have an added *'eteron asmatikon'* hymn in the First mode (229r).

Similarly in Iberon 971 (from 188r) and in Filotheou 122 (from 208r), we see an increase in the number of communion hymns, also in the authentic modes. For example in MS Filotheou 122, out of the fifty eight hymns represented no less then nineteen are composed in the authentic modes; many of these are from the hand of Ioannes Kladas. This trend is noticed in the Presanctified hymns too, with compositions by I. Kladas in *Tetraphonos* First (Filotheou 122, 235r) and by Demetrios Raidestinos in *Nenano* (id., 235v).

d) The *Amomos*

In the codex Athens 2458 the *Amomos*, ie. Psalm 118, is divided into three *staseis*[35]. In this Koukouzelean codex we find the *'Politikon'*, the *'Thettalikon'*, the *'Thessalonikeon'*, together with compositions by Koukouzeles, Ioannes Protopsaltes, Ethikos, Arkadios the Monk, Gregorios Glykys and Fardiboukes (125r-135v). The mode in which the three *staseis* are to be chanted are the Second mode, *Nenano* - Plagal Second, and, finally, Third mode - Plagal Fourth mode respectively. There are two further Amomoi designated for monastic use in two *staseis*, the first starts in Plagal Second, then it changes to Plagal First (135v), and the other composition is exclusively in Plagal First (136v).

Similarly in Koutloumousiou 457, the

Amomos (233v) is in the Second mode and then changes to Plagal Second (242r). Again we have the same names mentioned, with the addition of Athanasios the monk, Christophoros, Mystakonos, Manouel Panaretos, Daniel, Achrades the Monk, Kornelios, Korones, Fardiboukes and Longinos. An *Amomos* for the monks follows again in Plagal First (250r).

In the codex Iberon 973, we have an *Amomos* (123v) called 'new' and set to music by Ioannes the Lampadarios, in the Second mode ἔσω, but apart from his own composition, he includes melodies by others, i.e. Fardiboukes. It is atypical that this *Amomos* is placed between the *Polyeleos*. On folio 169v an *Amomos* - incomplete - for the burial of our Lord Jesus Christ and for the Dormition of the Theotokos and all the saints follows. The verses here, though, are accompanied by *ephymnia* or the *troparia* of the funeral lament (ἐπιτάφιος θρῆνος) i.e. to the first verse chanted in Plagal First is attached the *troparion* Ἡ ζωὴ ἐν τάφῳ...[36]. As to the composers, we have a particular reference to Germanos, patriarch of Constantinople, in the third stasis, the ἀλλάγματα. On folio 203v we have another *Amomos*, this time embellished by Fardiboukes, again in the Second ἔσω mode. Among the other composers which are mentioned here, but not in the two codices above, are Manougras Gabriel Keladinos the Priest, Ioannes Kladas the Lampadarios, Constantine Gauras the Priest, Manouel the Priest and the Theban. Many melodies are characterized as 'quick'. Then again we have an *Amomos* for monks (226r) in the Plagal Second mode.

In the codex Filotheou 122, the verses of the psalm *Amomos* (143r) are used as *stichoi* for the burial of Christ, the Dormition of the Theotokos and to all the Saints. The mode used here is Plagal First, the melody is a composition by Ethikos with variations by Patriarch Germanos of Constantinople. Then, the *Amomos* in the second mode is again

found (152v) as above, embellished by Fardiboukes. At the end of the second (163r) stasis there is a directive which states that this one and the last could also be chanted in Plagal First, or in the variation offered by Ioannes Kladas for these two *staseis* in *Nenano*. Finally, there is again an *Amomos* for the monks in Plagal First.

Concluding Remarks

In conclusion we can state that, having looked briefly at four codices and their use of Psalms, it is obvious that this period is characterized by its relaxed and florid style, as opposed to the modern liturgical practice where the chanted content of the service tends to be speeded up in order to keep pace with our modern lifestyle.

The *Papadike* as a codex, as we have seen, marks a zenith in the development of a particular type of melody, that of the *kalophony*. As a book it collected the contents of its two predecessors, the *Asmatikon* and the *Psaltikon*, but first of all it was enriched by Ioannes Papadopoulos Koukouzeles, his contemporaries and their predecessors. Although it was a new type of codex for the time, we have tried to show that it was not intended as a work of reform but rather one of codification and embellishment.

Remnants of the *Asmatike akolouthia*, are, as mentioned, present in the musical service books of the 14th and 15th centuries. Nonetheless, the predominance of the monastic tradition is quiet clear, Koukouzeles, in his codex Ms. Athens 2458, shows clearly the trend of his day, manifesting the overwhelming dominance of the monastic practice and the complete absence of a great number of Psalms that where otherwise sung, and not read, in the *Asmatike akolouthia*.

Other interesting and more technical features of the Psalms we have examined include particularly the second Psalm of the *Polyeleos*. Within the span of one century or so, covered by the codices examined, it changes mode. Further, the introduction of Psalm 44 for the feasts of Christ and the Theotokos should be noted, interestingly enough, with ascriptions to composers since long dead, in this way possibly showing the respect and continuity with the past, since these compositions stayed within the traditional parameters. This continuity is also proven by the numerous referrals to traditional or 'older' compositions. Even the changes made by Korones and Koukouzeles, for instance, did only affect the length of the pieces, and specifically they involved an addition of small doxologies or *kratemata*.

Bibliography

Alygizakis, A.E. 1985
Ἡ Ὀκταηχία στὴν ἑλληνικὴ λειτουργικὴ ὑμνογραφία. Thessalonike.

Alygizakis, A.E. 1990
Ἐκκλησιαστικοὶ ἦχοι καὶ ἀραβοπε
ρσικα μακάμια. Thessalonike.

Antoniades, E. 1949-51
"Περὶ τοῦ Ἀσματικοῦ ἢ
Βυζαντινοῦ Κοσμικοῦ τύπου τῶν
Ἀκολουθίων τῆς ἡμερονυκτίου προσευχῆς", Θεολογία" no. 20 704-724;no.
21 43-56, 180-200, 339-353 and 526-
540;no. 22 386-401

Bakalopoulos, A. 1989
"Γενικὴ Θεώρηση τῆς Παλαιολό-
γειας Ἐποχῆς", Χριστιανικὴ Θεσσαλονίκη Παλαιολόγειος Ἐποχή,
Κέντρο ἱστορίας Θεσσαλονίκης τοῦ
Δήμου Θεσσαλο-νίκης Αρ. 3, Thessalonike, 41-51

Chrysaphes 1985
'The Treatise of Manuel Chrysaphes, the
Lampadarios, Monumenta Musicae Byzantinae, Corpus Scriptorum de Re Musica II,
ed. Conomos, D.E., Vienna.

Conomos, D.E. 1985
The Late Byzantine and Slavonic Communion Cycle: Liturgy and Music. Dumbarton Oaks, Washington D.C.

Hatzegiakoumis, M.K. 1980
Χειρόγραφα ἐκκλησιαστικῆς
μουσικῆς 1453-1832. Athens.

Karas, S.I. 1970
"Γένη καὶ διαστήματα εἰς τὴν
Βυζαντινὴν Μουσικὴν", The 1st Inter-
national Congress for Byzantine Music in
Grottaferratta. Athens.

Meyendorff, J. 1974
A Study of Gregory Palamas. New York.

Stathis, G.Th. 1975
Τὰ Χειρόγραφα Βυζαντινῆς Μουσικῆς, Ἅγιον Ὄρος. Κατάλογος
περιγραφικὸς τῶν χειρογράφων
κωδίκων Βυζαντινῆς Μουσικῆς
τῶν ἀποκειμένων ἐν ταῖς Βιβλιοθήκαις τῶν ἱερῶν Μονῶν καὶ Σκητῶν
τοῦ Ἁγίου Ὄρους, Vol. I. Athens.

Stathis, G.Th. 1979
Οἱ ἀναγραμματισμοὶ καὶ τὰ μαθή-
ματα τῆς βυζαντινῆς μελοποιίας.
Athens.

Stathis, G.Th. 1986
"Ὁ μαίστωρ Ἰωάννης Παπαδόπουλος ὁ Κουκουζέλης. Ἡ ζωὴ καὶ
τὸ ἔργο του." Ἐφημέριος 34.

Stathis, G.Th. 1989
"Ἡ ἀσματικὴ διαφοροποίηση ὅπως καταγράφεται στόν Κώδικα ΕΒΕ 2458 τοῦ ἔτους 1336", Χριστιανικὴ Θεσσαλονίκη Παλαιολόγειος Ἐποχή, Κέντροι στορίας Θεσσαλονίκης του Δήμου Θεσσαλονίκης Αρ. 3, Thessalonike, 165-212

Stathis, G.Th. 1993
Τὰ Χειρόγραφα Βυζαντινῆς Μουσικῆς, Ἅγιον Ὄρος. Κατάλογος περιγραφικὸς τῶν χειρογράφων κωδίκων Βυζαντινῆς Μουσικῆς τῶν ἀποκειμένων ἐν ταῖς Βιβλιοθήκαις τῶν ἱερῶν Μονῶν καὶ Σκητῶν τοῦ Ἁγίου Ὄρους, Vol. III. Athens.

Strunk, O. 1956
"The Byzantine Office at Agia Sophia", Dumbarton Oaks Papers 9 and 10, 175-203

Strunk, O. 1965
Specimina Notationum Antiquiorum, Monumenta Musicae Byzantinae VII. Copenhagen.

Symeon of Thessalonike,
"Περὶ τῆς θείας προσευχῆς" (On Divine Prayer)" Migne, Patrologia Graeca 155, cols. 536-669.

Tillyard, H.J.W. 1935
Handbook of the Middle Byzantine Musical Notation, Monumenta Musicae Byzantinae, Subsidia I, Fasc. 1, Second impression 1970. Copenhagen.

Touliatos-Banker, D.H. 1984
The Byzantine Amomos Chant of the Fourteenth and Fifteenth Centuries, Πατριαρχικὸν Ἵδρυμα Πατερικῶν Μελετῶν, Ἀνάλεκτα Βλατάδων 46. Thessalonike.

Wellesz, E. 1961
A History of Byzantine Music and Hymnography. Oxford.

Williams, E.V. 1971
"The Treatment of Text in the Kalophonic Chanting of Psalm 2", Studies in Eastern Chant II, 173-193

Williams, E.V. 1979
"The Kalophonic Tradition and Chants for the Polyeleos Psalms 134", Studies in Eastern Chant IV, 228-241

Notes

NOTE 1
Our gratitude must at this point be expressed to our colleague, Mr. Philip Zymaris for proof-reading the final draft of this paper.

NOTE 2
Cf. Sthathis 1979 60-61, and particularly p. 89 where we have an important comment by Manuel Chrysaphes. A further remark by Manuel Chrysaphes along the same lines is the following: "And after all of these came the gracefully named Koukouzeles, who, even though he was indeed a very great teacher and had nothing to concede to any of his predecessors regarding his skill, he nevertheless followed closely in their footsteps and did not presume to innovate anything which was accepted and well-tested by them", cf. Chrysaphes lines 146-151.

NOTE 3
See Stathis 1979 44-45 for a discussion on the origin of the *Papadike* and its general contents; also the contents of its two predecessors. For a brief description of the content of the *Papadike* see Stathis 1975 35'. Also Manoles K. Hatzegiakoumis 1980 231. Although written by Ioannes Papadopoulos the Koukouzeles for the monastic setting, the *Papadike* was not limited to this alone. The Asmatic or 'city practice' was at this time in decline. Thus it is quite natural that the influence of monastic practices would also be felt outside of the monastic walls. Let us not forget that Koukouzeles before he became a monk on Mount Athos was a teacher of music in the capital of the empire. And although many elements of the *Asmatike akolouthia* remained in the monastic rubrics, the former had all but disappeared by the middle of the 15th century.

NOTE 4
Cf. Stathis 1989 165-211, all citations of the codex will be taken from this work.

NOTE 5
Cf. Stathis 1993 354-366. This codex is dated by Stathis around the second half of the 14th century.

NOTE 6
Stathis 1993 739-748. This codex is dated by Stathis at the beginning of the 15th century

NOTE 7
Stathis 1993 487-500. This codex is dated by Stathis at the first half of the 15th century.

NOTE 8
See Stathis 1989. For a recent account on the life and work of John Papadopoulos-Koukouzeles, see Stathis 1986.

NOTE 9
Cf. Wellesz 1961 262, where he states that he and the editors of M.M.B. accepted the following classification as to the subdivisions of the neumes:

1. Early Byzantine notation (Palaeobyzantine, 'Stroke-dot' or linear notation): 9th-12th cent.
2. Middle Byzantine notation (Hagiopolite, round): 12th-14th cent.
3. Late Byzantine notation (Koukouzelean, Hagiopolite-Psaltique): 14th-19th cent.

NOTE 10
Tillyard 1935

NOTE 11
Strunk 1965.

NOTE 12
Stathis 1979 48-49 and 55-59.

NOTE 13
Stathis 1989 167, the translation is ours.

NOTE 14
Tillyard 1935 14-15.

NOTE 15
See for instance H.J.W. Tillyard's comment that: "...The influence of the East was overwhelming: Greek musicians composed Turkish songs, while they naturally borrowed from Oriental sources much of the new melodic material used in the setting of Byzantine hymns", Tillyard 1935 15.

NOTE 16
Stathis 1979 50-51.

NOTE 17
Wellesz 1961 21-22.

NOTE 18
Wellesz 1961 22.

NOTE 19
Wellesz 1961 22.

NOTE 20
Wellesz 1961 22.

NOTE 21
Cf. Alygizakis 1985 31-54 and 203-210 for a discussion of the Chromatic and Enharmonic modes in the «Μέγα Ἴσον» by Koukouzeles and the Octaechos method of Ioannes Plousiadenos. See also Alygizakis 1990 and Karas 1970.

NOTE 22
Stathis 1989 168. Worthy of note is also that with this codex the tradition of assigning ones name to a work is increasing to a large extent. For further reading on this, consult Stathis 1979 63-64.

NOTE 23
See Stathis 1979 93, for discussion of ἀνα–φώνημα and ἄλλαγμα.

NOTE 24
Cf. Bakalopoulos 1987 43-51 for a discussion on the political, social and cultural events of this epoch.

NOTE 25
See Stathis 1989 193.

NOTE 26
Stathis 1993 354.

NOTE 27
Stathis 1993 355.

NOTE 28
This dispute had as its main protagonists, the Archbishop of Thessalonike St. Gregory Palamas on the one hand and Barlaam the Calabrian with Akindynos on the other. The main question at hand was that of the distinction in God between His Essence and energies. For a good study on the historical and theological issues on this dispute in English, see Meyendorff 1974.

NOTE 29
Stathis 1989 193-194. See further Williams 1971 173-193 and Williams 1979.

NOTE 30
The question of the antiphons is quite complex. Firstly because its original designation was not what it had come to be in the 14th and 15th centuries, and secondly because it was one of the major characteristics which distinguished the Akolouthia Asmatike or "city practice" from the monastic rite. For more details on this topic, see Antoniades 1949-51. See also Strunk 1951, 175-203.

NOTE 31
The use of Psalm 44 as an antiphon in this 15th century codex may give the impression that it is possibly an addition to the rubrics, but in another codex, Koutloumousiou 399 (see Stathis 1993, 235-237) - dated by Stathis at the middle of the 14th century - it is presented as an antiphon as well (65r). In this codex we even find Psalm 136 mentioned as an antiphon to be chanted on Cheesefare Sunday (71v).

NOTE 32
By the term 'Divine Liturgy' we mean here all three Liturgies of the Eastern Orthodox Church; namely that of St. John Chrysostom, that of St. Basil the Great and the Presanctified Liturgy.

NOTE 33
See table in Conomos 1985 48-51 for texts and times of celebration.

NOTE 34
This hymn (Psalm 33:8a "Taste and see that the Lord is good") is thought to be the oldest communion hymn of the Liturgy, Conomos 1985 6-16.

NOTE 35
The division into three staseis (at verses 1, 73, and 132) is the practice followed in the service of laymen. For the monastic funeral practice we have also divisions into two staseis (at verses 1 and 94) roughly from the 14th through the fifteenth centuries. Cf. Touliatos-Banker 1984 24 and 176-177.

NOTE 36
We find this practice of using Psalm 118 with ephymnia for the ἐπιτηάφιος θρῆνος in the Orthros of Holy Saturday in a codex of the 15th century. The two previous examples did not include this practice, indicating possibly an older usage. Further, one must keep in mind the fact that as more and more cities of the Eastern Empire were falling to the Turkish armies in the 14th and 15th centuries - with the ultimate fall of Constantinople - the only centers that were left to continue their work undisturbed were the monasteries. Thus, it is natural that the monastic practice would predominate and surpass even the last bastion of the Asmatike akolouthia, namely the church of Agia Sophia in Thessalonike and its last great representative, Archbishop Symeon (d. 1429). Cf. his work 'On Divine Prayer'. Nevertheless, the chanting of Psalm 118 was not restricted only to this one day. In the Asmatike akolouthia its daily usage at Orthros is evident. Even in the monastic rubrics of the Church of the Resurrection of Jerusalem of the 10th century, it is prescribed in the same position of the Orthros, i.e. after the hexapsalmos and before Psalm 50 on Palm Sunday, Holy Thursday and Holy Saturday, see Antoniades 1951 387-389.

Ἡ μελοποίηση στίχων τοῦ πολυελέου ἀπὸ τὸ μαίστορα Ἰωάννη Κουκουζέλη

Ἀχιλλέας Γ. Χαλδαιάκης

Προκείμενο θέμα τῆς παρούσης ἀνακοινήσεως[1], εἶναι ἡ μελοποίηση στίχων τοῦ πολυελέου – καὶ ἀντιφώνων τοῦ πολυελέου – ἀπὸ τὸ μαίστορα Ἰωάννη τὸν Κουκουζέλη. Ἀναφερόμενοι στὸ εἶδος αὐτὸ τῆς βυζαντινῆς μελοποιίας, πρέπει νὰ ἔχωμε κατὰ νοῦν ὅτι πρόκειται οὐσιαστικὰ γιὰ τοὺς ρλδ΄ καὶ ρλε΄ ψαλμοὺς τοῦ Δαβίδ, οἱ ὁποῖοι κατὰ κύριο λόγο συγκροτοῦν αὐτὸ ποὺ καλοῦμε *πολυέλεο* [2]. Μάλιστα, αὐτὴ ἀκριβῶς ἡ ὀνομασία, *πολυέλεος*, ὀφείλεται στὸ δεύτερο ἀπὸ τοὺς δύο ψαλμοὺς ποὺ ἀνωτέρου μνημονεύσαμε καὶ συγκεκριμένα στὸ ἐφύμνιο, ποὺ ἀνακλᾶται στὸ τέλος καθενὸς ἀπὸ τοὺς εἴκοσι ἕξι στίχους του, "τὸ ἔλεος αὐτοῦ". Ἡ συνεχὴς αὐτὴ ἐπανάληψη τῆς λέξεως "ἔλεος", τὴν ὁποία μὲ τὸν ἀκόλουθο χαρακτηριστικὸ τρόπο σχολιάζει ὁ ἱερὸς Χρυσόστομος σὲ σχετικὴ ὁμιλία του: "Οὐ ποτὲ μέν, φησίν, εὐεργετεῖ, ποτὲ δὲ ἀφίσταται, οὐδὲ ποτὲ μὲν ἐλεεῖ, ποτὲ δὲ παύεται, ὅπερ ἐπ᾽ ἀνθρώπων συμβαίνει... ἀλλὰ διηνεκῶς ἐλεεῖ, καὶ οὐδέποτε παύεται τοῦτο ποιῶν, κἂν διαφόρως καὶ ποικίλως ἐπιτελῇ. Ἀεὶ οὖν ἐλεεῖ καὶ οὐδέποτε ἵσταται τοὺς ἀνθρώπους εὐεργετῶν",[3] ὀνοματοδότησε ἐν τέλει τὸ ψαλμικὸ αὐτὸ εἶδος τῆς βυζαντινῆς μελοποιίας.

Ἡ ἐκτεταμένη χρήση τῶν ψαλμῶν τοῦ Δαβὶδ στὴ λατρευτικὴ ζωὴ τῆς ὀρθοδόξου ἐκκλησίας, ἀπὸ τοὺς πρώτους ἀκόμη χριστιανικοὺς χρόνους, διαζωγραφεῖται μὲ ξεχωριστὴ σαφήνεια καὶ εὐγλωττία ἀπὸ τὸν ἱερὸ Χρυσόστομο, στὰ λόγια του τοῦτα: "Τί οὖν εἰπεῖν ἔχω πρὸς τὸν μακά-

ριον Δαβίδ, ὅπως ἡ τοῦ Πνεύματος χάρις ᾠκονόμησε καθ᾽ ἑκάστην ἡμέραν τε καὶ νύκτα αὐτὸν ἀνακηρύττεσθαι; πάντες γὰρ αὐτὸν ἀντὶ μύρου διὰ στόματος φέρομεν. Ἐν ἐκκλησίᾳ παννυχίδες, καὶ πρῶτος καὶ μέσος καὶ τελευταῖος ὁ Δαβίδ· ἐν ὀρθριναῖς ὑμνολογίαις, καὶ πρῶτος καὶ μέσος καὶ τελευταῖος ὁ Δαβίδ· ἐν τοῖς σκηνώμασι τῶν νεκρῶν προπομπαί, καὶ πρῶτος καὶ μέσος καὶ τελευταῖος ὁ Δαβίδ· ἐν τοῖς οἰκίαις τῶν παρθένων ἱστουργίαι καὶ πρῶτος καὶ μέσος καὶ τελευταῖος ὁ Δαβίδ· Ὦ τῶν παραδόξων πραγμάτων! πολλοὶ μήτε γραμμάτων πεῖραν τὴν ἀρχὴν εἰληφότες, ἐκμαθόντες, ὅλον τὸν Δαβὶδ ἀποστηθίζουσιν. Ἀλλ᾽ οὐ μόνον ἐν ταῖς πόλεσι καὶ ταῖς ἐκκλησίαις οὕτω κατὰ πάντα καιρὸν καὶ κατὰ πᾶσαν ἡλικίαν ἐκλάμπει, ἀλλὰ καὶ ἐν ἀγροῖς καὶ ἐν ἐρημίαις καὶ εἰς τὴν ἀοίκητον γῆν μετὰ πλείονος τῆς σπουδῆς χοροστασίας ἱερὰς ἀνεγείρει τῷ Θεῷ. Ἐν μοναστηρίοις χορὸς ἅγιος ταγμάτων ἀγγελικῶν, καὶ πρῶτος καὶ μέσος καὶ τελευταῖος ὁ Δαβίδ· ἐν ἀσκητηρίοις παρθένων ἀγέλαι τῶν τὴν Μαριὰμ μιμουμένων, καὶ πρῶτος καὶ μέσος καὶ τελευταῖος ὁ Δαβίδ· ἐν ἐρημίαις ἄνδρες ἐσταυρωμένοι προσομιλοῦντες τῷ Θεῷ, καὶ πρῶτος καὶ μέσος καὶ τελευταῖος ὁ Δαβίδ. .... Ὦ μεγάλης κιθάρας, τὰς ψυχὰς τῶν ἀνθρώπων τῆς οἰκουμένης, ὥσπερ νευράς τινας, εἰς μίαν ἐξομολογίαν ἀνακρουομένης! "[4]

Ἐμφανέστατη λοιπὸν ἡ καταλυτικὴ παρουσία τῶν ψαλμῶν στὴν ᾀσματικὴ πράξη τῆς Ἀνατολικῆς Ἐκκλησίας, ἀλλὰ καὶ ἄξιον ἰδιαιτέρας προσοχῆς τὸ γεγονὸς ὅτι τὸ ψαλτήρι τοῦ Δαβίδ, ἀποτελεῖ τὸ ποιητικὸ ὑπόβαθρο ἑνὸς μεγάλου ποσοστοῦ τῶν μελῶν ποὺ ἀπαρτίζουν τὶς ἀκολουθίες τοῦ ἐκκλησιαστικοῦ νυχθημέρου – Ἀνοιξανταρίων, Κεκραγαρίων, Δοχῶν, Πολυελέων, Πασαπνοαρίων, Ἀλληλουιαρίων, Κοινωνικῶν κ. ἄ. – μελῶν ποὺ, ὅπως κανοναρχεῖ καὶ ὁ ἐκ Μαδύτων Χρύσανθος[5], ὁρίζουν τὸ παπαδικὸ γένος τῆς Ψαλτικῆς Τέχνης.[6]

Εἰδικώτερα τώρα γιὰ τὸν πολυέλεο τὸν "ἐν ὀρθριναῖς ὑμνολογίαις" δηλαδὴ μετὰ τὰ καθίσματα τῆς δευτέρας στιχολογίας τοῦ Ψαλτηρίου, ἀδόμενον, ἔχομε νὰ παρατηρήσωμε τὰ ἑξῆς:

Κατὰ τὴν ἐποχὴ τοῦ Ἰωάννου τοῦ Κουκουζέλη, ἡ μελοποίηση στίχων τοῦ πολυελέου ἐντάσσεται στὰ πλαίσια τῶν ἀκόλουθων ἑνοτήτων, ὅπως προκύπτει ἀπὸ τὶς συνθέσεις ποὺ, κατὰ κύριο λόγο, ἀνθολογοῦνται στὰ μουσικὰ χειρόγραφα τῆς Παπαδικῆς τοῦ ΙΔ´ καὶ ΙΕ´ αἰῶνος.[7]

– Πολυέλεος λεγόμενος "Λατρινός", ἦχ. α´ (Δοῦλοι Κύριον)
– Ἡ δευτέρα στάσις τοῦ Λατρινοῦ πολυελέου, ἦχ. β´ (Ἐξομολογεῖσθε τῷ Κυρίῳ)
– Πολυέλεος λεγόμενος "Κουκουμᾶς", ἦχ. α´ (Δοῦλοι Κύριον)
– Ἡ δευτέρα στάσις τοῦ πολυελέου "ὃς καλεῖται κουκουμᾶς", ἦχ. α´ (Ἐξομολογεῖσθε τῷ Κυρίῳ) ἢ "ὁ β´ ψαλμὸς τοῦ Κουκουμᾶ, ὃς λέγεται τετράστιχος", ἦχ. α´ (Ἐξομολογεῖσθε τῷ Κυρίῳ) (ὀκτάηχος)
– Ἕτερος πολυέλεος ὃν ψάλλουν οἱ μοναχοὶ συνοπτικόν, ἦχ. πλ. β´ (Δοῦλοι Κύριον)
– Ἕτερος ψαλμὸς καὶ αὐτὸς καλογερικός, ἦχ. πλ. β´ (Ἐξομολογεῖσθε τῷ Κυρίῳ)
– Ἀπὸ τὸν πολυέλεο στίχοι Καλοφωνικοί, ἦχ. α´ (ἐκ τοῦ ψ. ρλδ´)
– Ἀπὸ τὸν ἕτερο ψαλμὸ στίχοι Καλοφωνικοί, ἦχ. β´ (ἐκ τοῦ ψ. ρλε´)

Ἡ παραπάνω ἑνότητα τῶν συνθέσεων τοῦ πολυελέου, συμπληρώνεται ἀπὸ τὴν παράθεση τῶν λεγομένων Ἀντιφώνων τοῦ πολυελέου. Τὰ Ἀντίφωνα αὐτὰ δὲν εἶναι τίποτε ἄλλο, παρὰ στίχοι ἀπὸ διαφόρους ψαλμοὺς τοῦ Δαβίδ, στοὺς ὁποίους προσδίδεται ἰδιαίτερη, κατὰ περίπτωση, ἑορτολογικὴ χρεία πρὸς τιμὴν τῶν Ἁγίων Ἀγγέλων, Μαρτύρων, Ἱεραρχῶν ἢ Ὁσίων τῆς ὀρθοδοξίας, καθὼς καὶ λοιπῶν Δεσποτικῶν ἢ Θεομητορικῶν ἑορτῶν. Οἱ συνθέσεις τῶν Ἀντιφώνων ποὺ συνήθως ἀνθολογοῦνται στὶς Παπαδικὲς τοῦ ΙΔ´ καὶ ΙΕ´ αἰῶνος εἶναι οἱ ἀκόλουθες:

– Ἀντίφωνον ψαλλόμενον εἰς τὴν Ὑπεραγίαν Θεοτόκον, ἦχ. α´ (Λόγον ἀγαθόν)
– Ἀντίφωνον ψαλλόμενον τῇ μεγάλῃ Ἀπόκρεω καὶ τῇ Τυρινῇ, ἦχ. γ´ (Ἐπὶ τῶν ποταμῶν Βαβυλῶνος)
– Ἀντίφωνον ψαλλόμενον εἰς βασιλεῖς, ἦχ. α´ (Ἐπακούσαι σου Κύριος)
– Ἀντίφωνον ψαλλόμενον εἰς Ἱεράρχας, Ὁσίους καὶ Μάρτυρας, ἦχ. δ´ (Ὁ φοβούμενος τὸν Κύριον)
– Ἀντίφωνα εἰς τὴν Σύναξιν τῶν Ἀσωμάτων, ἦχ. πλ. β´ (Αἰνεῖτε τὸν Κύριον)
– Ἀντίφωνα εἰς τὴν Θείαν Μεταμόρφωσιν, ἦχ. βαρ. (Τὰ ἐλέη σου Κύριε)

Μορφολογικὰ σχόλια

Εἰσερχόμεθα εὐθὺς ἀμέσως σὲ ἐπὶ μέρους μορφολογικὰ σχόλια, ἀφορῶντα στὴ διάρθρωση τοῦ μέλους τῶν στίχων ποὺ ὁ μαΐστωρ Κουκουζέλης ἐμέλισε.

Καὶ πρῶτ᾽ ἀπ᾽ ὅλα, θὰ διαπραγματευθοῦμε τὶς συνθέσεις τοῦ πολυελέου, περὶ τοῦ ὁποίου σημειώνομε προοιμιακὰ τὴν ἀκόλουθη ὀφθαλμοφανῆ διαπίστωση: τὸ μελικὸ βάρος τῶν συνθέσεων τῶν στίχων τοῦ πολυελέου μεταπίπτει στὸ καταληκτήριο Ἀλληλούια, τὸ ὁποῖο ἐπαναλαμβάνεται συνήθως δύο ἢ τρεῖς φορές, ἀνάλογα μὲ τὶς μουσικὲς ἰδέες καὶ τὰ μελικὰ στοιχεῖα ποὺ θέλει νὰ παραθέση ὁ μαΐστωρ Κουκουζέλης.

Παρ᾽ ὅλ᾽ αὐτὰ μποροῦμε νὰ διακρίνωμε τὶς ἀκόλουθες περιπτώσεις μελοποιήσεως τοῦ *ψαλμικοῦ κειμένου* τῶν προμνημονευθέντων ψαλμῶν:

α) Στὸν πολυέλεον *Δοῦλοι Κύριον* τὸ ψαλμικὸ κείμενο μελίζεται χωρὶς ἐπιτηδεύσεις καὶ "περιττολογίες". Περιπτώσεις μουσικοῦ πλατυασμοῦ καὶ ἐκτενέστερη μελικὴ ἐπεξεργασία παρατηροῦμε ἀφ᾽ ἑνὸς μὲν κατὰ τὴν μελοποίηση τῆς τελευταίας λέξεως τοῦ ψαλμικοῦ κειμένου, ἀφ᾽ ἑτέρου δὲ κατὰ τὴ μελοποίηση κάποιας ἄλλης λέξεως τοῦ ψαλμικοῦ κειμένου σύμφωνα μὲ τὴν βούληση τοῦ μελουργοῦ.

β) Παρόμοια μελικὴ μεταχείρηση παρατηροῦμε ἐπίσης στὸ ψαλμικὸ κείμενο τοῦ πολυελέου *Ἐξομολογεῖσθε τῷ Κυρίῳ*, ὅπου καὶ πάλιν πλατυάζεται τὸ μέλος τόσο τῆς τελευταίας λέξεως, ὅσο καὶ κάποιας ἄλλης.

Καὶ ταῦτα μὲν ὅσον ἀφορᾶ στὸ μέλος ποὺ "ντύνει" τὸν ψαλμικὸ στίχο τῶν πολυελέων. Ἐρχόμενοι τώρα στὸ μέλος τῶν καταληκτηρίων *Ἀλληλούια*, διακρίνομε, ἔπειτα ἀπὸ προσεκτικὴ ἐξέταση, τὶς παρακάτω διαφοροποιήσεις στὴ μελικὴ ἐπεξεργασία τους, ἀρχικὰ στὸν πολυέλεο *Δοῦλοι Κύριον*.

Πρῶτον: ὅπως ἐκ προοιμίου ἤδη ἐπισημάναμε παρατηροῦμε μιὰ ξεχωριστὴ καὶ σαφῶς ἐκτενέστερη μελικὴ μεταχείρηση τοῦ *Ἀλληλούια* – οἱ διαστάσεις τοῦ ὁποίου εἶναι συχνὰ διπλάσιες ἢ τριπλάσιες σὲ σχέση μὲ τὸ μέλος τοῦ ψαλμικοῦ κειμένου – κατὰ τὴν ὁποία ὁ μελουργός, ἀποδεσμευμένος πλέον ἀπὸ τὰ νοήματα ποὺ πρέπει νὰ μεταδώση στοὺς πιστοὺς μέσω τοῦ ψαλμικοῦ κειμένου, ξεδιπλώνει τὶς μουσικές του ἰδέες φανερώνοντας τὴν τέχνη καὶ μαεστρία του. Προκειμένου νὰ ἐξαν-

τλήση τὰ μελικὰ τόξα ποὺ γεννᾶ ἡ φαντασία του, ἀναδιπλώνει τὸ κείμενο τοῦ *Ἀλληλούια* καὶ ἐπαναλαμβάνει αὐτὸ ὅσες φορὲς εἶναι ἀπαραίτητο, γιὰ νὰ ἐπιτευχθῆ τὸ ἐπιθυμητὸ ἀποτέλεσμα: Ἡ δημιουργία τέχνης ὑψηλῆς καὶ θαυμαστῆς.

Δεύτερον: ἀξιοπαρατήρητο στοιχεῖο, κατὰ τὴν μελοποίηση τοῦ καταληκτηρίου αὐτοῦ *Ἀλληλούια*, εἶναι ἡ ἐπιβολή, στὴν ἀρχὴ τῆς λέξεως, ἑνὸς μικροῦ κρατήματος, *τιτιτιρριτε*, τὸ ὁποῖο βέβαια παρατείνει ἀκόμε περισσότερο τὸ μέλος καὶ καθηδύνει μάλιστα τὶς ἀκοὲς τῶν ἀκροωμένων πιστῶν.

Τρίτον καὶ τελευταῖο στοιχεῖο ποὺ παρατηρεῖ κανεὶς κατὰ τὴ διαπραγμάτευση τῆς μελικῆς ἐπενδύσεως τοῦ *Ἀλληλούια*, τῆς κατακλεῖδος αὐτῆς τῶν στίχων τοῦ πολυελέου *Δοῦλοι Κύριον*, εἶναι ἡ προετοιμασία τῆς εἰσαγωγῆς του – τόσο γιὰ τὸν προσευχόμενο πιστό, ὅσο καὶ γιὰ τὸ χορὸ ψαλτῶν ποὺ μελωδεῖ τὴ σύνθεση – μὲ τὴν πρόταξη τῆς γνωστῆς παρακελευσματικῆς προσαγγῆς "λέγε", καὶ λέγομε προετοιμασία, διότι ἡ φράση αὐτή, γραμμένη πάντοτε στὰ χειρόγραφα μὲ κόκκινη μελάνη – ψάλλεται ἀπὸ τὸν μονοφωνάρη ἢ καλοφωνάρη ὡς μιὰ ἐπισήμανση γιὰ περισσότερη σπουδὴ καὶ προσοχὴ στὸ μέλος ποὺ θὰ ἀκολουθήση.

Στὴ δεύτερη στάση τοῦ πολυελέου, δηλαδὴ τὸν ψαλμὸ ρλε᾽ *Ἐξομολογεῖσθε τῷ Κυρίῳ*, τὰ πράγματα διαφοροποιοῦνται ὅσον ἀφορᾶ στὴ μελικὴ του κατακλείδα, καὶ τοῦτο διότι στὴν προκειμένη περίπτωση ἔχομε τὴν ὕπαρξη τοῦ ἀνακλώμενου ἐφυμνίου "ὅτι εἰς τὸν αἰῶνα τὸ ἔλεος αὐτοῦ.". Ἡ συνηθέστερη περίπτωση μελοποιήσεως τοῦ ἐφυμνίου τούτου – τὸ ὁποῖο, σημειωτέον, μελίζεται χωρὶς ἰδιαίτερη μουσικὴ ἀνάπτυξη σὲ λιτὲς καὶ ὡς ἐπὶ τὸ πολὺ ἁπλὲς μελικὲς γραμμές – προϋποθέτει τὴν παράθεση δύο μελισματικὰ ἐπιτηδευμένων *Ἀλληλούια* στὴν ἀρχὴ καὶ στὸ τέλος τοῦ ἀνακλωμένου. Ἀπὸ τὰ δύο αὐτὰ

Ἀλληλούια τὸ τελευταῖο καὶ καταληκτήριο, καταλαμβάνει – κατὰ τὴν
ἐκτύλιξη τοῦ μέλους του – σαφῶς
μεγαλύτερη ἔκταση, ἐνῷ πολλὲς φορὲς δὲν λείπουν καὶ οἱ ἐπαναλήψεις,
μὲ τὴν παρεμβολὴ τῶν ἐνηχηματικῶν
συλλαβῶν να, νε κτλ.

Ἡ περίπτωση ποὺ παραπάνω
περιγράψαμε, γίνεται πιὸ σύνθετη,
ὅταν τὰ "Ἀλληλουιάρια" – ἀνεξάρ-
τητα ἐὰν αὐτὰ εὑρίσκονται στὴν ἀρχὴ
ἢ τὸ τέλος τοῦ ἐφυμνίου – παρατίθενται πλέον περίτεχνα τῶν ἀνωτέρω, σχεδὸν διπλάσια σὲ σύγκριση μὲ
τὸ ψαλμικὸ κείμενο, ἐπαναλαμβανό-
μενα τοὐλάχιστον δύο φορές.

Τέλος σημειώνομε καὶ τὴν ἐκτενέ-
στατη μελικὴ μεταχείρηση τοῦ στίχου
Τῷ παντάξαντι βασιλεῖς, κατὰ τὴν
ὁποία ἔχομε ἀφ' ἑνὸς μὲν πρόταξη
τῆς παρακελευσματικῆς προσταγῆς
λέγε πρὸ τῶν, ἑκατέρωθεν τοῦ ἐφυμνίου, "Ἀλληλουιαρίων", ἀφ' ἑτέρου
δὲ ἐκτεταμένη μελισματικὴ ἐπιτή-
δευση, τόσο τῶν "Ἀλληλουιαρίων",
ὅσο καὶ τοῦ ψαλμικοῦ κειμένου τοῦ
ἀνακλωμένου:

"Τῷ παντάξαντι βασιλεῖς μεγά-
λους /λέγε- νααα... ἀλληηη... να-
λληλούια, α - να - λληηη.... να -
λληλούουου... ια ὅτι εἰς αἰῶνα τὸ
ἔλεεεε....εεε τὸ ἔλεος αὐτου λέγε -
νααα....λληη...να- λληλούιααααα....
να - λληηη.... να - λληλούουου, ια".[8]
Καὶ τοσαῦτα μὲν περὶ τῶν ὑπὸ τοῦ
Κουκουζέλους μελοποιηθέντων στίχων τοῦ πολυελέου.

Ἐὰν τώρα, θελήσωμε νὰ ἐπιχειρή-
σωμε μίαν ἀνάλογη ἐξέταση τῶν στίχων τῶν Ἀντιφώνων τοῦ πολυελέου
– ποιημάτων τοῦ Μαΐστορος, τὰ
ἀποτελέσματα τῆς ἔρευνας αὐτῆς δὲ
θὰ ἀφίστανται τῶν ὅσα παραπάνω
ἐκθέσαμε. Παρατηροῦμε δηλαδὴ καὶ
ἐδῶ τὰ ἑξῆς:

α) Τὸν πλατυασμὸ τῆς τελευταίας
ἢ ἄλλης λέξεως τοῦ ψαλμικοῦ κειμένου, μοναδική, θὰ λέγαμε "μουσικὴ
περιττολογία", στὶς συνήθως σύντο-
μες μουσικὲς γραμμὲς ποὺ τὸ χαρακτηρίζουν.

β) Τὴν ἐκτενῆ μελισματικὴ ἐπεξεργασία τοῦ τελικοῦ – καταληκτηρίου
Ἀλληλούια, τὸ ὁποῖο καταστρώνεται
σὲ ἐπαναλήψεις, τουλάχιστον τρεῖς
φορές, μὲ τὴν παρεμβολὴ ἐπίσης τῶν
ἠχηματικῶν συλλαβῶν να, νε, τα, χα,
κτλ.

γ) Τὴν ἐπιβολή, στὴν ἀρχὴ ἢ ἐνδιαμέσως τῶν ἀκροτελευτίων "Ἀλληλουιαρίων", βραχέως κρατήματος ἢ
ἠχήματος α να νε νε να, τὸ ὁποῖο
προσδίδει στὴ σύνθεση ἀκόμη ἐντο-
νώτερο μελισματικὸ χαρακτῆρα ἐκ-
τενοῦς μελικῆς μεταχειρίσεως.

δ) Τὴν παράθεση, τέλος, τῆς παρακελευσματικῆς–καλοφωνάρικης προσταγῆς "λέγε" πρὸ καὶ ἐνδιαμέσως
τῶν τελικῶν "Ἀλληλουιαρίων".

Τὰ στοιχεῖα αὐτὰ ποὺ διέπουν καὶ
χαρακτηρίζουν τὸ μέλος τῶν Ἀντιφώνων τοῦ πολυελέου ποὺ ἐμέλισε ὁ
περίφημος μαΐστωρ Ἰωάννης ὁ Κουκουζέλης, συνηγοροῦν, φρονοῦμε,
ὑπὲρ τοῦ χαρακτηρισμοῦ τῶν συνθέσεων τούτων ὡς "Ἀλληλουιαρίων"[9]
προσδιορισμοῦ, ποὺ συνοδεύει τὰ
ἀξιοθαύμαστα αὐτὰ φωνητικὰ μνημεῖα τῆς Ψαλτικῆς Τέχνης καὶ ὑπερ-
θεματίζει οὐσιαστικὰ τὸν χαρακτῆρα
καὶ κύριο λειτουργικό τους στόχο:
τὴν αἴνεση καὶ δοξολογία τοῦ Τριαδικοῦ Θεοῦ.

Κρίνομε σκόπιμο στὴ συνέχεια, ν'
ἀναφερθοῦμε διεξοδικώτερα σὲ δύο
ἰδιαίτερα σημαντικὲς περιπτώσεις
μελοποιήσεως τῶν στίχων τοῦ πολυελέου.

1) Ἡ περίπτωση τῆς ἐπιβολῆς κειμένου
Εὐρύτατα διαδεδομένη, κυρίως
στοὺς στίχους τοῦ λεγομένου "Λατρινοῦ" πολυελέου, εἶναι ἡ παροῦσα
περίπτωση τῆς ἐπιβολῆς κειμένου.[10]
Δύο εἶναι τὰ κύρια μορφολογικὰ
χαρακτηριστικὰ ποὺ διακρίνουν τὴν
πρὸς ἐξέταση περίπτωση:
Πρῶτον, βέβαια, ἡ ἐπιβολὴ στὸ τέλος τοῦ ψαλμικοῦ στίχου, ἄλλου κειμένου, ἐξωψαλμικοῦ, πεποιημένου σὲ
στίχους 15συλλάβους, 12συλλάβους,

10συλλάβους κτλ., κειμένου πού, ὡς ἐπὶ τὸ πολύ, ἀναφέρεται στὴν Ὑπεραγία Θεοτόκο, στὶς μνῆμες τῶν κυριοτέρων Δεσποτικῶν ἑορτῶν στοὺς Ἀρχαγγέλους ἢ στὴ Σύναξη τῶν Ἀσωμάτων Ταξιαρχῶν, καθὼς καὶ σὲ ἄλλες μνῆμες μεγάλων ἑορταζομένων Ἁγίων. Οἱ συνθέσεις αὐτὲς ἔχουν ὡς κύριο στόχο τὴν ἐξύμνηση καὶ τὸν ὑπερθεματισμὸ ἑνὸς συγκεκριμένου ἑορτολογιοῦ γεγονότος, καὶ προσαρτώμενες στοὺς στίχους τοῦ πολυελέου, προσδίδουν αὐτόματα σ' αὐτοὺς εἰδικὴ ἑορτολογικὴ χρεία, προκειμένου νὰ τονισθῇ ἡ ἑκάστοτε τρέχουσα ἑορτή.

Ἡ ἐπιβολὴ τῶν κειμένων τούτων – τῶν ὁποίων τὰ γράμματα περ' ἀπ' τὸ μέλος, προέρχονται, τὶς περισσότερες φορές, ἀπὸ τὸν κάλαμο τοῦ ἰδίου τοῦ μελουργοῦ – παρατηρεῖται στοὺς τελευταίους στίχους τοῦ Λατρινοῦ πολυελέου, Οἶκος Ἀαρών, Οἶκος Λευί, Οἱ φοβούμενοι τὸν Κύριον, καὶ κυρίως Εὐλογήσατε τὸν Κύριον.[11] Μὲ ἀφορμὴ τὴ διαπίστωση αὐτή, ἀναπόφευκτη εἶναι ἡ ἀκόλουθη παρατήρηση:

Στοὺς χειρόγραφους κώδικες τῆς Παπαδικῆς τοῦ ΙΔ' αἰῶνος καὶ ἐντεῦθεν, ποικίλλει ἡ κατάταξη τῶν ἐν λόγῳ ἐξωψαλμικῶν κειμένων σὲ ἀντιστοιχία μὲ τοὺς ἀνωτέρω ψαλμικοὺς στίχους.[12] Σύνηθες, γιὰ παράδειγμα, εἶναι τὸ φαινόμενο, κατὰ τὸ ὁποῖο τοῦ στίχου Εὐλογήσατε τὸν Κύριον ἔπεται ἡ παράθεση ὅλων ἢ ὁρισμένων μόνον ἐξωψαλμικῶν ἑορτολογικῶν κειμένων "αὐτονόμων" χωρὶς δηλαδὴ νὰ προτάσσεται αὐτῶν

κάποιος συγκεκριμένος ψαλμικὸς στίχος τοῦ πολυελέου.[13]

Ὅλα τοῦτα μᾶς ὁδηγοῦν στὸ ἑξῆς συμπέρασμα: ὁ ἀσματομελωδῶν στίχους τοῦ πολυελέου, εἶχε τὴ δυνατότητα, ἀνάλογα μὲ τὸ ἑορτολογικὸ θέμα πού ἤθελε νὰ προβάλῃ καὶ πανηγυρικὰ νὰ ἐξυμνήσῃ, νὰ ἐπιλέξῃ τὸ ἀνάλογο κείμενο, τὸ ὁποῖο ἔπρεπε νὰ προσαρτήσῃ σὲ κάποιον ἀπὸ τοὺς στίχους τοῦ Λατρινοῦ πολυελέου πού προσημειώσαμε. Μὲ τὸν τρόπο αὐτὸ ἐπετυγχάνετο ἄριστα τὸ ἐπιθυμητὸ ἀποτέλεσμα, νὰ ἐγκωμιασθῇ ὁ τιμώμενος ἅγιος ἢ νὰ ἀναπεμφθοῦν δοξολογικοὶ διθύραμβοι πρὸς τιμὴν τοῦ τυχόντος ἑορτολογικοῦ γεγονότος.

Πρὸς τὴν κατεύθυνση αὐτή, συνηγορεῖ καὶ τὸ δεύτερο μορφολογικὸ χαρακτηριστικὸ πού διακρίνει τὶς ἐν λόγῳ συνθέσεις: ἡ μελικὴ μεταχείρηση τοῦ κειμένου τοῦ ψαλμικοῦ στίχου εἶναι ἰδιαίτερα ἁπλή, χωρὶς ἐξάρσεις καὶ ἐπιτηδεύσεις. Ὁ μελοποιός, μετατοπίζει τὸ κύριο βάρος τῆς μελουργικῆς του δεινότητος στὸ ἐξωψαλμικὸ κείμενο – ἀκριβῶς γιὰ νὰ ὑπερθεματισθῇ τὸ ἐπιθυμητὸ ἑορτολογικὸ γεγονός – ἐνῷ τὸ ψαλμικὸ κείμενο μελίζεται σχεδὸν "περιγραφικὰ" ὡς "πρόλογος" ἢ "εἰσαγωγὴ" τῆς ὅλης συνθέσεως.[14]

Ἀπὸ μιὰ λεπτομερέστερη, πλέον ἐξειδικευμένη ἐξέταση τοῦ μέλους τοῦ στίχου Εὐλογήσατε τὸν Κύριον ἐξάγομε – ὀφελιμώτατα συμπεράσματα, στὸν κώδικα ΕΒΕ 2406 φ. 95v, σημειώνεται ὁ στίχος Εὐλογήσατε τὸν Κύριον, καὶ ἀκολουθεῖ ἡ παρά-

Ex. 1

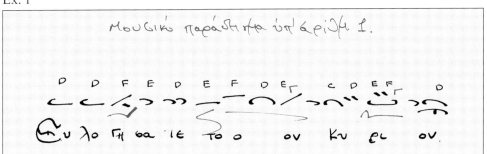

177

θεση τῶν κειμένων *Δεῦτε τῇ Πανάγ-νῳ, Ἐμμανουὴλ παιδίον, Ἄγγελοι ὑμήσατε, Αἰνοῦσι σε στρατιαί*. Στὴ συνέχεια τοῦ ἰδίου κώδικος (φ. 96ῖ) παρατίθεται καὶ πάλι ὁ στίχος *Εὐλο-γήσατε τὸν Κύριον* τοῦ ὁποίου ἔπον-ται τὰ κείμενα *Ἀλλαλάξατε τῷ Θεῷ* καὶ *Ἐλπὶς ἁπάντων ἄχραντε*. Συγ-κρινόμενο τὸ μέλος τῶν δύο αὐτῶν στίχων *Εὐλογήσατε τὸν Κύριον* εἶναι πανομοιότυπο, τονισμένο ὡς ἑξῆς: (ex.1)

Ἐπιπλέον, ὁ στίχος αὐτὸς τονισμέ-νος στὸ ἴδιο ἀκριβῶς μέλος, παρα-τίθεται καὶ στὸν κώδικα EBE 2458, φ. 93v (ὅπου φέρει τὴν ἔνδειξη: "ἕτε-ρον τοῦ μαΐστορος κὺρ Ἰωάννου Κου-κουζέλους") μὲ τὴν ἐπιβολὴ αὐτὴ τὴ φορὰ τῶν κειμένων, *Ἀγνὴ Παρθένε, Τοὺς ὀρθοδόξους ἄνακτας, Παντάνασ-σα πανύμνητε* καὶ *Ἄγγελοι ὑμήσατε*.

Τέλος, γιὰ νὰ προχωρήσωμε περισ-σότερο τὸν παρόντα συλλογισμὸ καὶ πρὸς ἐπίρρωση τῶν ἀνωτέρων ἐκτε-θέντων, σημειώνομε ὅτι καὶ τὸ μέλος τοῦ στίχου *Οἶκος Ἀαρών* [15]– καὶ συγκεκριμένα ἡ κατακλεῖδα του *Εὐλογήσατε τὸν Κύριον* – ταυτίζεται μὲ τὸ μέλος τοῦ στίχου *Εὐλογήσατε τὸν Κύριον*. Ἰδοὺ τί ἀποδεικνύει μιὰ παράλληλη πράθεση τῶν δύο στίχων: (ex.2)

Ἂς σημειωθῇ ἀκόμη ἐδῶ ὅτι καὶ οἱ ὑπόλοιποι στίχοι ποὺ χρησιμεύουν ὡς "πρόλογοι" τῶν ἐξωψαλμικῶν αὐ-τῶν κειμένων διαφοροποιοῦνται

ἐλάχιστα, κυρίως στὸ μέλος ποὺ ἐπ-ενδύει τὴν κατάληξη "τὸν Κύριον",[16] τὸ ὁποῖο προοδευτικὰ ἐπιμηκύνεται ὡς ἑξῆς (Βλ. EBE 2406, φ. 95r–v): (exx.3-5)

Ἐν πολλοῖς λοιπὸν ὅμοιο τὸ μέλος τοῦ – προτασσομένου τῶν πρὸς ἐξ-έταση ἐξωψαλμικῶν συνθέσεων – ψαλμικοῦ κειμένου τῶν τελευταίων στίχων τοῦ *Λατρινοῦ* πολυελέου, μελισμένο σὲ ἀδρὲς καὶ "περιγρα-φικὲς" μελωδικὲς γραμμές, ἀρκετὸ μὲν γιὰ νὰ ἐπιβάλλη τὸν ἦχο καὶ τὴν ὅλη σύνθεση, κατάλληλο δὲ γιὰ νὰ μεταθέση τὴν προσοχὴ στὸ ἀκολου-θοῦν – ἐπιτηδευμένο μελικά – κείμε-νο τὸ ἀναφερόμενο σὲ συγκεκριμένο ἑορτολογικὸ γεγονὸς τῆς Ὀρθοδόξου Ἀνατολικῆς Ἐκκλησίας.

2) Ἡ περίπτωση τῶν καλοφωνικῶν στίχων

Ἀνεπανάληπτα καὶ ἀξεπέραστα φω-νητικὰ μνημεῖα ἀπαράμιλλου μου-σικοῦ κάλλους καὶ μελουργικῆς δει-νότητος, οἱ πρὸς ἐξέταση καλοφωνι-κοὶ στίχοι τοῦ πολυελέου, ἀποτελοῦν ἀναντίρρητα τὸ ἀποκορύφωμα τῆς ψαλτικῆς τέχνης καὶ βυζαντινῆς με-λοποιίας.

Εἶναι προφανὲς ὅτι στὴν περί-πτωση αὐτὴ ἔχομε νὰ κάνωμε μὲ τὴν ᾀσματικὴ πράξη τῆς καλοφωνίας τῆς ὁποίας τὰ βασικὰ γνωριστικὰ στοι-χεῖα εἶναι τρία:[17]

Ex. 2

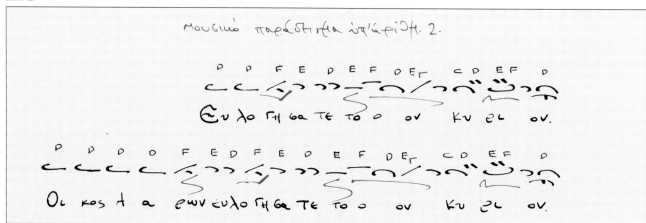

Ex. 3

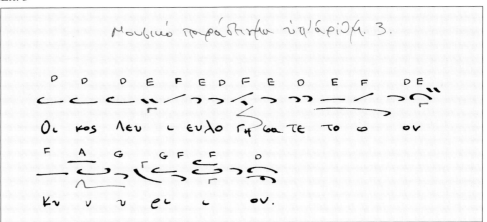

Ex. 4

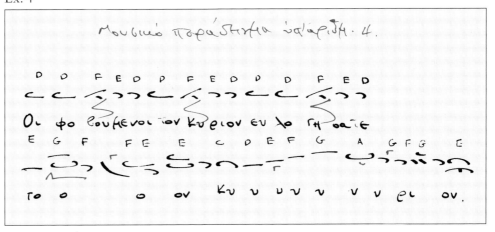

Ex. 5

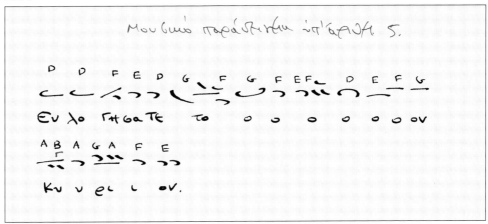

Πρῶτον, αὐτὸ καθ᾽ ἑαυτὸ τὸ καλοφωνικὸ μέλος, μὲ τὴν ἔννοια τῆς πεποικιλμένης μελικῆς ἐπιτηδεύσεως καὶ τοῦ ἐντόνου μελισματικοῦ χαρακτῆρος. Ἡ καλοφωνικὴ μελοποιία διακρίνεται γιὰ τὶς πλατιὲς μελωδίες, τὰ εὐρηματικὰ μελικὰ τόξα, τὸ "κεκαλωπισμένον" μέλος μὲ τὶς συχνὲς ἐναλλαγὲς καὶ μεταπτώσεις ἀπὸ ἦχον εἰς ἦχον, τὴν παράθεση ποικίλων θέσεων τῆς βυζαντινῆς μελοποιίας. Διακρίνεται, μὲ λίγα λόγια, γιὰ τὸν εὐρύτατο πλατυασμὸ τοῦ μέλους.[18]

Δεύτερον, ἡ ὕπαρξη τῶν λεγομένων ἀναγραμματισμῶν ἢ ἀναποδισμῶν. Ἡ ἀνακατάστρωση δηλαδὴ τοῦ οἰουδήποτε ψαλμικοῦ κειμένου ἢ ἄλλου ὑμνογραφήματος, σὲ τέτοιο σημεῖο ὥστε νὰ διαφοροποιῆται τελικὰ τὸ ἀρχικὸ κείμενο, καὶ νὰ καθοδηγῆ πλέον ὁ μελουργὸς τὰ νοήματα πρὸς τὴν κατεύθυνση ποὺ ὁ ἴδιος ἐπιθυμεῖ νὰ προβάλλη ἢ νὰ ἐξάρη ἰδιαίτερα. Συχνὰ φαινόμενα στὴν περίπτωση αὐτὴ, εἶναι οἱ ἐπαναλήψεις συλλαβῶν ἢ καὶ ὁλοκλήρων λέξεων καὶ φράσεων, καθὼς καὶ ὁ ἀναποδισμὸς τῶν ψαλμικῶν στίχων. Δὲν λείπει ἀκόμη ἡ παρεμβολὴ διαφόρων στίχων ἀπὸ τὸν ἴδιο ψαλμὸ ἢ ἀπὸ ἄλλο ὑμνογράφημα καὶ ἡ παράθεση ἐξωψαλμικοῦ κειμένου, πεποιημένου πρὸς τοῦτο ὑπὸ τοῦ ἰδίου τοῦ μελουργοῦ.[19]

Τρίτον, ἡ ἐπιβολὴ βραχέων ἢ ἐκτενῶν κρατημάτων καὶ ἠχημάτων στὴν ἀρχή, στὴ μέση καὶ κυρίως στὸ τέλος τῆς ὅλης συνθέσεως. Μὲ τὸν τρόπο αὐτό, σφραγίζεται καταλυτικὰ ἡ ἀξεπέραστη αὐτὴ μουσικὴ δημιουργία, μὲ τὸ ἀπόκυημα τῆς μελουργικῆς φαντασίας τοῦ μελοποιοῦ. Οἱ ἄσημες συλλαβὲς τεριρέμ, νενά, χιχί, τιτί, κτλ. εἴτε λειτουργοῦν ὡς προοίμιο καὶ εἰσαγωγὴ – preludio κατὰ τὴν διεθνῆ μουσικὴ ὁρολογία – τῆς συνθέσεως, εἴτε ὡς ἀνάπαυλα καὶ ἐνδιάμεση στάση εἴτε τέλος ὡς δυναμικὴ καὶ ἐκτενὴς κατακλείδα αὐτῆς, προσδίδουν τόνο πανηγυρικό, ἐπιμηκύνουν τὴ μελωδία, δημιουργοῦν ποικίλα συναισθήματα καὶ ἐξασφαλίζουν ὅλους ἐκείνους τους ὅρους ποὺ πρέπει νὰ πληροῖ μιὰ σύνθεση γιὰ νὰ χαρακτηρισθῆ μουσικὴ πανδαισία.[20]

Ἡ λαμπρὴ αὐτὴ πράξη τῆς καλοφωνίας, ἂν καὶ χαρακτηρίζεται ἀναμφισβήτητα ὡς ἡ "Ars Nova" τῆς Βυζαντινῆς μελοποιίας κατὰ τὸν ΙΔ´ αἰῶνα, εἶχε ἤδη ἀναπτυχθῆ καὶ διαμορφωθῆ ἐνωρίτερα ἀπὸ τὶς ἀρχὲς ἀκόμη τοῦ ΙΓ´ αἰῶνος.[21] Ὁ δὲ μαΐ-

στωρ Ἰωάννης ὁ Κουκουζέλης, "εἰ καὶ μέγας τῷ ὄντι διδάσκαλος ἦν καὶ οὐδενὶ τῶν πρὸ αὐτοῦ παραχωρεῖν εἶχε τῆς ἐπιστήμης"[22], ἀκολούθησε τοὺς προγενεστέρους του διδασκάλους κατὰ τὴ διακονίαν τοῦ "δρόμου τῆς αὐτῆς ἐπιστήμης"[23] "εἵπετο δ᾽ οὖν ὅμως κατ᾽ ἴχνος αὐτοῖς καὶ οὐδέν τι τῶν ἐκείνοις δοξάντων καὶ δοκιμασθέντων καλῶς δεῖν ᾤετο καινοτομεῖν· διὸ οὐδὲ ἐκαινοτομεῖ."[24]

Τοῦτο καθίσταται πλέον σαφέστερο ἀπὸ μιὰ εἰς βάθος ἐξέταση τῶν καλοφωνικῶν στίχων ποὺ ἐμέλισε ὁ Κουκουζέλης, ὅπου κανεὶς διαπιστώνει ὅτι διαφυλάσσονται ὅλα ἐκεῖνα τὰ, ἀφοριστικὰ τῆς καλοφωνίας, στοιχεῖα ποὺ ἀνωτέρω κατονομάσαμε.

Χωροῦντες ἤδη σὲ διεξοδικώτερη ἀνάλυση τῆς παρούσης περιπτώσεως τῶν καλοφωνικῶν στίχων, σημειώνομε ὅτι ἀντικείμενο καλοφωνικῆς μεταχειρίσεως ἀποτελοῦν οἱ στίχοι αὐτοὶ τοῦ ρλδ´ ψαλμοῦ, Δοῦλοι Κύριον, ποὺ ἀναφέρονται στὰ εἴδωλα τῶν ἐθνῶν. Θέμα ἰδιαίτερα πρόσφορα στὸν ὀρθόδοξο μελουργὸ ποὺ ἐπιθυμεῖ νὰ καταδείξη τὴν ἀσημαντότητα καὶ οὐτιδανότητα τῶν εἰδώλων, σὲ ἀντίθεση πρὸς τὴ μεγαλειότητα τοῦ Τριαδικοῦ Θεοῦ: "Στόμα ἔχουσι καὶ οὐ λαλήσουσιν, ὀφθαλμοὺς ἔχουσιν καὶ οὐκ ὄψονται, ὦτα ἔχουσι καὶ οὐκ ἐνωτισθήσονται, οὐδὲ γάρ ἐστι πνεῦμα ἐν τῷ στόματι αὐτῶν."

Μιὰ συνεξέταση καὶ ἀντιπαράθεση τῶν ψαλμικῶν αὐτῶν στίχων πρὸς τοὺς μετὰ ταῦτα διαμορφωμένους καλοφωνικούς, ἀποτελεῖ ἰδιαίτερα ἔγκυρο καὶ εὔγλωττο πειστήριο γιὰ τὴν ἀλήθεια τῶν ὅσα παραπάνω ἐκθέσαμε.

Ἔτσι, γιὰ παράδειγμα ὁ στίχος Στόμα ἔχουσι, μετατρέπεται κατὰ τὴν καλοφωνική του μεταχείρηση ὡς ἑξῆς:

(ἦχ. α΄)	*"Στόμα ἔχουσι καὶ οὐ λαλήσουσι*
	στόμα ἔχουσι καὶ οὐ λαλήσουσι
	τὰ εἴδωλα - τὰ εἴδωλα τῶν ἐθνῶν
	οὐ λαλήσουσι τὰ εἴ - τὰ εἴδωλα
	οὐ λαλήσουσι τὰ εἴδωλα τῶν ἐθνῶν
	ἀργύριον καὶ χρυσίον, ἔργα χειρῶν ἀνθρώπων
	στόμα ἔχουσι καὶ οὐ λαλήσουσι
	τὰ εἴδωλα τῶν ἐθνῶν
(ἦχ. πλ. α΄)	*Τοτοτοροτο - τεριρεμ (ἐκτενὲς κράτημα)*
	Ἀλληλούια"[25]

Παρόμοιο εἶναι καὶ τὸ ἀποτέλεσμα τῆς καλοφωνικῆς ἐπιτηδεύσεως τῶν δύο ἐπομένων στίχων Ὀφθαλμοὺς ἔχουσι καὶ Ὦτα ἔχουσι. Ὁ κολοφώνας ὅμως τῆς καλοφωνίας εἶναι σίγουρα ὁ στίχος Οὐδὲ γὰρ ἐστὶ πνεῦμα, ἀπὸ τὶς πλέον σπουδαῖες καὶ χαρακτηριστικὲς περιπτώσεις τῶν καλοφωνικῶν στίχων ποὺ ἐξετάζομε:

(ἦχ. α΄)	*"Οὐδὲ γὰρ ἐστὶ πνεῦμα ἐν τῷ στόματι αὐτῶν*
	καὶ οὐ λαλή - λαλήσουσι τὰ εἴ - τὰ εἴδωλα τῶν ἐθνῶν
	στόμα ἔχουσι τὰ εἴδωλα καὶ οὐ λαλή - λαλήσουσι
	οὐ λαλήσουσι τὰ εἴδωλα [πάλιν] τὰ εἴδωλα τῶν ἐθνῶν
	ἀργύριον - ἀργύριον καὶ χρυσίον
	ἔ - χε ἔργα χειρῶν ἀνθρώπων
	οὐ λαλή - λαλήσουσι τὰ εἴδωλα [τῶν ἐθνῶν]
	τὰ εἴδω - χωχω λα - χαχα τῶν ἐθνῶν
	στόμα ἔχουσι καὶ οὐ - καὶ οὐ λαλή - λαλήσουσι
[Ἀναποδισμός]	
(ἦχ. α΄)	*Ὀφθαλμοὺς ἔχουσι τὰ εἴδωλα*
	καὶ οὐκ ὄψονται τὰ εἴδωλα
	καὶ οὐ λαλήσουσι
(ἦχ. πλ. α΄)	*οὐδὲ γὰρ ἐστὶ πνεῦμα ἐν τῷ στόματι αὐτῶν*
	οὐ λαλήσουσι τὰ εἴδωλα τῶν ἐθνῶν
	καὶ πάντες οἱ πεποιθότες ἐπ' αὐτοῖς
	στόμα ἔχουσι καὶ οὐ λαλή - λαλήσουσι
(ἦχ. α΄)	*Ἀλληλούια, Ἀχαναχα - Ἀλληλούια*
(ἦχ. πλ. α΄)	*Ἀλλη - τιριτιριτι.... (κράτημα)*
	Ἀλληλούια, - Ἀλλη - κικι να - λληλούια
	Ἀλληλούια."[26]

Στοιχεῖο ἄξιο ἰδιαίτερης προσοχῆς στὸν ἀνωτέρω στίχο, περ' ἀπ' τοὺς ἀναγραμματισμούς, τοὺς ἀναποδισμοὺς καὶ τὴν ἐπιβολὴ κρατημάτων, εἶναι ἡ χρήση ἀναφωνημάτων σχετλιαστικῶν, συγκεκριμένα στὴ λέξη "τὰ εἴδωλα"[27]: "τὰ εἴδω- χωχωλα- χαχα". Τὰ ἀναφωνήματα αὐτά – μιμούμενα κραυγὲς γέλωτος ὑπὸ τὴ μορφὴ ἠχημάτων – ὑποκρύπτουν μιὰ σαφέστατη ἐμπαικτικὴ διάθεση διακωμωδήσεως τῆς λέξεως "εἴδωλα" καὶ κατ' ἐπέκτασιν, μιὰ προσπάθεια στηλιτεύσεως τῆς ἐπαράτου καὶ ποικιλοειδοῦς εἰδολολατρίας.

Καὶ σὲ στίχους ὅμως "τῆς δευτέρας στάσεως τοῦ πολυελέου", τοῦ ψ. ρλε', Ἐξομολογεῖσθε τῷ Κυρίῳ, ἐπιφυλάσσει ὁ μαΐστωρ Ἰωάννης καλοφωνικὴ μεταχείριση, μὲ ἰδιαίτερη πάντοτε φροντίδα γιὰ διατήρηση ὅλων τῶν, γνωστῶν ἤδη σὲ᾿ μᾶς, στοιχείων, ποὺ συνιστοῦν καὶ ὁρίζουν τὴν καλλιφωνία.

Ἀπὸ τὰ ποικίλα, πρὸς τὴν κατεύθυνση αὐτή, παραδείγματα ἀναφέρομε ἐδῶ τὴν περίπτωση τοῦ στίχου Τῷ καταδιελόντι τὴν ἐρυθρὰν θάλασσαν, ὁ ὁποῖος ὡς καλοφωνικὸς ἐμφανίζεται μὲ τὴν ἀκόλουθη μορφή:

(ἦχ. πλ. β') "Τῷ καταδιελόντι τὴν Ἐρυθρὰν θάλασσαν εἰς διαιρέσεις
καὶ διαγαγόντι τὸν Ἰσραὴλ διὰ μέσου αὐτῆς.
Ἐξομολογεῖσθε τῷ Κυρίῳ, τῶν κυρίων
τῷ καταδιελόντι τὴν θάλσσαν
καὶ ἐκτινάξαντι Φαραὼ καὶ τὴν δύναμιν αὐτοῦ,
εἰς θάλσσαν Ἐρυθράν, Ἀλληλούια
ὅτι εἰς τὸν αἰῶνα τὸ ἔ- χε- τὸ ἔλεος αὐτοῦ, Ἀλληλούια
α νε να νε - ριτερετε (ἐκτενὲς κράτημα)
Ἀλληλούια"[28]

Θὰ ὁλοκληρώσωμε τὴν παράγραφο αὐτὴ καὶ τὴν ἀναφορὰ μας στοὺς καλοφωνικοὺς στίχους τοῦ πολυελέου μὲ τὴν παράθεση ἑνὸς ἰδιαίτερη χαρακτηριστικοῦ καλοφωνικοῦ στίχου ἀπὸ τὸν Λατρινὸ πολυέλεο, ὁ ὁποῖος ἀνθολογεῖται συνήθως στοὺς χειρόγραφους μουσικοὺς κώδικες μὲ

τὴν ἔνδειξη "᾿Αναποδισμὸς" ἢ "᾿Αναγραμματισμός". Πρόκειται γιὰ τὸν στίχο Εὐλογητὸς Κύριος ἐκ Σιῶν, λαμπρὸ δεῖγμα τῆς ὑψηλῆς συνθετικῆς τέχνης καὶ τῆς ἀνυπερβλήτου μουσικῆς ἰδιοφυΐας τοῦ μαΐστορος Ἰωάννου τοῦ Κουκουζέλους. Ἰδοὺ τὸ κείμενο τοῦ ἐν λόγῳ ᾿Αναποδισμοῦ:

"Εὐλογητὸς Κύριος ἐκ Σιῶν ὁ κατοικῶν Ἰερουσαλήμ.
Κύριος ἐκ Σιῶν εὐλογητός.
Εὐλογητὸς Κύριος ἐκ Σιῶν, ὃς ἐπάταξεν ἔθνη πολλὰ καὶ
ἀπέκτεινε βασιλεῖς κραταιούς.
Ὁ Κύριος εὐλογητός·
Κύριος ὃς ἐπάταξεν τὰ πρωτότοκα Αἰγύπτου,
ἀπὸ ἀνθρώπου ἕως κτήνους·
καὶ ἔδωκεν τὴν γῆν αὐτῶν κληρονομίαν Ἰσραὴλ
λαῷ αὐτοῦ.
Ὁ κατοικῶν Ἰερουσαλὴμ Κύριος·
κύριος πάντα ὅσα ἠθέλησεν ἐποίησεν,
ἐν τῷ οὐρανῷ καὶ ἐν τῇ γῇ
τιτιτιριρι - τετερερουτε (κράτημα)
Εὐλογητὸς ἐκ Σιῶν Κύριος
ὁ κατοικῶν Ἰερουσαλὴμ Κύριος, Ἀλληλούια"[29]

Δὲν ἀπομένει τίποτε ἄλλο πλέον, παρὰ νὰ τερματίσωμε τὸ λόγο μας μὲ τούτη ἀναστροφή, παραφράζοντας τὴ

ρήση τοῦ Μανουὴλ Δούκα τοῦ Χρυσάφη καὶ Λαμπαδαρίου: Μὴ τοίνυν νόμιζε ἁπλῆν εἶναι καὶ μονοειδῆ τὴν

- τῶν τοῦ πολυελέου στίχων - μεταχείρισιν, ἀλλὰ ποικίλην τε καὶ πολυσχιδῆ καὶ πολύ τι διαφέρειν ἀλλήλων γίνωσκε οἵ τε καλοφωνικοὶ στίχοι καὶ τὰ ἀλλάγματα, Θεοτοκία καὶ ἑόρτια, καὶ τὰ τοῦ πολυελέου Ἀντίφωνα καὶ τὰ λοιπά, περὶ ἃ ἡ τέχνη καταγίνεται, κατὰ τὰς μεταχειρήσεις αὐτῶν. Ὥστε τὸν μὲν ποιήσαντα καὶ ἐντέχνως συνθέσαντα ταῦτα, χαριτώνυμον Ἰωάννην Παπαδόπουλον τὸν Κουκουζέλην, ἐπαξίως προσαγορεύσαι - ὡς τοιοῦτον ὄντα τῇ ἀληθείᾳ - θαυμασιώτατον, γλυκύτατον, διδάσκαλον τῶν διδασκάλων, ὡς ἀληθῶς μαΐστορα.[30]

Bibliography

Conomos, D. 1985
The Treatise of Manuel Chrysaphes the
Lampadarios, Monumenta Musicae Byzan-
tinae, Corpus Scriptorum de Re Musica, 2,
Vienna

Καράς, Σ. 1993
Ἰωάννης Μαΐστωρ ὁ Κουκουζέλης καὶ ἡ
ἐποχή του, Ἀθῆναι

Migne
Patrologia Graeca (PG)

Morgan, M.M. 1972
The musical setting of Psalm 134, The Poly-
eleos, Studies in Eastern Chant, 3, 112-25,
Oxford

Μπεκάτωρ, Γ. 1966 (-67)
"Πολυέλεος", Θρησκευτικὴ καὶ Ἠθικὴ
Ἐγκυκλοπαιδεία, τόμ. 10, Ἀθῆναι

Στάθης, Γ. 1977
Ἡ δεκαπεντασύλλαβος ὑμνογραφία ἐν
τῇ βυζαντινῇ Μελοποιΐα, Ἀθῆναι

Στάθης, Γ. 1979
Οἱ ἀναγραμματισμοὶ καὶ τὰ μαθήματα
τῆς βυζαντινῆς μελοποιίας, Ἀθῆναι

Στάθης, Γ. 1980
Μορφολογία καὶ ἔκφραση τῆς
βυζαντινῆς μουσικῆς, Ἀθῆναι

Στάθης, Γ. 1986
Ὁ Μαΐστωρ Ἰωάννης Παπαδόπουλος ὁ
Κουκουζέλης (1270 περίπου- αˋ ἥμ. ιδˋ
αἰ.) Ἡ ζωὴ καὶ τὸ ἔργο του, Ἐφημέριος
12-14 (1986), Ἀθῆναι

Στάθης, Γ. 1989
Ἡ ἀσματικὴ διαφοροποίηση στὸν
κώδικα ΕΒΕ 2458 τοῦ ἔτους 1336,

Χριστιανικὴ Θεσσαλονίκη –
Παλαιολόγειος ἐποχή, Θεσσαλονίκη

Χρύσανθος 1832
Θεωρητικὸν Μέγα τῆς Μουσικῆς,
Τεργέστη (Trieste)

Χρυσοχοΐδης, Ν.Α.
"Πολυέλεος", Μεγάλη Ἑλληνικὴ
Ἐγκυκλοπαιδεία, τόμ. 20, Ἀθῆναι

Williams, E.V. 1971
The Treatment of Text in the Kalophonic
chanting of Psalm 2, Studies in Eastern
Chant, 2

Williams, E.V. 1979
The kalophonic Tradition and Chants for
the Polyeleos Psalm 134, Studies in Eastern
Chant, 4

Notes

NOTE 1
Τὸ κείμενο ποὺ ἀκολουθεῖ, ἀποτελεῖ ἀνακοίνωση κατὰ τὸ *Dano/Hellenic symposium on Byzantine chant* ποὺ διοργάνωσε τὸ Ἰνστιτοῦτο τῆς Δανίας στὴν Ἀθήνα (11-14 Νοεμ. 1993). Βεβαίως, ἀπὸ τὴ συνολικὴ μελέτη γιὰ τὴ μελοποίηση, ἀπὸ τὸν Κουκουζέλη, στίχων τοῦ πολυελέου καὶ τῶν ἀντιφώνων τοῦ πολυελέου, ἀναγκασθήκαμε νὰ παραλείψωμε ἱκανὰ στοιχεῖα λόγω τῆς ἐλλείψεως χρόνου τότε καὶ τῆς "στενότητος" χώρου τώρα. Σημειώνομε πάντως, πὼς ἡ παροῦσα ἀνακοίνωση, ἀποτελεῖ ἐπὶ μέρους ἑνότητα τῆς γενικώτερας περὶ τῶν πολυελέων ἐρεύνης μας – γιὰ τὴν ἐκπόνηση διδακτορικῆς διατριβῆς μὲ θέμα "Ὁ πολυέλεος στὴ Βυζαντινὴ καὶ Μεταβυζαντινὴ Μελοποιία"– ὁπότε τὰ ἀνωτέρω ἀναφερθέντα στοιχεῖα θὰ ἐκτεθοῦν, κατὰ πᾶσαν πιθανότητα, στὰ πλαίσια τῆς προειρημένης διατριβῆς μας.

NOTE 2
Περὶ τοῦ πολυελέου γενικῶς βλέπε Μπεκάτωρ 1966, Χρυσοχοίδης καὶ Morgan 1972.

NOTE 3
Βλ. Migne PG 55,399

NOTE 4
Βλ. Migne PG 64,12-13, *Περὶ τῆς μετανοίας, καὶ εἰς τὸ ἀνάγνωσμα περὶ τῆς τοῦ Οὐρίου*. (Τὴν ὑπόδειξη περὶ τῆς ὀρθῆς παραπομπῆς στὸ ἀνωτέρω παράθεμα ὀφείλομε στὸν ἀγαπητὸ καθηγητὴ κ. Christian Troelsgaard, τὸν ὁποῖον καὶ εὐχαριστοῦμε θερμῶς). Σημειωτέον ὅτι ἡ μνημονευθεῖσα ὁμιλία συγκαταλέγεται στὰ νόθα ἔργα τοῦ "χρύσου τῇ γλώττῃ" πατρός.

NOTE 5
Χρύσανθος 1832 179,404 "Τὸ δὲ παπαδικὸν μέλος εἶναι τοιοῦτον, οἷον εὑρίσκεται εἰς τὰ κοινωνικὰ καὶ χερουβικά. Μελίζονται λοιπὸν μὲ τοιοῦτον μέλος ἀνοιξαντάρια, κεκραγάρια, δοχαί, πολυέλεοι, πασαπνοάρια, οἶκοι, μεγαλυνάρια, ἀσματικὰ μαθήματα, εἰσοδικά, τρισάγια, ἀλληλουιάρια, χερουβικά, κρατήματα"

NOTE 6
Ἄκρως ἐνδιαφέρουσα καὶ ἰδιαίτερα σημαντικὴ εἶναι νομίζομε ἡ παρατήρηση ὅτι ἀφοριστικὸ στοιχεῖο γιὰ τὴν κατάταξη ἑνὸς μέλους στὸ παπαδικὸ γένος εἶναι τὸ ποιητικὸ κείμενο τῶν ψαλμῶν τοῦ Δαβίδ.

NOTE 7
Γιὰ τὴ σύνταξη τῶν πινάκων ποὺ ἀκολουθοῦν καὶ περιλαμβάνουν τὶς ἑνότητες τῶν συνθέσεων τοῦ πολυελέου ἀλλὰ καὶ τῶν ἀντιφώνων του, ὅπως αὐτὲς παρατίθενται στὶς Παπαδικές, εἴχαμε ὑπ᾽ ὄψιν μας τοὺς ἑξῆς κώδικες: ΕΒΕ 2458, Κουτλ. 399 καὶ 457 τοῦ ΙΔ´ αἰῶνος καθὼς καὶ ΕΒΕ 2406, Κωνστ. 86, Ἰβηρ. 973, 974 καὶ 985 τοῦ ΙΕ´ αἰῶνος.

NOTE 8
Βλ. ΕΒΕ 2406 φ. 136v

NOTE 9
Πρβλ. καὶ Στάθης 1986 36

NOTE 10
Γιὰ τὴν ἀσματικὴ αὐτὴ πράξη τῆς ἐπιβολῆς κειμένου στοὺς τελευταίους στίχους τοῦ λατρινοῦ πολυελέου, βλέπε καὶ Στάθης 1977 77-8 καὶ 197-8, Στάθης 1979 69-70 καὶ 137, Στάθης 1989 193-8, Καρᾶς 1993 28-9

NOTE 11
Βλ. πρόχειρα τοὺς κώδικες ΕΒΕ 2406, φφ. 95r - 96r καὶ ΕΒΕ 2458 φφ. 93v-94r

NOTE 12
Πρβλ. Στάθης 1977 197-8

NOTE 13
Βλ. γιὰ παράδειγμα τοὺς κώδικες ΕΒΕ 2406 φφ. 95v-96r καὶ ΕΒΕ 2458 93v-94r

NOTE 14
Αὐτὸ καὶ μόνο τὸ γεγονὸς προσφέρει στὸν ψάλλοντα τὴν δυνατότητα νὰ προκρίνη τὸν ψαλμικὸ στίχο ποὺ ἐπιθυμεῖ, χωρὶς νὰ κινδυνεύη νὰ ἀλλοιωθῆ ὁ χαρακτήρας τῆς συνόλου συνθέσεως.

NOTE 15
Βλ. ΕΒΕ 2406 φ. 95r

NOTE 16
Παρόμοιο φαινόμενο παρατηροῦμε καὶ στὶς μεταγραφὲς τῶν συνθέσεων τούτων στὴ Νέα Μέθοδο κατὰ τὴν ἐξήγηση τοῦ Χουρμουζίου Χαρτοφύλακος. Ἔτσι, γιὰ παράδειγμα, οἱ πέντε διαφορετικοὶ στίχοι *Εὐλογήσατε τὸν Κύριον* ποὺ παραθέτει ὁ Χουρμούζιος στὸν αὐτόγραφο κώδικα τοῦ ΜΠΤ 704 φφ. 77v, 78v, 79r, καὶ 80r-v, παρουσιάζονται μὲ πανομοιότυπο προοίμιο *Εὐλογήσατε* καὶ διαφοροποιοῦνται ὀλίγον ὡς πρὸς τὴν καταληκτήρια φράση *τὸν Κύριον*. Ἐπαληθεύει λοιπὸν ὅ, τι ἀνωτέρω σημειώσαμε. Ἡ μελῴδηση πρὸ τῶν ἐξωψαλμικῶν ἑορτίων κειμένων τούτου ἢ τοῦ ἄλλου στίχου διόλου παραλλάσσεται ἢ διαφοροποιεῖ τὸν χαρακτήρα ποὺ ἀπνέει ἡ ὅλη σύνθεση.

NOTE 17
Βλ. διεξοδικὴ διαπραγμάτευση τοῦ θέματος σὲ Στάθης 1979 66-79. Εἰδικώτερα γιὰ τὴν καλοφωνικὴ μεταχείριση τοῦ ψ. 134, βλ. Williams 1979 228-41

NOTE 18
Βλ. Στάθης 1979 68-9

NOTE 19
Βλ. Στάθης 1979 69-70 καὶ Williams 1971 179-80

NOTE 20
Βλ. καὶ Στάθης 1979 70

NOTE 21
Βλ. Στάθης 1979 67 καὶ γιὰ τὶς ἀπαρχὲς
τοῦ καλοφωνικοῦ μέλους 71-79

NOTE 22
Βλ. Conomos 1985 lines 147-8

NOTE 23
Βλ. "Τὸ μνημόσυνον" τοῦ Κουκουζέλη,
ποὺ χαράσσει ὁ Ἰωάννης Πλουσιαδηνὸς
στὸν αὐτόγραφο του κώδικα Διον. 570
φ. 216r. Πρβλ. Στάθης 1976 711

NOTE 24
Conomos 1985 lines 149-51

NOTE 25
Τὸ κείμενο δημοσιεύεται ἀπὸ τὸν
κώδικα ΕΒΕ 2458 φφ. 100r-101r. Ὁ
ἴδιος στίχος, παρατίθεται ἐπίσης στὰ
φύλλα 101 Ἀλληλούια- 102r τοῦ ἰδίου

κώδικος, προσηρμοσμένος στὸ κείμενο
τοῦ στίχου ᾽Οφθαλμοὺς ἔχουσι, ὅπου
καὶ παρουσιάζεται μὲ διαφορετικὴ
ἀνακατάστρωση τοῦ ποιητικοῦ
κειμένου, ὡς ἑξῆς: (ἦχ. α᾽)Στόμα ἔχουσι
καὶ οὐ λαλήσουσι / τὰ εἴδωλα τῶν ἐθνῶν
οὐ λαλήσουσι / τὰ εἴδωλα τῶν ἐθνῶν /
στόμα ἔχουσι καὶ οὐ λαλήσουσι τὰ
εἴδωλα / στόμα ἔχουσι καὶ οὐ λαλήσουσι
τὰ εἴδωλα τῶν ἐθνῶν / ἀργύριον καὶ
χρυσίον ἔργα χειρῶν ἀνθρώπων / καὶ οὐ
λαλήσουσι τὰ εἴδωλα - τὰ εἴδωλα τῶν
ἐθνῶν / ἀργύριον - ἀργύριον καὶ
χρυσίον, ἔργα χειρῶν ἀνθρώπων / στόμα
ἔχουσι καὶ οὐ λαλήσουσι / (ἦχ. πλ. α᾽)
Ἀλληλούια, Ἀλληλούια, Ἀλλη- τιτιριτι
(βραχὺ κράτημα) / Ἀλληλούια.

NOTE 26
Τὸ κείμενο δημοσιεύεται ἀπὸ τὸν
κώδικα ΕΒΕ 2458 φφ. 102r-103v. Τὸ
ἴδιο κείμενο δημοσιεύει ὁ Στάθης 1979
69-70. Ἐπίσης, τὸ μέλος τοῦ παρόντος
καλοφωνικοῦ στίχου – ἐξηγημένο στὴ

Νέα Μέθοδο ἀπὸ τὸν Χουρμούζιο
Χαρτοφύλακα – παρατίθεται στὸν
κώδικα ΜΠΤ 704 φφ. 39r-41v. Οἱ λέξεις
δὲ ποὺ ἐντὸς ἀγκυλῶν θέτομε, ἀπαντοῦν
μόνο στὸν ἀνωτέρω, αὐτόγραφο τοῦ
Χουρμουζίου, κώδικα.

NOTE 27
Βλ. Στάθης 1979 70

NOTE 28
Ἀπὸ τὸν κώδικα ΕΒΕ 2458, φφ. 111r-
112r

NOTE 29
Ἀπὸ τὸν κώδικα ΜΠΤ 704, φφ. 81v-83v,
ὅπου παρατίθεται ὁ παρὼν στίχος,
ἐξηγημένος στὴ Νέα Μέθοδο παρὰ τοῦ
Χουρμουζίου Χαρτοφύλακος.

NOTE 30
Πρβλ. Conomos 1985 lines 96-8, 104-9,
124, 467-8, 348-9, 416-7

Summary:
The setting of verses for the Polyeleos from the maistor Ioannis Koukouzeles

Achilleas
G. Chaldeakis

From the great amount of verses for the Polyeleos and the Polyeleos' *Antiphona* composed by Byzantine and post-Byzantine composers, the manuscript tradition of the art of chant attributes (as it follows from the research made so far) 66 verses of the Polyeleos and 43 verses of the Polyeleos' *Antiphona* to Ioannis Papadopoulos Koukouzeles.

After a careful examination of the melody of these verses we underline the following:

a) The weight of the melody falls from the Psalm verse that is composed without any special effects - except extension of the last or another of its words - onto the final "Allelouia".

b) The "Allelouia" is twice or three times longer than the Psalm text and is repeated twice, three times, or as many times as the composer wants, with the insertion of the sonorous syllables α, να, νε, νε, να etc.

c) Sometimes, in the introduction of the final "Allelouia", there is a slight "kratima" τι τι ρρι τε.

d) The singing of "Allelouia" is sometimes preceded by the command "λέγε"

Furthermore, it is worth mentioning the following two cases:

a) The case of adding a text. In the final verses of the *"latrinos"* Polyeleos, non-psalmic texts devoted to a specific celebration of the Orthodox Church year are added and comprise the major part of the composition.

b) The case of "kalophonic" verses. The verses of Psalm 134 which refer to the "idols of the heathens" constitute an object of "kalophonic" process and, following, their form is clearly differentiated because of:

   i) The variation and strong melismatic character of the melody.

   ii) The rearrangement of the Psalm text through the *anagrammatismoi* or *anapodismoi*.

   iii) The addition of short or long "kratimata" and "ichimata" at the beginning, at the middle or at the end of the composition.

Ἡ Μέθοδος τῶν θέσεων τοῦ Ἰωάννου Κουκουζέλη καί ἡ ἐφαρμογή της

Γρ. Θ. Στάθης

"εἰς μνήμην Jørgen Raasted, + 5. 5. 1995"

Τό θέμα πού ἐπέλεξα ὡς συμβολή στό διμερές αὐτό ἑλληνο-δανικό μουσικολογικό Συμπόσιο, δηλαδή *"Ἡ Μέθοδος τῶν θέσεων τοῦ Ἰωάννου Κουκουζέλη καί ἡ ἐφαρμογή της"*, ἀποτελεῖ τήν καίρια ὑπόθεση τῆς σημειογραφίας τῆς Ψαλτικῆς Τέχνης καί τήν κρίσιμη θεώρηση τῆς ὀρθῆς ἑρμηνείας τῆς σημειογραφίας. Τό θέμα, ὡς κεντρικό τῆς ὑποθέσεως τῆς Ψαλτικῆς, εἶναι μέγα καί σύνθετο καί πολύπλοκο. Ἀσχολοῦμαι μέ αὐτό, ἐδῶ καί πολύν καιρό· καί μέ τό ἐνδιαφέρον τοῦ ἱστορικοῦ καί θεωρητικοῦ τῆς βυζαντινῆς καί μεταβυζαντινῆς μελοποιίας, ἀλλά καί ἀπ' τήν ἀνάγκη τῆς προσεγγίσεως τῆς ποικίλης δομῆς τῆς σημειογραφίας καί τῆς ἐξηγήσεώς της καί ἀναλυτικῆς καταγραφῆς της. Ἡ φύση τοῦ προκειμένου θέματος ἀπαιτεῖ σύνολη θεώρηση τῶν γραπτῶν μαρτυριῶν, τῶν θεωρητικῶν ἐπεξηγήσεων, τῆς ψαλτικῆς πρακτικῆς. Ἡ θεώρηση αὐτή δέν μπορεῖ νά γίνει τώρα, μέ βάση μόνο τή 'μέθοδο τῶν θέσεων' τοῦ Κουκουζέλη. Μέ τήν εὐκαιρία ὅμως αὐτοῦ τοῦ Συμποσίου θά ἤθελα νά θίξω, μέ μιά προδρομική ἀνακοίνωση, τά βασικά σημεῖα, γιά νά συνεισφέρω ἐδῶ στή σύναξή μας, καί προσφέρω ἀφορμή γιά συζήτηση καί ἀνταλλαγή ἀπόψεων.

Α΄. Ὀνομασία τῆς Συνθέσεως.

Ἡ 'Μέθοδος τῶν Θέσεων τῶν σημαδίων' τοῦ Ἰωάννου Παπαδοπούλου τοῦ Κουκουζέλη καί Μαΐστορος εἶναι ἡ γνωστότερη καί πλέον διαδεδομένη στή χειρόγραφη

παράδοση, ἀπ' τίς ἄλλες παρεμφερεῖς μεθόδους, τῆς βυζαντινῆς καί μεταβυζαντινῆς ἐποχῆς. Τοῦτο ὀφείλεται κυρίως στό ὅτι ὁ πρῶτος κώδικας, καί ὁ ἀρχαιότερος τοῦ τύπου τῆς Παπαδικῆς, χρονολογημένος μάλιστα τό ἔτος 1336, ὁ ΕΒΕ 2458[1], πού περιέχει αὐτήν τή 'μέθοδο' στήν πρώτη της καταγραφή, χρησίμευσε ὡς βάση γιά ἀντιγραφή σέ δεκάδες ἄλλους κώδικες μέ τήν ἴδια ἐπιγραφή· *"Ἀκολουθίαι συντεθειμέναι παρά τοῦ μαΐστορος κύρ Ἰωάννου τοῦ Κουκουζέλη, ἀπ' ἀρχῆς τοῦ μεγάλου Ἑσπερινοῦ μέχρι καί τῆς συμπληρώσεως τῆς θείας Λειτουργίας"*. Κατά τήν ἀναγραφή, φυσικά, δέν παραλείφθηκε, ἐκτός ἀπό λίγες ἐξαιρέσεις, ἡ μέθοδος αὐτή τῶν σημαδίων. Ἡ συχνή της ἀνθολόγηση, ὁπωσδήποτε εἶχε καί τήν ἔννοια τῆς χρησιμότητάς της γιά τήν ἐκμάθηση τῆς Ψαλτικῆς, καί ἐπομένως τήν ἰδιαίτερη ἐνασχόληση τῶν μεταγενεστέρων διδασκάλων, καί τήν περίπτωση ἐξηγήσεώς της ἀπ' τόν Πέτρο Πελοποννήσιο καί στή συνέχεια ἀπ' τόν Γρηγόριο Πρωτοψάλτη καί τόν Ματθαῖο Βατοπεδηνό.

Ἐδῶ εἶναι ἐνδιαφέρον νά παρακολουθήσουμε τήν ὀνομασία μέ τήν ὁποία παραδίδεται στά χφφ. αὐτή ἡ 'μέθοδος τῶν θέσεων'.

Στήν πρώτη της καταγραφή, στόν κώδικα ΕΒΕ 2458 τό ἔτος 1336 [2], φέρει τήν ἐπιγραφή (φ. 3α): *"Σημάδια ψαλλόμενα κατ' ἦχον· ποίημα τοῦ μαΐστορος κυρίου Ἰωάννου τοῦ Κουκουζέλη· ἦχος α΄ ""Ἴσον, Ὀλίγον, Ὀξεῖα"".

Στόν κώδικα τοῦ Μανουήλ Βλατηροῦ, Ἰβήρων 985 τό ἔτος 1425, φέρει τήν ἴδια σχεδόν ἐπιγραφή (φ. 7α): "Σημάδια ψαλλόμενα κατ᾽ ἦχον· συντεθέντα παρά τοῦ μαΐστορος κυρίου Ἰωάννου τοῦ Κουκουζέλη".[3]

Στόν κώδικα Κωνσταμονίτου 86 (α᾽ ἥμισυ ιε᾽ αἰ., φ. 22α): "Σημάδια συντεθέντα καί μελισθέντα κατ᾽ ἦχον παρά τοῦ μαΐστορος κυρίου Ἰωάννου τοῦ Κουκουζέλη".[4]

Στόν σπουδαῖο κώδικα τοῦ Ἰωάννου Πλουσιαδηνοῦ, Διονυσίου 570 (τέλη ιε᾽ αἰ.) ἀναγράφεται (φ. 77α): "Ἑτέρα μέθοδος, δηλονότι τῶν αὐτῶν σημαδίων ψαλλομένων μετά μέλους, ποίημα τοῦ θαυμαστοῦ μαΐστορος κυρίου Ἰωάννου τοῦ Κουκουζέλη". Στό τέλος τῆς μεθόδου (φ. 79α) σημειώθηκε τό μνημόσυνο τοῦ Κουκουζέλη. "Αἰωνία σου ἡ μνήμη Κουκουζέλη. Ἀμήν, ἀμήν, ἀμήν".[5]

Ὁ Κοσμᾶς Ἰβηρίτης καί Μακεδών, ὁ σπουδαιότατος κωδικογράφος τοῦ ιζ᾽ αἰῶνος, στό χφ. Ἰβήρων 970 τοῦ ἔτους 1686, προσφέρει τήν ἐπιγραφή (φ. 6α): "Ἀρχή τῶν σημαδίων τῆς Μουσικῆς Τέχνης, ἅ συνετέθησαν παρά κυρίου Ἰωάννου μαΐστορος τοῦ Κουκουζέλου, κάλλιστά τε καί ἔντεχνα, ψαλλόμενα κατ᾽ ἦχον".[6]

Στόν κώδικα Ἰβήρων 987 (πρό τοῦ 1731) συναντᾶμε τήν ἐνδιαφέρουσα διατύπωση (φ. 7α): "Σημάδια ψαλλόμενα κατ᾽ ἦχον μετά πάσης χειρονομίας καί συνθέσεως, ποιηθέντα παρά τοῦ μαΐστορος...",[7] κλπ.

Ἕνας ἄλλος κώδικας, ὁ Ξηροποτάμου 307, χφ. τοῦ Ἀναστασίου Βάϊα στά 1767, μᾶς προσφέρει τόν χαρακτηρισμό 'πάνυ ἔντεχνα' (φ. 17β): " Σημάδια ψαλλόμενα εἰς τούς ὀκτώ ἤχους, πάνυ ἔντεχνα, συντεθέντα παρά τοῦ μαΐστορος κύρ Ἰωάννου τοῦ Κουκουζέλη...".[8]
Καί ὁ Δημήτριος Λῶτος, ἕνας δοκιμώτατος κωδικογράφος, στόν κώδικα Ξηροποτάμου 330, τό ἔτος 1781,

μᾶς προσφέρει ἕναν ἄλλο τίτλο (φ. 8α): "Τό Μέγα Ἴσον τοῦ κύρ Ἰωάννου μαΐστορος τοῦ Κουκουζέλη, ἐξηγηθέν παρά κύρ Πέτρου λαμπαδαρίου τῆς Μεγάλης Ἐκκλησίας, ὀκτάηχον, ἀρχομένου ἀπό τόν πλ. δ᾽ (sic) [= α᾽] ".[9]

Εὔκολα παρατηροῦμε, ὅτι στή χειρόγραφη παράδοση δέν ἀπαντᾶ ἡ ὀνομασία "Μέθοδος τῶν Θέσεων", μέ ἐξαίρεση μόνο τόν κώδικα Διονυσίου 570, ὅπου ὁ ὅρος 'Μέθοδος' ἤ 'Μέθοδος τῶν Θέσεων', ἀναγράφεται στήν ἀρχή αὐτοῦ τοῦ κειμένου τοῦ Κουκουζέλη καί ἄλλων παρομοίων κειμένων - μεθόδων. Ὁ Ἀναστάσιος Βάϊας (Ξηροποτάμου 307) ἀμέσως μετά τά "Σημάδια ψαλλόμενα" τοῦ Κουκουζέλη, ἀναγράφει (21β): "Ἑτέρα μέθοδος τῶν θέσεων τοῦ αὐτοῦ [Πλουσιαδηνοῦ] ὀκτάηχος· Τόν πρῶτον τόν λεγόμενον Κουκουμᾶν".

Τόν τίτλο "Μέθοδος τῶν Θέσεων" τόν πρωτογράφει ὁ Μανουήλ λαμπαδάριος ὁ Χρυσάφης, στήν θεωρητική του συγγραφή, καί μάλιστα σέ συνάφεια καί μέ τίς ἄλλες παρεμφερεῖς μεθόδους. Γράφει: "... οὐδεμία ἦν ἄν χρεία οὐδ᾽ ἀνάγκη τοῦ τόν μέν Γλυκύν Ἰωάννην πεποιηκέναι τάς μεθόδους τῶν κατά τήν Ψαλτικήν θέσεων, τόν δέ μαΐστορα Ἰωάννην μετ᾽ αὐτόν τήν ἑτέραν μέθοδον καί τά σημάδια ψαλτά, εἶτα μετ᾽ αὐτόν πάλιν τόν Κορώνην τάς ἑτέρας δύο μεθόδους τῶν κρατημάτων καί τήν ἑτέραν τῶν στιχηρῶν".[10]

Καί πρέπει νά παρατηρηθῆ ἐδῶ ὅτι δέν ἦταν δυνατόν νά ἀναγραφῆ "μέθοδος τῶν θέσεων" πρό τοῦ Μανουήλ Χρυσάφη, ἀφοῦ αὐτός πρῶτος καί σέ θεωρητικό κείμενο χρησιμοποίησε τόν ὅρο "θέσις", ἀλλά καί τόν ὅρο "μέθοδος". Κι᾽ ἦταν ὁ ἁρμοδιώτερος νά τό πράξει, καί πολύ ὀρθά διατύπωσε ὅτι πρόκειται γιά "μέθοδο θέσεων τῶν σημαδίων". Ὁ Μανουήλ Χρυσάφης στήν προκείμενη περίπτωση λειτούργησε ὡς μουσικολόγος. Ὁ κοινότερος τίτλος, πάντως, εἶναι "Σημάδια ψαλλόμενα κατ' ἦχον". Οἱ μεταγενέστεροι προσδιορισμοί, ὅπως "συντεθέντα καί μελισθέντα κατ' ἦχον", "ψαλλόμενα μετά μέλους", "ἀρχή τῶν σημαδίων τῆς Μουσικῆς Τέχνης, ἅ συνετέθησαν,... κάλλιστά τε καί ἔντεχνα, ψαλλόμενα κατ' ἦχον", "μετά πάσης χειρονομίας καί συνθέσεως", "πάνυ ἔντεχνα", ἤ "τό Μέγα Ἴσον τοῦ κύρ Ἰωάννου μαΐστορος τοῦ Κουκουζέλη, ἐξηγηθέν..." κλπ, μᾶς βοηθοῦν νά διαπιστώσουμε ὑπό ποιό πρίσμα εἶδαν οἱ κατά καιρούς διδάσκαλοι τό κείμενο αὐτό καί ποιό εἰδικό βάρος τοῦ προσέδωκαν. Δυό προσδιορισμοί ἔχουν ἰδιάζουσα σημασία "συντεθέντα" ἤ "συνετέθησαν" καί "μετά πάσης χειρονομίας καί συνθέσεως". Κι' ἄς προσαχθῆ ἐδῶ καί ὁ προσδιορισμός "κάλλιστά τε καί ἔντεχνα" ἤ "πάνυ ἔντεχνα". Ἐδῶ σαφῶς μαρτυρεῖται ὅτι πρόκειται γιά ὁριοθέτηση, μέχρι ἕνα βαθμό, τῆς συνθέσεως τῶν σημαδίων τῆς Μουσικῆς Τέχνης· καί ὑπονοεῖται, βέβαια, καί ὁ κανονισμός τῆς ὀρθογραφίας κατά τήν σύνθεση, ὅπως ὑπαγορεύει ἡ χειρονομία καί ἡ διάκριση τῶν σημαδίων σέ σώματα καί πνεύματα. Εἶναι χρήσιμη ἐδῶ ἡ ἀναγραφή στόν κώδικα Κωνσταμονίτου 86, (φ. 46α): "Τά σώματα ὁμοῦ μετά τῶν πνευμάτων χειρονομοῦνται οὕτω".

Β΄. Κοινότητα τῶν μεθοδων τοῦ Γλυκέος καί τοῦ Κουκουζέλη.

Ὁ Μανουηλ Χρυσάφης μαρτυρεῖ, ὅπως εἴδαμε, ὅτι ὁ Κουκουζέλης "ἐποίησε τήν ἑτέραν μέθοδον καί τά σημάδια ψαλτά" μετά τόν Ἰωάννην Γλυκύ τόν Πρωτοψάλτη. Τό γεγονός αὐτό ἐπιβεβαιώνεται ἀπ' τήν χειρόγραφη παράδοση, ὅπου συναντᾶται, σέ εὐάριθμες περιπτώσεις, ἡ 'Μέθοδος τῶν Θέσεων' τοῦ Ἰωάννου Γλυκέως. Τό πρᾶγμα ἔχει μεγάλη σημασία, ἄν συνδυασθῆ καί μέ τή μαρ-

τυρία τοῦ κώδικος Κουτλουμουσίου 457, ὅπου ὁ Ἰωάννης Κουκουζέλης χαρακτηρίζεται "διάδοχος καί μαθητής" τοῦ Ἰωάννου Γλυκέως, μαζί μέ τόν συνομήλικό του Ξένο Κορώνη. Κι' εἶναι πολύ ἐνδεικτική καί ἡ ἀπεικόνιση τῆς τριανδρίας αὐτῆς μέ τήν ἐπιγραφή "Ἰωάννης ὁ Πρωτοψάλτης μανθάνων τόν Κορώνην καί τόν Κουκουζέλην"[11]. Ὡς μέγας διδάσκαλος τῆς Ψαλτικῆς ὁ Ἰωάννης Γλυκύς ὁ Πρωτοψάλτης παρέδωκε πρῶτος τήν "Μέθοδο τῶν θέσεων τῶν σημαδίων". Κι' αὐτή ἡ Μέθοδος ἔχει ὡς ἐπιγραφή· "Ἀρχή τῶν σημαδίων τῆς Παπαδικῆς Τέχνης, ψαλλόμενα κατ' ἦχον"[12]. Ὁ Ἰωάννης Κουκουζέλης, δεύτερος μετά τόν Ἰωάννη Γλυκύ, παρέδωκε παρόμοια Μέθοδο τῶν θέσεων τῶν σημαδίων. Οἱ δυό αὐτές Μέθοδοι εἶναι σπουδαιότατες γιά τήν Ψαλτική Τέχνη. Ἔχουν μεγάλη κοινότητα μεταξύ τους, ἀλλ' ἔχουν καί πολυσήμαντες διαφορές. Οἱ δυό μαζί ἀλληλοσυμπληρώνονται κι ἀποτελοῦν τήν βασική πηγή γιά τήν ὀνομασία τῶν σημαδίων καί τῶν θέσεων τῆς "Μέσης πλήρους βυζαντινῆς σημειογραφίας" (1177-1670 περίπου).[13]

Ὁ Κουκουζέλης, ὡς δεύτερος, παρέλαβε καί διατήρησε τό μεῖζον μέρος, σχεδόν τά τέσσερα πέμπτα, τοῦ περιεχομένου τῆς Μεθόδου τοῦ Ἰωάννου Γλυκέος. Ἡ ἀποδοχή εἶναι αὐτούσια, ὅσον ἀφορᾶ στή σύνθεση τῶν σημαδίων. Παρέλειψε κάποιες θέσεις καί δημιούργησε, ἀντ' αὐτῶν, καινούργιες, δίνοντας αὐτός καί τά ὀνόματά τους. Κατ' αὐτόν τόν τρόπο, ἔχει μεγάλη σημασία γιά τήν ὀνοματοδοσία τῶν σημαδίων καί τῶν θέσεων, ἐκεῖνο τό τμῆμα τῶν δύο Μεθόδων πού δέν εἶναι κοινό.

Στή σειρά αὐτή τῆς συγκρίσεως τώρα ὑπεισέρχεται κι ἕνας τρίτος παράγοντας· ὁ πίνακας "τῶν μελωδημάτων". πού πρωτογράφηκε στό φ.159α τοῦ κώδικος τῆς Μεγιστης Λαύρας τοῦ Ἁγίου Ὄρους Γ 67, τοῦ ι΄ αἰῶνος[14]. Ἕνας συγκριτικός πίνακας σέ τρεῖς στῆλες παρουσιάζει καθαρά τήν κοινότητα καί τίς διαφορές μεταξύ τῶν Μεθόδων τῶν σημαδίων καί τῶν θέσεων τοῦ Ἰωάννου Κουκουζέλη, Ἰωάννου Γλυκέος καί τοῦ ἀδήλου κωδικογράφου τοῦ κώδικος Μεγίστης Λαύρας Γ 67.

Μέθοδοι τῶν θέσεων ἤ "μελωδημάτων"

Ἰωάννου Κουκουζέλη (ΕΒΕ 2458, φ.3α)	Ἰωάννου Γλυκέος (Κωνσταμονίτου 86, φ.13β)	Ἀδήλου, ι΄ αἰ. (Λαύρας Γ 67, φ.159α)
Ἴσον	Ἴσον	Ἴσον
Ὀλίγον	Ὀλίγον	Ὀλίγον
Ὀξεῖα	Ὀξεῖα	Ὀξεῖα
καί Πεταστή	καί Πεταστή	
Διπλῆ	Διπλῆ	
Κράτημα		
Κρατημοκατάβασμα	Κρατημοϋπορροοκατάβασμα	
Τρομικόν	Τρομικόν	Τρομικόν
Στρεπτόν	Στρεπτόν	
Θές καί Ἀπόθες	Θές καί Ἀπόθες	
καί Θεματισμός {ἔσω}	Θεματισμός ἔσω	
Ὄρθιον σύν τούτοις	Ὄρθιον - χορείαν	
Οὐράνισμα	Οὐράνισμα	Οὐράνισμα
Σεῖσμα	Σεῖσμα	Σεῖσμα
Ἀνατρίχισμα	Ἀνατρίχισμα	Ἀνατρίχισμα
Σύναγμα	Σύναγμα	Σύναγμα
Κύλισμα	Κύλισμα	
Στραγγίσματα	Στραγγίσματα	Στραγγίσματα
Κροῦσμα ἄλλον	Κροῦσμα ἕτερον	
Ἀνάβασμα καί Κατάβασμα	Κατάβασμα καί Ἀνάβασμα	

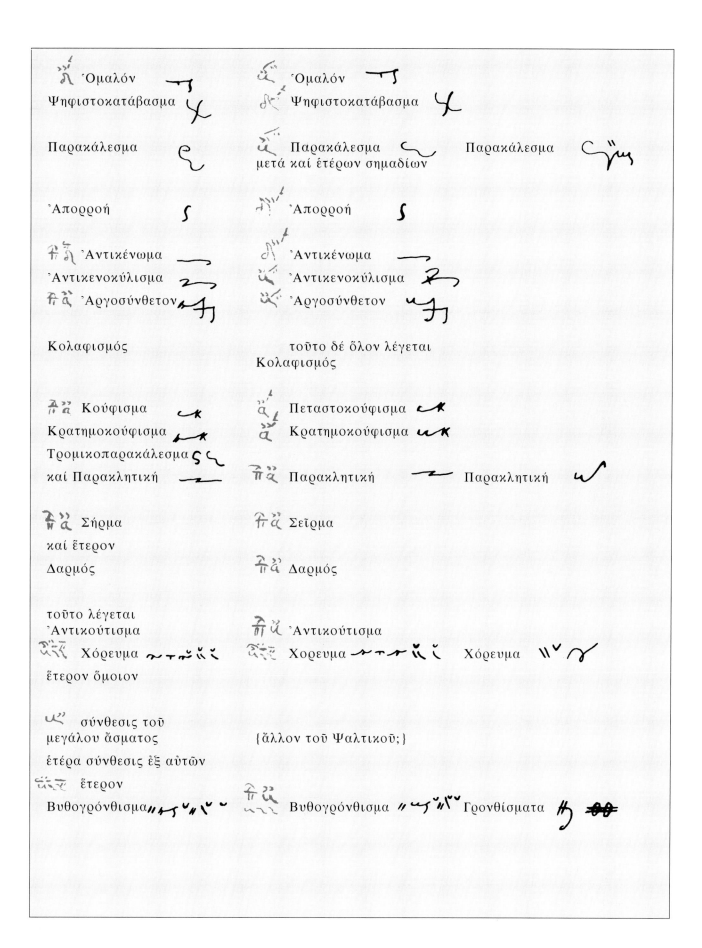

Ὁμαλόν

Ψηφιστοκατάβασμα

Παρακάλεσμα

Ἀπορροή

Ἀντικένωμα
Ἀντικενοκύλισμα
Ἀργοσύνθετον

Κολαφισμός

Κούφισμα
Κρατημοκούφισμα
Τρομικοπαρακάλεσμα
καί Παρακλητική

Σήρμα
καί ἕτερον
Δαρμός

τοῦτο λέγεται
Ἀντικούτισμα
Χόρευμα
ἕτερον ὅμοιον

σύνθεσις τοῦ
μεγάλου ἄσματος
ἑτέρα σύνθεσις ἐξ αὐτῶν
ἕτερον
Βυθογρόνθισμα

Ὁμαλόν

Ψηφιστοκατάβασμα

Παρακάλεσμα
μετά καί ἑτέρων σημαδίων   Παρακάλεσμα

Ἀπορροή

Ἀντικένωμα
Ἀντικενοκύλισμα
Ἀργοσύνθετον

τοῦτο δέ ὅλον λέγεται
Κολαφισμός

Πεταστοκούφισμα
Κρατημοκούφισμα
Παρακλητική   Παρακλητική

Σεῖρμα

Δαρμός

Ἀντικούτισμα

Χόρευμα   Χόρευμα

{ἄλλον τοῦ Ψαλτικοῦ;}

Βυθογρόνθισμα   Γρονθίσματα

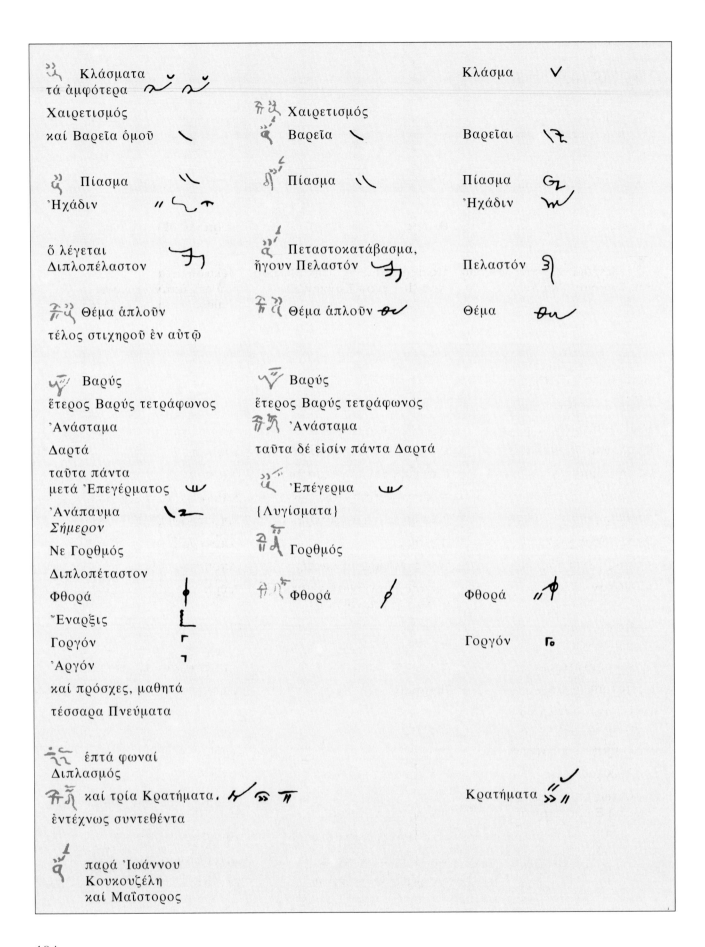

Κλάσματα
τά ἀμφότερα

Κλάσμα

Χαιρετισμός
καί Βαρεῖα ὁμοῦ

Χαιρετισμός

Βαρεῖα

Βαρεῖαι

Πίασμα
Ἠχάδιν

Πίασμα

Πίασμα
Ἠχάδιν

ὅ λέγεται
Διπλοπέλαστον

Πεταστοκατάβασμα,
ἤγουν Πελαστόν

Πελαστόν

Θέμα ἁπλοῦν
τέλος στιχηροῦ ἐν αὐτῷ

Θέμα ἁπλοῦν

Θέμα

Βαρύς
ἕτερος Βαρύς τετράφωνος
Ἀνάσταμα
Δαρτά
ταῦτα πάντα
μετά Ἐπεγέρματος
Ἀνάπαυμα
Σήμερον
Νε Γορθμός
Διπλοπέταστον
Φθορά
Ἔναρξις
Γοργόν
Ἀργόν
καί πρόσχες, μαθητά
τέσσαρα Πνεύματα

Βαρύς
ἕτερος Βαρύς τετράφωνος
Ἀνάσταμα
ταῦτα δέ εἰσίν πάντα Δαρτά
Ἐπέγερμα
{Λυγίσματα}
Γορθμός
Φθορά

Φθορά

Γοργόν

ἑπτά φωναί
Διπλασμός
καί τρία Κρατήματα.
ἐντέχνως συντεθέντα

Κρατήματα

παρά Ἰωάννου
Κουκουζέλη
καί Μαΐστορος

194

Σημειογραφικές Παρατηρήσεις

Ἡ Μέθοδος τοῦ Ἰωάννου Κουκουζέλη	Ἡ Μέθοδος τοῦ Ἰωάννου Γλυκέος	Ὁ Πίνακας τῶν Μελωδημάτων
δέν περιέχει τίς ἀκόλουθες	δέν περιέχει τίς ἀκόλουθες	(Λαύρα Γ 67, τοῦ ι΄ αἰ.)
Θέσεις	Θέσεις	περιέχει τά ἀκόλουθα
τίς περιεχόμενες στήν Μέθοδο τοῦ Ἰωάννου Γλυκέος	τίς περιεχόμενες στήν Μέθοδο τοῦ Ἰωάννου Κουκουζέλη	Μελωδήματα πού δέν ἀπαντοῦν στίς Μεθόδους τοῦ Ἰω. Γλυκέος καί Ἰω. Κουκουζέλη
Πεταστοκατάβασμα (ἀντίστοιχο μέ Διπλοπελαστόν)	Κράτημα	Ψιλόν
Ἕτερον τοῦ Ψαλτικοῦ	Τρομιχοπαρακάλεσμα	Χαμηλόν
Θεματισμός ἔξω	καί ἕτερον {Σεῖρμα}	Βαθύ
Ὁμαλόν μετά Θέματος	ἕτερον ὅμοιον {Χόρευμα}	Σαξίματα
Λαρύγγισμα	σύνθεσις τοῦ μεγάλου ἄσματος	Πάρηχον
Δίπλωμα	ἑτέρα σύνθεσις ἐξ αὐτῶν	Σταυρός ἀπό δεξία
Σταυρός	Κλάσματα τά ἀμφότερα	Ἀπόστροφος
ἄλλος {Σταυρός}	Ἠχάδιν	Ἀπόδερμα
ὁ αὐτός {Σταυρός}	τέλος στιχηροῦ ἐν αὐτῷ	Ἀπόθεμα
Ἀπόθετον	Ἀνάπαυμα (εἶναι ἀντίστοιχο μέ τά Λυγίσματα)	Ρεῦμα
Ἀνάβασις καί Κατάβασις	Σήμερον	Τίναγμα
Τρομιχοσύναγμα	Διπλοπέταστον	μετά Σταυροῦ {Σύναγμα}
Ψηφιστοσύναγμα	Ἔναρξις	Λεμοί
Λυγίσματα (ἀντίστοιχο πρός τό Ἀνάπαυμα)	Γοργόν	Τρία
καί ἕτερα{Λυγίσματα}	Ἀργόν	Τέσσαρα
Ξηρόν Κλάσμα	καί πρόσχες μαθητά	Ἀπ᾽ ἔσω ἔξω
καί οὕτως καί ἄλλως (δηλαδή Ξηρόν Κλάσμα)	τέσσερα Πνεύματα	Δύο
	ἑπτά φωναί Διπλασμός	Ἡμίφθορα
	καί τρία Κρατήματα	Καταβατρομιχόν
	ἐντέχνως συντεθέντα	Ψηφιστόν

παρά Ἰωάννου	Κόνδευμα
τοῦ Κουκουζέλη	Ράπισμα
καί Μαΐστορος.	Νανά
	Πέτασμα
	Κόνδευμα (ἄλλο).

καί ὑπάρχουν μελισμένα
τά ἐνηχήματα τῶν ἤχων,
ἀπ᾽ τόν β΄ Νεανές καί ἑξῆς

Σέ μελλοντική φάση ὁ συγκριτικός αὐτός πίνακας πρέπει νά συμπληρωθῆ καί μέ ἄλλες στῆλες, ὅπου θά ἀναγράφονται καί οἱ 'θέσεις' τῶν Μεθόδων τῶν θέσεων τῶν μεταγενεστέρων διδασκάλων.

Ἐδῶ πρέπει νά σχολιασθῆ ὅτι τά σημάδια στόν κώδικα Λαύρας Γ 67 δέν χαρακτηρίζονται σημάδια, ἀλλά 'μελωδήματα'. Ὁ κωδικογράφος σαφέστατα ἀπέβλεψε στό μελικό περιεχόμενο πού ὑπεδήλωναν τά σημάδια αὐτά κι ὄχι στό σχῆμα τους. Μελώδημα {- τα} δέν εἶναι ποτέ μιά φωνή, ἕνας φθόγγος, ἀλλά μιά μελική φράση.

Οἱ πολυσήμαντες διαφορές πού παρατηροῦνται, ἀναφέρονται στόν ἦχο, κατά τόν ὁποῖο ψάλλονται οἱ ἴδιες, πανομοιότυπες θέσεις. Σέ ἄλλον ἦχο τίς χρησιμοποιεῖ ὁ Ἰωάννης Γλυκός καί σέ ἄλλον ὁ Ἰωάννης Κουκουζέλης. Ὑπάρχει, βέβαια, καί ταυτότητα ἤχου γιά πολλές θέσεις, κυρίως στούς ἤχους πλάγιο β΄ καί βαρύ.

Ἡ παρατήρηση αὐτή σχετικά μέ τήν διαφορά ἤχου ἐπικυρώνει τό γεγονός ὅτι οἱ ἴδιες θέσεις ἔχουν ἄλλο μέλος στόν ἕνα ἦχο καί ἄλλο στόν ἄλλον[15]. Ἀκόμα, ἡ παρατήρηση αὐτή προσδιορίζει καί τήν ἀξία αὐτῶν τῶν Μεθόδων στίς πραγματικές τους διαστάσεις· εἶναι δυό Μέθοδοι Θέσεων ἀπ᾽ τίς πολλές πού θά ἦταν δυνατό νά παραδοθοῦν ἀπό αὐτούς ἤ καί ἀπό ἄλλους διδασκάλους (Κι ἐγώ, ἄν ζοῦσα τότε, γιά διδακτικούς σκοπούς θά μποροῦσα νά συντάξω μιά Μέθοδο τῶν θέσεων· παρόμοια κι ὁ καθένας ἀπό σᾶς).

Κι ἡ ὕπαρξη, ἀκριβῶς, καί ἄλλων Μεθόδων τῶν θέσεων ἀπό μεταγενεστέρους διδασκάλους[16], ἀποδεικνύει "τοῦ λόγου τό ἀσφαλές". Γιατί, ἡ Ψαλτική εἶναι πέλαγος καί ὠκεανός ὁλόκληρος καί δέν χωρεῖ μέσα σέ δυό ἤ τρεῖς σελίδες μεμβράνης ἤ χαρτιοῦ τῶν κωδίκων, γιά νά μετρήσουμε μέ "Μέθοδο" ἤ "Κανόνα" τό μέγεθός της.

Γ΄. "Πολλαί εἰσι σημαδίων θέσεις".

Ἡ ἀκροτελεύτια παρατήρηση στήν προηγούμενη παράγραφο καθιστᾶ ἀναγκαία τήν ἀναφορά στό λεγόμενο, δυό φορές μάλιστα, " πολλαί εἰσι σημαδίων θέσεις, ἀλλ᾽ οὐ δεῖ καί ὀνόματι λέγειν", πού ἀπαντᾶ σέ θεωρητικό κείμενο ἀποδιδόμενο στόν Ἰωάννη Πλουσιαδηνό[17]. Στό ἴδιο κείμενο, ὑπάρχει ἡ ἀκόλουθη ἐκτενέστερη διατύπωση· "Ἠδυνάμην γράψαι πλείονας σημαδίων θέσεις, ἤτοι χειρονομίας, ἀλλά διά τήν τῶν ἀρχαρίων ἀγανάκτησιν καί τῶν πολλῶν σημαδίων τόν κόρον ἔγραψα τήν μικράν ταύτην προγυμνασίαν " (Ἰβήρων 1192). Ἐπισημαίνω στό παράθεμα αὐτό τήν ἰσό-

196

τητα "θέσεις ἤτοι χειρονομίαι "·
γίνεται δηλαδή λόγος γιά ὀρθή –
ὀρθογραφημένη – ἕνωση καί σύνθεση τῶν σημαδίων, φωνητικῶν καί
ἀφώνων, πρός ἀπαρτισμό συγκε-
κριμένης θέσεως.

Κοιτάζοντας καί μέ αὐτό τό δε-
δομένο τή Μέθοδο τῶν Θέσεων τοῦ
Κουκουζέλη, καί τοῦ Γλυκέος βέβαια, ἀλλά καί τῶν μεταγενεστέρων, κατανοοῦμε εὐκολώτερα γιατί
οἱ θέσεις παραδίδονται μέ δύο τύ-
πων ὀνομασίες· μέ τό ὄνομα κάποι-
ου ἀφώνου σημαδίου ἤ ὑποστάσεως
χειρονομίας, ὅπως προσφυῶς λέ-
γονται, καί μέ τό ὄνομα τοῦ σχημα-
τισμοῦ τοῦ μέλους, πού ἡ ἁρμόδια
συμπλοκή τῶν σημαδίων ὑποδηλώ-
νει. Γιά παράδειγμα· θέση Στραγγίσματα, ἤ Κολαφισμός, ἤ ᾽Αντι-
κούτισμα, ἤ ᾽Ανάσταμα. Ἡ δυσκο-
λία, βέβαια, στήν ὀνοματοδοσία
τῶν θέσεων ὡδήγησε γιά δάνεια
στήν ψαλτική πράξη. Κι ἔχουμε,
ἔτσι, θέση Χαιρετισμός, ἤ Σήμερον,
᾽Ανάβασμα καί Κατάβασμα, ἤ "τέλος στιχηροῦ ἐν αὐτῷ ", ἤ "Λαρύγγισμα ", κλπ. Καί καταλαβαίνουμε
τώρα τήν ἀλήθεια τοῦ λεγομένου·
"πολλαί εἰσι σημαδίων θέσεις, ἀλλ᾽
οὐ δεῖ καί ὀνόματι λέγειν ". Καί
μένει ἔτσι εὐρύ πάντοτε κι᾽ ἐλεύ-
θερο πεδίο γιά τήν δημιουργία
"νεοφανῶν θέσεων", "ὡς ἀσματομε-
λωδεῖται " ἑκάστοτε[18]. Ἡ δημιουργία θέσεων εἶναι τό ἄπαν στή μελοποιία, γιατί εἶναι ἕξη ποιητική. Οἱ
ποιητές - κι οἱ μελοποιοί - θά πεθάνουν τελευταῖοι ἀπ᾽ τό ἀνθρώπινο
γένος, καί θά πεθάνουν μ᾽ ἕνα ποίημα, ὅ,τι κι ἄν εἶναι αὐτό, στό
στόμα.

Δ´. Οἱ Θέσεις τῆς Μεθόδου εἶναι στιχηραρικές.

Ἡ μορφολογία τῶν Θέσεων τῶν
δυό αὐτῶν Μεθόδων τίς διακρίνει
καί τίς κατατάσσει, σχεδόν ἀπο-
κλειστικά, στό Στιχηραρικό Γένος
Μελῶν. Στή Μέθοδο τοῦ Κουκουζέλη ὑπάρχει ἡ σαφής ἀναφορά

"τέλος στιχηροῦ ἐν αὐτῷ ". Ἡ ἄλλη
ἀναφορά "σύνθεσις τοῦ μεγάλου
ἄσματος ", στήν Μέθοδο τοῦ Κουκουζέλη, ἤ "Ἄλλον τοῦ Ψαλτικοῦ "
στή Μέθοδο τοῦ Γλυκέος, προσφέ-
ρουν τά κριτήρια τῆς διακρίσεως
τῶν θέσεων σέ στιχηραρικές καί
παπαδικές. Ἕνας ἀριθμός θέσεων
εἶναι κοινές στά δύο Γένη μελῶν.
Οἱ θέσεις πού προσδιορίζονται ἀπό
μιά μεγάλη ὑπόσταση χειρονομίας
εἶναι κυρίως στιχηραρικές. Οἱ θέσεις πού ὀνομάτίζονται περιγρα-
φικά εἶναι κυρίως παπαδικές, καί
κάποιες ἀπ᾽ αὐτές κοινές καί στό
Στιχηραρικό Γένος.

Μιά προσεκτική παρατήρηση στή
Μέθοδο τοῦ ᾽Ιωάννου Γλυκέος στόν
κώδικα Κωνσταμονίτου 86 ἀνακα-
λύπτει κάτω ἀπ᾽ τά σημάδια τῶν
θέσεων, μέ κόκκινο μελάνι ἀπό ἕνα
χέρι σχεδόν σύγχρονο τοῦ κωδικογράφου, τίς συλλαβές ᾽ανεεεε᾽ ἤ
᾽κεχεχε᾽, κυρίως, γιά μιά ὑποβοή-
θηση στήν ψαλμώδηση τῶν θέσεων,
καί σέ μερικές περιπτώσεις φράσεις
ἀπό σχετικά στιχηρά ἰδιόμελα· ὅ-
πως " ὅθεν ", στή θέση ῾Ομαλόν μετά θέματος᾽, "οὔτε οὗτος ἥμαρτεν "
στή θέση ᾽τοῦτο δέ ὅλον λέγεται
Κολαφισμός᾽, "χαῖρε- χαίρετε" στίς
θέσεις ᾽Χαιρετισμός᾽ καί ῾Βυθο-
γρόνθισμα᾽, "σήμερον" στή θέση
᾽Σύρμα᾽, "ἄρχοντες" στή θέση
᾽᾽Ανατρίχισμα᾽, "χαρισάμενος" στή
θέση ᾽᾽Ανάσταμα, "πάλιν ἡμῖν" στή
θέση ᾽Φθορά᾽, καί ἡ χαρακτηριστική
λέξη "διό" στή θέση ᾽Γοργμός᾽.

Κι᾽ ὑπάρχει καί ἡ ἀκόλουθη κα-
ταπληκτική περίπτωση. Στόν ἴδιο
αὐτόν σπουδαῖο κώδικα Κωνσταμονίτου 86, μετά τήν Μέθοδο τῶν
θέσεων τοῦ Κουκουζέλη, ἀναγράφεται στήν ἀρχή ἑνός ποιήματος
(φ.23α): Λόγοι παρακλητικοί εἰς
τήν ἁγίαν Θεοτόκον· ποίημα Μάρ-
κου ἱερομονάχου τοῦ Βλατῆ· τό δέ
μέλος ἐστίν ἀπό τῶν σημαδίων τῶν
ψαλτῶν τοῦ μαΐστορος κυροῦ ᾽Ιω-
άννου τοῦ Κουκουζέλη· ἦχος α´
Μόνη Παρθένε καί μήτηρ τοῦ ποιη-

τοῦ μου ἀγνή"[19]. Τό κείμενο δέν ἔχει τήν αὐστηρή δομή ἑνός στιχηροῦ ἰδιομέλου, καί εἶναι ἀρκετά ἐκτενές, ἐκτενέστερο ἀπό ὁποιοδήποτε στιχηρό ἰδιόμελο τοῦ Στιχηραρίου, προσιδιάζει περισσότερο μέ τά παρακλητικά ὑμνογραφήματα σέ 15συλλάβους στίχους, μέ τή διαφορά ὅτι ἐκεῖνα ἔχουν σαφῆ μελική μεταχείριση τοῦ παπαδικοῦ μέλους τοῦ Μαθηματαρίου.

Ε΄. Ἐφαρμογή τῆς ῾Μεθόδου τῶν Θέσεων᾽.

῎Υστερ᾽ ἀπ᾽ τήν ἐξέταση τῆς Μεθόδου τοῦ Κουκουζέλη, καί παρεμφερῶς τῆς ἀντίστοιχης τοῦ Ἰωάννου Γλυκέος, δέν ὑπάρχει ἀμφιβολία, ὅτι πρόκειται, - πέρ᾽ ἀπ᾽ τήν δηλοποίηση τοῦ σχήματος καί τοῦ ὀνόματος τῶν σημαδίων – , γιά μιά σοβαρή προσπάθεια κωδικοποιήσεως τῶν κυριωτέρων θέσεων τῆς Ψαλτικῆς Τέχνης τῆς ἐποχῆς τους, καί συγχρόνως γιά μιά ἀνάγκη ὁριοθετήσεως τῆς συνθέσεως τῶν σημαδίων τῆς μουσικῆς, φωνητικῶν καί ἀφώνων. Κι᾽ ἐδῶ ἔγκειται ἡ μεγάλη σπουδαιότητα αὐτῆς τῆς Μεθόδου. Μεταγενέστεροι διδάσκαλοι τῆς μουσικῆς, στίς διάφορες παραλλαγές τῆς Προθεωρίας, προσπάθησαν, ἄλλος μέ περισσότερη εὐστοχία, κι᾽ ἄλλος μέ ἁπλοϊκότερη ἀντίληψη καί διατύπωση, νά ἑρμηνεύσουν αὐτά πού παρέδωκε ὁ Κουκουζέλης – καί οἱ ἄλλοι-, χωρίς σέ καμιά περίπτωση νά τά ἀμφισβητοῦν. Στό σημείο αὐτό οἱ ἀναφορές θά ἦταν πολλές καί μακρές.

Δύο μεγάλοι θεωρητικοί δάσκαλοι, ὁ Γαβριήλ ἱερομόναχος ἐκ τῶν Ξανθοπούλων καί ὁ Μανουήλ λαμπαδάριος ὁ Χρυσάφης, ἀσχολήθηκαν εἰδικότερα γιά τήν ἐτυμολογία τῶν σημαδίων καί τήν σύνθεσή τους. Μιά σύνθεση τῶν ἀπόψεών τους, ἐξάγει τό ἀκόλουθο συμπέρασμα. Ὁ Μανουήλ Χρυσάφης κανονίζει· "Θέσις ἐστίν ἡ τῶν σημαδίων ἕνωσις, ἥτις ἀποτελεῖ τό μέλος"[20].

Κι᾽ ὁ Γαβριήλ διευκρινίζει· "Διά γάρ τῶν ῥηθέντων φωνητικῶν καί ἀφώνων σημαδίων ποιεῖ ἡ Ψαλτική τάς θέσεις ... ταύτας δέ διακρίνειν καί θεωρεῖν εἴτε καλῶς ἔχουσιν εἴτε καί μή ἡ χειρονομία ".[21]

Ἡ ἕνωση τῶν σημαδίων, φωνητικῶν καί ἀφώνων, πρέπει νά γίνεται "ἐπιστημόνως", κατά τόν Μανουήλ Χρυσάφη. Καί μόνον ἔτσι ἐννοοῦμε τή διαφορά πού ὑπάρχει ἀνάμεσα στά φωνητικά σημάδια, ἕξ συνολικά[22], πού δείχνουν ἀνάβαση μιᾶς φωνῆς· κι ἀκόμα περισσότερο, ἔτσι μόνο ὑποπτεύουμε τήν χρησιμότητα τῶν μεγάλων ὑποστάσεων χειρονομίας, πού φανερώνουν ὄχι μόνο μιά φωνή, δέν εἶναι αὐτή ἡ φύση τους, ἀλλά μέλος ὁλόκληρο, ἕνα μελώδημα, γιά νά θυμηθοῦμε τόν πρῶτο χαρακτηρισμό τους στόν ι΄ αἰῶνα. Μέλος, στήν Ψαλτική, δέν "ποιοῦν", δέν κάμουν μόνα τους τά φωνητικά σημάδια, καί μάλιστα ὅταν δέν ἔχουν ὀρθή ἕνωση, ὅπως δέν κάνουν ψηφιδωτό οἱ σκόρπιες ψηφίδες. Καί γιά τήν ὀρθή ἕνωση εἶναι ἀπαραίτητη ἡ διάκρισή τους σέ σώματα καί πνεύματα. Μέλος ἀποτελεῖ ἡ ἐπιστημονική ἕνωση τῶν φωνητικῶν καί τῶν ἀφώνων χειρονομικῶν σημαδίων, ὡς τόνισμα τοῦ νοήματος τοῦ λόγου.

Τούς προσδιορισμούς πού ἀπέδωσε ἡ παράδοση στή σύνθεση τῶν θέσεων, δηλαδή ὅτι "ἐμελίσθησαν", ὅτι "ψάλλονται μετά μέλους", ἤ ὅτι εἶναι "κάλλιστα καί ἔντεχνα", τούς κατανοοῦμε μέσα στό πλαίσιο καί τήν ἔννοια τῆς Προθεωρίας τῆς Ψαλτικῆς καί τῆς Μεθόδου, ἀκριβῶς, ἐξασκήσεως τῆς μνήμης τῶν ψαλτῶν. Οἱ ψάλτες πρέπει νά ἐκπαιδεύονται στήν ὀρθή συμπλοκή τῶν σημαδίων πρός ἀπαρτισμό θέσεων συγκεκριμένων μελῶν καί στήν πιστή ἀπομνημόνευση τοῦ μέλους αὐτῶν τῶν θέσεων, στόν ἕνα ἤ στόν ἄλλο ἦχο. Κατ᾽ αὐτόν τόν τρόπο ἐξασφαλίζεται ἡ συνέπεια καί ἡ ὁμοιογένεια στήν παράδοση τῶν διαφόρων μελῶν τῶν τριῶν βασικῶν Γενῶν τῆς Ψαλτικῆς, τοῦ Στιχηραρικοῦ, τοῦ Παπαδικοῦ καί τοῦ Εἱρμολογικοῦ. Ἡ Μέθοδος τοῦ Κουκουζέλη, καί ἡ ἄλλη τοῦ Γλυκέος, εἶναι κυριολεκτικά ὀπτικομνημονική μέθοδος, ἀντίστοιχη μέ τίς σημερινές ὀπτικοακουστικές μεθόδους ἐκμαθήσεως τῶν ξένων γλωσσῶν. Ὁ ψάλτης βλέπει τή θέση καί ἀπομνημονεύει τό μέλος, ὅπως τό ὑπαγορεύει ἡ παράδοση μέ τούς διαφόρους διδασκάλους, οἱ ὁποῖοι μιμοῦνται κατά διαδοχή τούς πρό αὐτῶν "τῇ ἐπιστήμῃ ἐνδιαπρέψαντας", ὅπως κανοναρχεῖ ὁ Μανουήλ Χρυσάφης.[23]

Τό θέμα, τώρα, τῆς ἐξηγήσεως τῶν θέσεων καί τῆς καταγραφῆς τοῦ μέλους τους ἀναλυτικά καί μέ σαφήνεια, πού μᾶς ἐξασφαλίζει ἡ μεταρρυθμισμένη σημειογραφία τῶν Τριῶν Διδασκάλων στά 1814, δέν χωρεῖ ἐδῶ, καί σχεδόν δέν ἐξαρκεῖ ὁ χρόνος μιᾶς ζωῆς.

Σᾶς λέω μόνο αὐτό πού διάβασα στόν κώδικα Ξηροποτάμου 333 (μέσα ιη΄ αἰ.),[24] στό τέλος τῆς Προθεωρίας (φ. 6α)·

"Καί ταῦτα μέν πρός μικράν διδασκαλίαν, ὦ μαθητά. διδάξει δέ σε ἀκριβέστερόν τε καί ἐντελέστερον ἡ μάθησις, διά τῆς διαφόρου συνθέσεως τῶν ποιητῶν, παλαιῶν τε καί νέων ".

Bibliography

Chrysanthos of Madytas, 1832
Θεωρητικόν Μέγα τῆς Μουσικῆς, Trieste

Conomos D., 1985
The Treatise of Manuel Chrysaphes, the Lampadarios, MMB, Corpus Scriptorum de Re Musica, Vienna

Hannick C. and Wolfram G., 1985
Gabriel Hieromonachos, MMB, Corpus Scriptorum de Re Musica, Vienna

Stathis G., 1975 - 93
Τά Χειρόγραφα Βυζαντινῆς Μουσικῆς - Ἅγιον Ὄρος, (ἔκδ. Ἵδρυμα Βυζαντινῆς Μουσικολογίας), I - III, Athens

Stathis G., 1979
Οἱ ἀναγραμματισμοί καί τά μαθήματα τῆς βυζαντινῆς μελοποιίας, Ἵδρυμα Βυζαντινῆς Μουσικολογίας, III, Athens

Stathis G., 1989
Ἡ ἀσματική διαφοροποίηση ὅπως καταγράφεται στόν κώδικα ΕΒΕ 2458 τοῦ ἔτους 1336", Χριστιανική Θεσσαλονίκη - Παλαιολόγεια Ἐποχή, 169- 88, Thessaloniki

Strunk O., 1965
Specimina notationum antiquiorum, MMB, VII, Copenhagen

Notes

NOTE 1.
Τήν πλήρη ἀναλυτική περιγραφή τοῦ σπουδαιοτάτου αὐτοῦ κώδικος βλ. Στάθης, 1989 169-188.

NOTE 2.
Ὅπου παραπάνω 170.

NOTE 3.
Στάθης 1993 817.

NOTE 4.
Στάθης 1975 657.

NOTE 5.
Στάθης 1976 703.

NOTE 6.
Στάθης 1993 717.

NOTE 7.
Στάθης 1993 828.

NOTE 8.
Στάθης 1975 107.

NOTE 9.
Στάθης 1975 190.

NOTE 10.
Πρβλ. Conomos 1985 40.

NOTE 11.
"Ἀρχή σύν Θεῷ ἁγίῳ τοῦ Μεγάλου Ἑσπερινοῦ, ἀπό χοροῦ, περιέχει δέ ἀλλάγματα παλαιά τε καί νέα, τοῦ τε θαυμαστοῦ πρωτοψάλτου τοῦ Γλυκύ καί τῶν διαδόχων αὐτοῦ καί φοιτητῶν κυροῦ Ξένου τοῦ Κορώνη καί τοῦ Παπαδοπούλου κυροῦ Ἰωάννου καί μαΐστορος τοῦ Κουκουζέλη, σύν αὐτοῖς καί ἐτέρων πολλῶν", μαρτυρεῖται στό φ. 1α τοῦ κώδικος Κουτλουμουσίου 457. Βλ. Στάθης 1993 354.

NOTE 12.
Ὁ πλήρης τίτλος στόν κώδικα Κωνσταμονίτου 86, φ. 13β εἶναι· "Ἀρχή τῶν σημαδίων τῆς Παπαδικῆς Τέχνης, ψαλλομένων κατ᾽ ἦχον. Ἀρχή μέση καί τέλος, σύστημα πάντων τῶν σημαδίων, τῶν ἀνιόντων καί κατιόντων, τό ἴσον ἐστί· χωρίς γάρ τοῦ ἴσου ὅλα ἄφωνα· ποιηθέντα παρά τοῦ πρωτοψάλτου κυροῦ Ἰωάννου τοῦ Γλυκέος· ἦχος α´ Ἴσον, Ὀλίγον, Ὀξεῖα, Πεταστή". Βλ. Στάθης 1975 656. - Εἰδικότερο λόγο γιά τήν Μέθοδο τοῦ Ἰωάννου Γλυκύ κάνει ὁ Christian Troelsgaard, στό Συμπόσιο αὐτό ἐδῶ.

NOTE 13.
Βλ. σχετικά γιά τόν καθορισμό τῆς Β´ περιόδου ἐξελίξεως τῆς βυζαντινῆς σημειογραφίας, μέ τή μετακίνηση τῶν ὁρίων ἀπ᾽ τόν ιε´ αἰῶνα στό "1670 περίπου", βάσει τῶν ἐσωτερικῶν ἀφοριστικῶν καί ἀσφαλῶν κριτηρίων τῆς σημειογραφίας, εἰς Στάθης 1979 48-55.

NOTE 14.
Βλ. Strunk 1965, specimen 12.

NOTE 15.
Τό ἀναμφισβήτητο αὐτό γεγονός διδάσκουν ὅλοι οἱ δάσκαλοι τῆς Ψαλτικῆς καί ἐπικυρώνει ὁ Χρύσανθος λέγοντας: "οἱ εἰρημένοι χαρακτῆρες καί αἱ ὑποστάσεις ὅταν ἀλλάζωσι τόνους ἤλλαζον καί τήν δύναμιν". Χρύσανθος 1832 181.

NOTE 16.
Ἐκτός τοῦ Ἰωάννου Πλουσιαδηνοῦ καί ὁ Θεόδουλος μοναχός Αἰνίτης καί Ἁγιορείτης, στά μέσα τοῦ ιη´ αἰῶνος ἐποίησε "μεθόδους τῶν θέσεων". Βλ. κώδικα Ἰβήρων 1083 (μέσα ιη´ αἰ.), φ. 260α- β.

NOTE 17.
Βλ. κώδικα Ἰβήρων 1192, φφ. 207α-210α.

NOTE 18.
Πρόδηλη καί ἀποφασιστική περίπτωση εἶναι ὁ "καλλωπισμός" τοῦ στιχηραρικοῦ μέλους ἀπ᾽ τόν Χρυσάφη τόν νέο καί πρωτοψάλτη καί τόν Γερμανό ἐπίσκοπο Νέων Πατρῶν. Βλ. Στάθης 1979 52-53.

NOTE 19.
Βλ. Στάθης 1975 659.

NOTE 20.
Πρβλ. Conomos 1985 40.

NOTE 21.
Βλ. Hannick/Wolfram 1985 72.

NOTE 22.
Βλ. σχετικά τήν διδασκαλία τοῦ Γαβριήλ ἱερομονάχου, ὅ.π. , 42, 48 καί 50.

NOTE 23.
Βλ. Conomos 1985 46.

NOTE 24.
Πρβλ. Στάθης 1975 209.

Summary:
Ioannes Koukouzeles' "Method of Theseis" and its Application

Gr. Th. Stathis

In memory of Jørgen Raasted

The theme of this contribution is a central issue of the Psaltic Art as it addresses both the history of Byzantine/Postbyzantine chant and its theory. The "Method of *Theseis* of the musical signs" by Ioannes Papadopoulos Koukouzeles, the Maïstor, is the most widespread and well-known method of Byzantine Chant ever since its appearance in the earliest dated Koukouzelean Akoluthiai MS, EBE 2458 (AD 1336). *Exegeseis* of the method were later made by Petros Peloponnesios (+ 1778), Gregorios Protopsaltes (+ 1821) and Matthaios of Vatopedi (+ 1849).

In the MSS a variety of titles for this method are found, many of them including the expression "The musical signs, sung through the eight modes". The wording "Method of the *theseis*" is first documented in the treatise by Manuel Chrysaphes (mid 15th c.), who actually coined "*thesis*" as a technical term, but it is also found in the MSS Dionysiou 570 (end of 15th c.) and Xeropotamou 307 (ca. 1767-70).

Manuel Chrysaphes tells that Ioannes Koukouzeles followed Ioannes Glykys in composing a method of musical signs, and this statement is confirmed by many occurrences of a method ascribed to Glykys in the musical manuscripts. Although there are many similarities between these two important methods, they differ in many respects as well. Together they constitute the main source for the nomenclature of the neumes and *theseis* in the period of fully developed Middle Byzantine Notation (1177 - ca. 1670). In addition, the old anonymous list of signs from MS Laura GAMMA 67 (10th c.) should be included in a comparative study, for which a table in three columns is presented above. It is worth noticing that the signs in Laura GAMMA 67 are called "*melodemata*" (meaning "whole musical phrases"), not just "*semadia*" ("signs"). Evidently, Glykys and Koukouzeles set some of the theseis in different modes, but especially in modes Second plagal and Barys there are many correspondences. These two methods have inspired many teachers through the centuries and will probably continue to do so.

The 15th c. theoretician Ioannes Plousiadenos stated that "there are many *theseis* of the musical signs". The nomenclature of signs and theseis (or *cheironomiai*) is manifold, referring either to the graphic shape of the signs, to the movement of the melody implied by the sign, or to other features of the chant practice, and, as the Byzantine chant tradition is a living one, new theseis were continuously created.

The *theseis* of Koukouzeles' and Glykys' methods belong primarily to the Sticheraric style, especially the ones named after a 'great sign' (*hypostasis*), whereas the theseis with descriptive names mostly are common to the Papadic (*Asmatikon/Psaltikon*) and the Sticheraric styles. In the MS Kostamonitou 86 (first half of 15th c.), a second row of text in red ink offers mnemonical help for the singer through "asmatic" syllables and brief quotations from suitable stichera. In the same MS, a kind of sticheron in honour of the Mother of God, reminding of the poetry of the fifteenth-syllable verses, is adapted to the melody of Koukouzeles' method by Markos Blates.

Gabriel Hieromonachos and Manuel Chrysaphes have in their treatises dealt with the etymology and grouping of the musical signs, stressing the unity of the interval signs and the *hypostaseis*, which together produce the actual melody (= *melos*). Founded on the basic manuals of the Art of Chanting (the *Protheoria* or *Papadike*) and Koukouzeles' Method, the singers have been trained to put the *theseis* correctly together in each mode, and therefore the characteristics of each of the three great genres, the Sticheraric, the Papadic, and the Heirmologic, have been preserved through the centuries. The pedagogic force of the method is that a singer learned a *thesis* by seeing it before his eyes and remembering the melody (= *melos*) at the same time.

The theme of *exegesis* of the *theseis* and the analytic transcription of the melodies into the notation of the Three Teachers in 1814 is vast in itself, and can – due to the limits of time and space – not be dealt with here.